POTEMKIN

POTEMKIN

Soldier, Statesman, Lover and
Consort of Catherine of Russia

by GEORGE SOLOVEYTCHIK

POTEMKIN

*Soldier, Statesman, Lover and
Consort of Catherine of Russia*

By GEORGE SOLOVEYTCHIK

W · W · NORTON & COMPANY · INC · *New York*

First Edition

PRINTED IN THE UNITED STATES OF AMERICA
FOR THE PUBLISHERS BY THE VAIL-BALLOU PRESS

TO THE MEMORY

OF

MY FATHER

CONTENTS

ILLUSTRATIONS

PREFACE

POTEMKIN, who for seventeen years was the most powerful man in Russia and as such one of the most powerful men in Europe, has been overlooked by the historians. For a long time he was considered merely as one of Catherine's many favorites, a particularly unsavory and extravagant character who bamboozled the Empress during her trip to the Crimea by putting up cardboard villages on the way and importing thousands of peasant serfs with their implements and cattle in order to create a picture of sham prosperity. The origin of all these stories, which resulted in Potemkin being handed down to history as a villain and an unscrupulous charlatan, was established many years ago. They can all be traced back to his anonymous biography, the author of which is known to have been the Saxon diplomat Helbig. It appeared in the years 1797 to 99 in the *Minerva*—a German review, published in Hamburg. This German biography was also translated into French (1808), English (1811 and 1813), and various other languages, being published with occasional additions and alterations, but always anonymously and with the bulk of Helbig's crude inventions incorporated in the narrative.

In the words of the best British authority on this period of Russian history, the late Robert Nisbett Bain, these stories are 'absolutely worthless'. Yet only shortly before the war a German book appeared bearing the odd title *From Silly Fool to First Man in the Realm,* and purporting to be a new biography of Potemkin. Its author follows more than closely the French version of Helbig's work, and not only repeats the absurdities this contains but, having obviously misunderstood the meaning of a French word, proceeds to refer to Potemkin's memoirs or reminiscences.

The fact is that Potemkin left no such, or any other, reminiscences, but a very large number of his Russian and foreign contemporaries did. From these fascinating documents, as well as from the mass of state, diplomatic, and private papers bearing on Catherine's reign and published in Russia or other countries throughout the last century and also in the present one, Potemkin's figure emerges in a very different light. Indeed, students of the period have for some time past been constrained, on the strength of that evidence, to revise the established opinion about him, and to admit his undoubted gifts, even though his faults and eccentricities still seemed to attract more attention than his positive achievements. An intriguing sketch of Potemkin was drawn by Waliszewsky in his brilliant but superficial book *Autour d'un Trône,* which appeared in Paris in 1894. Yet for some strange reason no professional historian, whether of Russian or other nationality, has taken the trouble to write a full-size life story of Potemkin on the basis of the vast documentary evidence that is now available. Almost the same applies to the case of Catherine herself; though the name of her biographers is legion, no scholar of standing has yet given us a scientifically written biography covering the whole of her reign, and founded on the immense wealth of facts that have gradually come to light. If such a book existed, Potemkin's place in history would have been established before now.

In attempting to write the story of his life, I was severely handicapped by the impossibility of access to the libraries and archives of Russia. To my surprise and gratification, however, I found both in Paris and in London some invaluable sources of material. During a protracted visit to Poland, the Baltic countries, and Finland—all of them formerly parts of the Russian Empire—I was able to extend my researches still further. Finally, in Stockholm, I found a great deal that was essential for my work, and I wish to express my thanks to Mr. Walter Singer of that city for the assistance rendered me in connection with some of these books and as yet unpublished papers. Other friends have also been good enough to put their libraries as well as their advice at my disposal, for which I am profoundly grateful. Portions of the first chapter have appeared, in a somewhat different form, in my *Russia in Perspective* (W. W. Norton & Company, Inc., 1947).

All the statements made in my book are based on documentary evidence. Where this has been contradictory, I have naturally taken those facts that agreed with my own interpretation of the persons or events in question. To obviate irritating footnotes I have occasionally added a few words of explanation in square brackets, and have translated practically all foreign quotations into English. It also seemed to me of the utmost importance to give as a background of Potemkin's or Catherine's story a general picture of the Russian scene, without which it would be hard to see that story in its true perspective.

There is just one word I must add about the spelling of Russian names. While using throughout the book the modern method of transliteration, I did not wish to alter anything in the quotations or on the map, and have left the contemporary spelling intact. I hope that no confusion will result, since all the names are easily recognizable.

Throughout my work I was constantly reminded of Voltaire's famous dictum on the happiness reserved for future authors dealing with the life of Catherine the Great. Perhaps one of the principle causes that made me enjoy this work so much was that it took me back to the days of a very happy youth and childhood spent in St. Petersburg and Tsarskoe Selo, both of them the scenes of Catherine's greatest glory. It was at Tsarskoe Selo, in the magnificent park bearing Catherine's name, that my father remarked to me during a walk nearly twenty-five years ago, that some day I should write Russian history. Of course, I have not attempted anything so ambitious. But if he were still alive to read my book I hope he would have agreed that I did not pervert the facts of a great story that needed telling.

POTEMKIN

1

THE RUSSIAN SCENE

IN THE panorama of eighteenth-century Europe, which includes some of the foremost events of modern history, the Russian scene occupies a very special place. The spectacular rise and consolidation of the Russian Empire, accompanied as it was by tremendous territorial expansion; the significance acquired by the newly built and rapidly growing, truly cosmopolitan capital city of St. Petersburg; the sumptuousness of the imperial court, which exceeded in magnificence even that of Versailles—on which it was modeled—all this is something unique even for so rich and varied an epoch, when practically every scene enacted on the European stage was a major drama and when most of the actors were stars of unusual caliber.

Europe in the eighteenth century offered a rare spectacle of progress and reaction, extravagant splendor and squalid misery somehow being made to exist side by side; but nowhere was this paradox more striking and more deeply rooted than in Russia.

Two parallel processes were at work: on the one hand, the emancipation of the nobility, and, on the other, the further enslavement of the peasant class—this latter process reaching quite unprecedented and unbelievable forms.

The empire of the *Tsars* had traveled a long road within a remarkably short time since the day when Peter the Great, not without violence, had forced the old Muscovite noblemen to shave off their beards and adopt a West-European mode of living. During the half century that elapsed between his reforms and the accession of Catherine II, the transformation of the ruling class had become almost complete. Indeed, the ground to which the tastes and manners of western Europe were originally transplanted by force, proved so fertile that the results soon acquired alarming proportions. European refinement blended with Asiatic pomp became an unhealthy growth on the body of the Russian people.

'Prepared as I was for the magnificence and parade of this court,' writes Great Britain's ambassador, the future Lord Malmesbury—as yet plain Mr. James Harris—in his very first dispatch from St. Petersburg on January 5, 1778, 'yet it exceeds in everything my ideas: to this is joined the most perfect order and decorum.' Most other foreign visitors to Russia at the time also recorded their amazement at the picture they saw. They were all of them dazzled by the grandeur of the court and the noblemen with whom they came into contact, and they certainly had every reason to be so impressed. A more eccentric, extravagant, and profligate society it would have been hard to find.

The Empress Catherine herself, who considered 'penny economies' to be 'indecent' was setting the pace, and all those around her were going out of their way to keep up with, or if possible excel, the general standard; slave labor had to provide the funds for their life of Sardanapalian luxury, comparable only to the mode of living of oriental potentates.

Catherine, who—to use her own words—had come to Russia at the age of fifteen, 'a poor and ambulant princess' from a provincial German court, developed a capacity for spending money on a scale hitherto unknown to her new country, and, after all, squandering has always been, and still is, a national Russian characteristic. The value of the ruble in those days was approximately a dollar and a quarter. Catherine spent millions not only on building palaces and country houses for herself, on assembling art collections of the greatest value, on clothes and jewels, and other luxuries, but also on dispensing fortunes with equal prodigality to her favorites and other privileged people. On one occasion she presented Orlov with a gold-embroidered coat worth the unbelievable sum of 1,000,000 rubles. The palaces she built for him and later for Potemkin, or the estates she gave away with hundreds of thousands of 'souls' or peasant serfs, attached for the 'amusement' of the happy recipients, mount up to quite fabulous sums. Following the Empress' example, the rich nobility were also erecting magnificent town and country palaces, villas, hothouses, stables and riding schools, private theaters; laying out the choicest of parks and gardens, embellished by lakes and fountains; collecting jewels and various treasures, indeed, sparing no efforts to surround themselves with an atmosphere of almost unreal luxury. Most of the building was done by French and Italian masters, and within a remarkably short time not only St. Petersburg and its suburbs, but also the country, and of course the various imperial residences, like Tsarskoe Selo, Peterhof, and Gatchina, became filled with the choicest palazzos, many of which have survived to the present day.

A contemporary author, writing in 1788, compared St. Petersburg to 'the glorious Versalia', and another observed a few years later that St. Petersburg society was 'the exact reflection of the court; it can be compared to the entrance hall of a huge temple, where all those present concentrate their looks solely on the deity sitting on the throne, to whom they make their sacrificial offerings and burn incense.'

Not only the courtiers and the rich noblemen living in the capital, but even the poorer landed gentry soon became affected by an utterly crazy quest for pleasure and diversion. To keep up with the general trend they frequently had to sell or mortgage their property; and many of them—formerly simple and sober people—ruined themselves; but the standards of 'the glorious Versalia' had to be emulated at any price. And just as the imperial 'deity' in St. Petersburg was setting the pace to her entourage of rich noblemen and courtiers whom she really despised, so the latter in their turn were the local little gods of their poorer and humbler neighbors, whom they, of course, also despised and not infrequently humiliated.

It was fashionable to have as large a staff as possible, and social standing was considerably influenced by it. To display the greatest number of servants was to enhance one's credit. They kept five or six times as many domestics as people of similar rank in Europe. The very rich frequently had a staff of anything from 300 to 800, while 100 to 150 for a person of standing was considered rather moderate. Even the poor noblemen indulged in a dozen or a few score servants and invariably drove coach and four.

Most of these servants were recruited by the gentry among the peasant serfs belonging to them, with just an occasional cook or barber or other menial—quite often a Frenchman or an Italian—imported from the world outside and hired as a free agent, though seldom treated as such. Sometimes, either in punishment or for reasons of domestic economy, these peasants were put back on the land again or used part of the year as laborers and the rest of the time in domestic service. As to their functions, it must be remembered that in those days a rich Russian nobleman kept his own tailors, shoemakers, saddlers, carpenters, grooms, stable boys, dairymaids, apothecaries, musicians, actors and actresses, poets, architects, painters, and a whole army of more personal servants such as cooks, bakers, pastry makers, dishwashers, laundresses, footmen, butlers, carvers, coffee servers, maids, valets *et hoc genus omne*. Usually there were several people for each of these jobs, with assistants and underassistants supporting them. Moreover, as most of the wealthier noblemen possessed not only a number of large town houses, but also innumerable estates in the country, each residence was richly endowed with a staff of its own. Some people kept a private guard of their own to protect them against brigands in the country or escort them while traveling, and this was by no means a superfluous precaution. Again, many of these gentlemen had special hobbies which necessitated an army of slaves for their gratification. Thus Count Sheremetiev kept twelve 'Hussars' with a 'commander', who used to parade for his and his guests' delectation; another famous nobleman had several hundred 'huntsmen' with two thousand hounds, just to amuse himself; yet another used to stage regular cavalry encounters between a special troupe of armored knights. Not infrequent were those who kept a private theologian or even an astronomer.

This latter mania seems to be a special national kink, for not so many years ago the present author met in a French spa a famous Russian millionaire who was accompanied by an enormous staff that included a private astronomer. Inquiring why the services of the gentleman were required, he got the classical reply: 'Let the bastard look at the stars: I can well afford it.' And this was not in the eighteenth, but well in the twentieth century.

The functions of each servant were laid down in most precise manner, and in a well-kept house minutely written instructions by the master himself were issued at regular intervals. Even the best educated people of their day spent much time and energy in drawing up endless documents as to who should light the candles and who should blow them out, while somebody else was to trim the wicks, and yet another flunky collect the melted wax, not to mention such serious points, as who should answer what bell, open what door or attend to what requirements of the masters or their guests. The possibilities foreseen or the cases envisaged in some of these instructions leave nothing to chance or imagination; failure to carry out these fantastic orders was punished with flogging or even torture. In the antechamber of one gentleman seventeen footmen had to sit day and night, of whom one was to fetch the master's pipe, another a glass of water, the third a book, and so forth. The established ritual in the house of another, who kept 300 servants, included a daily dinner of forty courses. Each was brought in by a separate chef wearing a white apron and a tall cap, who had to put his dish on the table, raise his cap, and retire after a deep bow, while twelve butlers and carvers in red uniforms and powdered wigs attended at the table. The same gentleman, by the way, also had seven cats, which were tied for the night to a table with seven legs, and, if one of them happened to break loose, the special staff of maids who were in charge of these cats were severely punished. This maniac was no exception, for there were many hundreds of others with equally crazy wishes that also had to be gratified by their slaves. Thus, Count Skavronsky, an influential and fabulously rich nobleman, who was passionately fond of music, and fancied himself a great composer, made it compulsory for all his servants to address him or to converse with each other in recitative.

It pleased another gentleman, whenever he wanted to punish one of his slaves, first to stage a mock trial, himself to pronounce several speeches for both the prosecution and the defense, and only then to send the bewildered victim to be flogged or otherwise punished. There was really no limit to the eccentricities and fancies of this incredible society, and little or no protection against their quite pathological abuse of power. The servants' duties were not always limited to purely domestic work or personal attendance. Like the ancient Romans who had their slave actors or slave musicians, many rich Russian noblemen in the eighteenth century kept their own theaters and orchestras, some of them numbering more than a hundred performers. It must be realized that, spending as they did a great deal of their time in the country, frequently separated from their nearest neighbor by huge distances, with bad roads that at different periods of the year (especially in the spring when the snow begins to melt) were practically unusable, these people were bored and had to do something to entertain themselves and the huge house parties it was customary to have.

Traditional Russian hospitality on a most lavish scale survived all social and political transformations. What was there for the hosts and guests to do, particularly during the long winter months? These private theaters and orchestras must have been to them the equivalent of the modern radio, or phonograph, or movies, or other means of obtaining entertainment in the country.

They were most particular, too, about their artistic pleasures, and spared no efforts and no money to get their serfs properly trained; often French or Italian masters were imported to teach them singing, or deportment on the stage, or some difficult musical instrument, or ballet dancing. Several noblemen even sent their peasant actors or musicians abroad to improve their artistic propensities, and not infrequently it happened that these wretched people having enjoyed comparative freedom while abroad, took to drink or even committed suicide on being once more reduced to slavery after their return. Here again not only casting, but every other sort of directions was carefully thought out by the masters, who supervised everything themselves. One gentleman invariably attended all the rehearsals of his private opera, and wearing just a dressing gown and a night-cap, he would come up on the stage to encourage his performing serfs with words or gestures. But one night during the performance of 'Dido' he did not like the singing of the principal artist, and jumping over the footlights he slapped her face with great vigor, and yelled: 'I always said I would catch you out, you sow! After the performance you will go to the stables to get your reward!' After the performance! He did not wish his pleasure to be interrupted, and poor 'Dido' had to pull herself together and start again.

When they moved from one estate to another, or from town to country, they usually took their private theaters and orches-tras with them. No less than twenty large carriages full of actors and musicians invariably accompanied a certain nobleman on his travels to entertain him wherever he stopped for the night;

nowadays people like that travel with a portable phonograph or radio.

Entertainments on a large scale were fashionable, courtiers and others competing with each other in extravagance. Count Kamensky spent 30,000 rubles on staging a play, the *Caliph of Baghdad*, for his guests; to celebrate the termination of the Turkish War, Leo Narishkin, Catherine's Master of the Horse, gave a party at which the whole war with its main battles was reproduced. Count Sheremetiev's theater at the village of Kouskovo—perhaps the most famous of the lot, and frequently attended by Catherine, the Emperor Joseph II of Austria, the King of Poland, and other potentates—had a repertoire of no less than forty operas; at Prince Youssoupov's theater a ballet was danced by several hundred maidens in the nude. Potemkin's parties, as will be seen, eclipsed even the most lavish festivities at the court itself.

Each 'Grand Seigneur' took a snobbish pride in inventing for his guests some new form of entertainment or offering them some special new dish. Count Rasoumovsky suddenly decided that it would be nice to hear a nightingale sing at the very time when the local river had flooded the whole region, and promptly thousands of peasants were made to build barrages and warping banks so that he and his guests might pass. Turning a field into a lake or a mountain practically overnight, putting up a pavilion, or a tower, or triumphal arch, or some other architectural adornment, almost within a few hours, was a popular pastime. One gentleman was famous for his 'Island of Love', where the loveliest girls from the village were placed at his guests' disposal; another provided the best artistic and musical entertainments. Orlov treated his guests to asparagus as large as a cudgel. Potemkin invariably got the choicest delicacies from France and other distant foreign lands. Harris reports that at the palace, meals were sometimes served on plates that were not merely of massive gold, but also actually set in jewels.

Money, time, effort, or human life counted little with the Empress or with Russia's eighteenth-century nobleman. As far as his peasants were concerned, he did not feel it was a question of human life. He viewed his serfs very much like cattle, perhaps not quite so valuable, and as something only fit to be whipped and made to work for him till they dropped dead. This applies not only to the 'die-hard' landlords whose name is legion, and who represented an almost clinical case of sadistic power psychosis. To these people the martyrology of the Russian peasant is a monument of eternal shame. But the significant thing is that even the more enlightened or decent kind of representatives of the upper class, even those who lived on terms of comparative affection with their peasants and servants, still considered these as mere cattle. The benign Andrew Bolotov, who in his fascinating memoirs has stigmatized both the spirit and practices of his epoch, or the great Field Marshal Souvorov who had a profound sympathy with the underdog and who as a landlord surpassed in simple humanity most of his contemporaries, are interesting cases in point. Not only were their dealings with their own peasants quite 'patriarchal', but both sincerely believed these were no better than cattle and that they should be treated as such. Perhaps a parallel may be found in the attitude of American families to their negro servants and retainers, to the 'black mammies' who are allowed to nurse their children, but who, despite a certain appreciation or even affection, are definitely considered as an altogether different and lower type of animal.

It was the established practice of the day in Russia to sell, mortgage, or exchange peasant serfs. An idea of values can be gathered from the advertisements to be found in the Moscow and St. Petersburg papers of those days. A good borzoi puppy could fetch 3,000 rubles, while a young peasant girl was worth anything from two and one-half to thirty-three rubles; it was even possible to buy a child for ten kopecks. But if the quality of a serf was superior, he could fetch very substantial prices; a good cook or a good musician was worth 800 rubles or even more. Count Kamensky gave in exchange for a troupe of actors he fancied a whole village with 250 inhabitants; another gentleman sold twenty musicians for 10,000 rubles. Serfs or 'souls' were advertised together with household goods or, in fact, any other commodities. Here are a few specimens: 'To be sold: a barber, and in addition to that four bedsteads, an eiderdown and other domestic chattels'; 'To be sold: banqueting tablecloths and also two trained girls and a peasant'; 'To be sold: a girl of sixteen of good behavior and a second-hand slightly-used carriage.'

. At no time in Russian history was this revolting commerce so active as in the 'enlightened' days of Catherine, just as at no other period was the quest of pleasure allowed to take more extravagant forms.

The contradiction between these sordid realities and the liberal ideas professed by the Empress, or the outward appearance of Russia's glory, is staggering.

The long reign of Catherine (1762–1796), who has been labeled an 'enlightened despot', is often described as Russia's Golden Age. And there is no doubt that she herself was most anxious that the world—both her contemporaries and posterity —should look upon her person and her work in that light. She spared no effort to create a favorable impression, and in a large measure succeeded. This was due to a variety of reasons. Her talent for publicizing herself was unique. She considered publicity to be an essential part of the craft of government and she can be said to have possessed that art in a supreme degree. Throughout her reign she excelled not only in skillfully conducting her own publicity on both a national and an international scale, but in getting others to do it for her. Her innumerable manifestoes and ukases to the people of Russia—for instance those issued after she deposed her husband and seized the throne—are a model for any modern press campaign.

Foreign opinion was a matter of constant concern to her.

Frequently she had such of her speeches or projected legislation as she wanted to make an impression outside Russia
translated into foreign languages and distributed abroad. But
she was clever enough to realize the limitations of self-advertise-
ment and knew that her monologues, however eloquent, could
not alone carry all the weight she wanted. Before long she succeeded in winning a whole chorus of enthusiastic supporters in
all the leading countries who added their authoritative voices
to her own. This she obtained by entering into regular correspondence with some of the greatest and most influential
men of her day, an intellectual intercourse with whom no doubt
gave her much pleasure, but whom she also deliberately used
as the willing or unsuspecting distributors of her publicity.
With astonishing energy and prolixity she would write to
them at frequent intervals expounding her ideas, arguing with
them about the fashionable political creeds of the day and,
above all, describing to them in the minutest details her own
actions or proposed activities. In addition to this regular flow
of information, she asked them from time to time to publish
or spread on her behalf quite openly certain definite statements, and they did. Moreover, through them she liked to 'tell
Europe' what she thought of it. The mere enumeration of her
regular correspondents is sonorous with great names like a roll
of French drums: Voltaire, Diderot, D'Alembert, the cosmopolitan and ubiquitous Prince de Ligne, Madame Geoffrin,
Madame Bjelke, Frederick the Great of Prussia, the Emperor
Joseph II of Austria, and many others. But the principal correspondent and eighteenth-century equivalent of a personal
press agent was Frederick Melchior Grimm, a German domi-
ciled in Paris, a bore operating on an international scale.
Grimm published a circular or periodical called *Literary Correspondence*, which he sent to a few privileged and influential
subscribers for a handsome fee, and for many years Catherine
was by far his best client; he even spent some time at her court
in St. Petersburg.

Among these correspondents of the Russian Empress there were some who were definitely mercenary, while others acted out of enthusiasm or for political purposes of their own. But it must be said that whereas Catherine's innumerable and truly brilliant letters to them are full of the greatest historical value, and even allowing for their specific character as publicity and deliberate make-believe, are documents of supreme interest, the epistles of her various foreign friends and 'philosophical masters' make pitiful reading. It would be hard to find specimens of more repulsive and mendacious flattery, of more crude and cynical adulation, the bad taste of which is all the more surprising when they are signed by the foremost representatives of independent and enlightened thought of the day. The fascination the 'Minerva' or 'Semiramis' of the North exercised on them at a distance of many thousand miles, especially when she not only dispensed epigrams but rubles as well, and sent expensive fur coats or jeweled snuffboxes as tokens of her admiration, was great indeed. But when, as happened in the case of Diderot, some of these fervent admirers visited Russia and could not help telling Catherine their real impressions, the spell was broken and the mutual glorification was immediately replaced by a temporary chill. These passing estrangements, however, never lasted long, for Catherine knew how to laugh them off, and how to evade critical and searching questions on the rare occasions anybody dared to ask them; it was not for nothing that wit—*esprit*—was the rule of the day. This capacity for getting out of a difficult situation, for making the best of given circumstances, and finding the right compromise to avoid open conflict stood Catherine in good stead throughout her long life. Her dexterous triumph over the many serious obstacles and difficulties of her political career—from the early unpleasantness at the court of the Empress Elizabeth, who very nearly sent this intriguing little German princess back home again, to the internal, diplomatic, and military complications of her own reign—reveals Catherine as a woman of striking intelligence and infinite resource. Where the stormy genius of Peter the Great would not have feared to challenge the elements, daring a frontal attack, fighting, retreating, and finally conquering, Catherine displayed boundless subtlety and preferred to move towards the achievement of her object by a less daring process. To pursue the line of least resistance; not to destroy her enemies but to render them harmless; to follow people and trends rather than to lead them; to negotiate, cajole, and, if need be, bluff or bully; such were the methods that were best suited to her nature, and which enabled her to achieve so many of her successes.

These qualities, which presuppose a cold and calculating character, may sound oddly paradoxical in a woman of Catherine's passionate temperament. Yet the key to the astonishingly wide range of genuine triumphs and achievements of her spectacular reign will be found in precisely that combination of faculties which usually appear to exclude each other: passionate desires and unique self-control in bringing about their realization.

Passion, both mental and physical, was a dominating feature in that woman. The shape and extent favoritism acquired in her time is a sufficient proof of that. This particular counterpart of the royal mistresses famous at Versailles and other courts, was inaugurated in Russia by the Empress Anna Ioannovna in 1730, when she openly made her equerry Johann Ernst Bühren, called Biron, her favorite, and allowed herself to be completely dominated by this ignorant and revolting Courlander. Her female successors on the throne followed the precedent she had established, and favoritism thus became a recognized institution. The Empress Elizabeth even appears to have been married to the Ukrainian village shepherd and choirboy Alexis Rasoumovsky, whom she made a count, and for a time the most influential man in the realm. When many years later Catherine for a while seriously contemplated marrying Grigory Orlov, she sent her chancellor, Count Michael

Vorontsov to Rasoumovsky to find out whether he and Elizabeth really had been married; to induce the old man to let her
peruse all the documents she cunningly suggested raising him
to the title of Imperial Highness as the widowed Prince Consort, if he could show his marriage certificate. But Rasoumovsky refused to talk. Getting up from the fireside, where he had
been sitting when Vorontsov arrived, he took out of a locked
ebony chest a parcel wrapped up in pink silk and containing a
number of papers which he carefully read in complete silence.
Then he kissed the papers, made the sign of the cross, and
threw the parcel into the blazing fire. After that he turned to
Vorontsov and said, visibly moved: 'I have never been anything else but the late Empress' most faithful slave. Now you
can see for yourself I have no documents of any kind.'

Under Catherine the favorite assumed the status of a high
state dignitary. A complicated ritual in connection with his
selection and installation was soon established. The outward
sign of his peculiar office was the rank of 'General Aide-de-
Camp', bestowed on him as soon as the final choice had been
made. He was also made the titular holder of a number of important military commands and was allowed to wear a selection
of uniforms. Special quarters were provided for him in the
palace, immediately below the private rooms of the Empress,
and connected with them by a secret staircase. Upon his installation, the favorite invariably received a handsome inaugural
cash present—usually 100,000 rubles—discreetly placed in a
drawer of his desk. Further monetary presents, estates in the
country, jewels, fur coats, and similar luxuries—as well as Russian and, if possible, foreign orders and decorations or titles and
honors duly followed suit, until one day the favorite received
a final and generous farewell gift on his being superseded by
someone else in that office.

His expenses were defrayed by the state, and he was also
given handsome emoluments, in connection with the various

government positions to which he was almost automatically appointed.

The favorite's private duties included constant personal attendance on the Empress, and indeed he was not allowed to leave the palace without her special permission. Nor was he free to talk too familiarly with any other women at the various court and private entertainments to which he had to escort the Empress. At the same time, he had to be careful about the way he behaved to her in public; she would never stand nor herself betray any signs of the true relationship that existed between them. Her reticence on this point almost amounted to prudishness.

Needless to say, not all her favorites were prepared to abide by that strict discipline which virtually made them prisoners in a golden cage, and many of her romances came to a premature end for that very reason. Yet, with all these qualifications, the office of favorite was definitely a key position in Catherine's Russia. In their struggle for power the various parties and court cliques made the Empress' alcove one of their main objectives, sponsored or fought rival candidates, and even continued the struggle long after the 'vacancy'—if there happened to be one— had been filled.

History knows only two favorites of the Empress Elizabeth: Alexis Rasoumovsky and Ivan Ivanovitch Shouvalov—one of the most learned and interesting men of his day, a patron of the arts and curator of Moscow University. But in the case of Catherine, according to the most reliable calculations, there were twenty-one favorites in forty-four years. From early youth to her last day she was animated by sexual desire which she gratified without restraint or consideration. In the years 1752– 1758—as yet the unhappy wife of the heir to the throne—she had two lovers: Saltykov and Poniatowsky. She was 23–29 years of age then. In her thirties, from 1761–1772, she lived for eleven years with Grigory Orlov. But between 1772 and 1780,

in her forties, she changed no less than nine lovers: Wassiltchikov, Potemkin, Zavadovsky, Zoritch, Korsakov, Stakhiev, Strak-
hov, Levashov, Rantzov. During the next ten years, when she
was 50–60, eight lovers follow each other in rapid succession:
Vissotsky, Mordvinov, Lanskoy, Ermolov, Mamonov, Stoya-
nov, Miloradovitch, and Miklashevsky. Finally, during the last
ten years of her life this passionate sexagenarian was completely
spellbound by her handsome young lover Plato Zoubov.

It would be wrong to attribute this incredible galaxy of lovers
—as long as it is varied in type, age, and station, but Russian
throughout, with the solitary exception of Zoritch, who was a
Serbian, and in her early youth the Pole Poniatowsky—to
sensuality only. Of course, Catherine indulged in a regular
orgy of it, and never more so than in the years 1776–1789—
the period between her liaison with Potemkin and Zoubov's
contemptible domination over this aging woman. But sex was
not the only thing. Catherine, despite her brilliant entourage,
was a lonely woman. These lovers had to replace not only the
husband, but to all intents and purposes the whole family,
since her relations with her son the Tsarevitch Paul were
strained from the very first, and she did not see much of her
three illegitimate children by Orlov. Only with her grandchildren, the youthful Grand Dukes Alexander and Constantine, did she experience any family joys; otherwise her longing
for giving and getting affection had to be satisfied by her
favorites. She was constantly worrying about their happiness,
their mood, their health, and their recreations, and intellectual
pursuits. It is no mere coincidence that most of them were
younger than herself, and when questioned about that she replied that instead of reproaches she deserved praise for 'edu-
cating and polishing capable young men, thus turning them
into useful servants of the fatherland'. This was no mere excuse,
and no doubt she genuinely believed what she said; there was
something of the maternal instinct in all that. Herself a born
statesman, she tried to instruct her lovers, mostly young of-

ficers or court officials, in the art of government, and wanted them to help her in her arduous task of administering the country's affairs.

When the help was not direct, it was indirect: experience revealed that whenever she was happy with her favorite, she did her work best. Lovers' quarrels or the temporary absence of a favorite, on the other hand, interfered with her brain and her temper; on such occasions she found it hard to concentrate and lost much of her habitual verve. Throughout her life she had a truly insatiable desire to love and to be loved. Her attachment to most of her favorites was genuine and deep; she loved them not only passionately but tenderly as well, revealing herself as a sentimental woman rather than a cynical Messalina. In all cases she was wholeheartedly in love, infinitely patient and forebearing, always ready to forgive and forget the faults of her men, who were sometimes anything but nice to her. In love, as indeed in everything else, Catherine was never petty or mean. But she had no luck with her lovers, for those who meant most to her were either forced by circumstances to leave her, like Poniatowsky, or deceived her with other women, like Orlov, Potemkin, and Mamonov, or died, like Lanskoy. She insisted on personally nursing this young man through his fatal illness, and when he died she had a complete nervous breakdown. For many days she was incapable of attending to work or seeing anybody, she was in tears all the time, she had lost her sleep, and the only remedy that finally cured her was the study of philology, in which she buried herself. After plowing her way through the many heavy tomes of the French philologist Court-de-Gébelin's work she conceived the idea of composing a comparative dictionary of all languages. She piled up a regular mountain of dictionaries, filled reams of paper with her preliminary notes, and although the results were of no particular value this effort enabled her to forget her bereavement.

Reading was always one of her main hobbies, especially philosophy and history. This unsuccessful and characteristic attempt of the Empress to compile a universal dictionary was but one of her never-ending literary efforts. A more prolific writer it would be hard to find. She wrote plays and proverbs; she was a hard-working journalist; she tried to give a modern interpretation of the ancient Russian chronicles; she composed her memoirs and drafts for various other books, such as a history of Russia from its origins; as a letter writer she was inexhaustible, carrying on a voluminous private and business correspondence, not only with the foreign celebrities already mentioned, but with all her leading statesmen, soldiers, scholars, diplomats, provincial governors, and innumerable other men and women both inside and outside Russia. At the same time she was an untiring lawmaker, writing out herself not only the actual laws, but arguments in their favor, philosophical commentaries on them, instructions in connection with them, and a mass of other state papers, bearing on or arising from her proposed legislation. She spent her life with a pen in her hand, and it seems hard to conceive how she found time or commanded the necessary energy for this prodigious literary output. Just as she was a passionate lover, she was a passionate writer. But her writings, interesting though they are, and especially for their light on her character, are those of a gifted dilettante. Moreover, despite her frantic efforts, she never succeeded in fully mastering the Russian language, which she spoke with a strong German accent, and wrote with both grammatical and spelling mistakes.

From her early years on the throne of Russia Catherine was animated by a legislative mania, which apart from the occasional interruptions caused by war and other vicissitudes, lasted to the end, producing many new laws and projecting a still greater number. Setting out to make her reign brilliant, and herself the initiator of a liberal era in Russia, she sought inspiration for her reforms in Montesquieu and Beccaria, but upon encountering the opposition of the gentry to any attempted curtailment of their powers over the serfs she promptly

changed her course and turned without struggle into a friend
and protector of the privileged class. After the French Revolution she became a frank reactionary, persecuting the liberalism
and advanced opinion that had developed in the early days of
her 'enlightened' reign. But some of her purely administrative
legislation was extremely good and stood the test of time, till
the reforms of Alexander II nearly a century later put Russia
on an altogether different basis, and finally, in 1861, did away
with the disgraceful serfdom of the peasants.

It is remarkable how hard Catherine worked throughout
her reign, and what a keen interest she took in absolutely everything that came within the wide range of her almost unlimited
interests. Endowed with an iron constitution, a brilliant intellect, an over abundance of temperament and vitality, this ambitious and extravagant woman had qualities that transcended
both her immorality and her unforgivable condonation, or
even encouragement of the worst type of slavery in modern
history.

Her real triumphs must be sought not in her domestic
policy, but in her diplomatic activities. Here she was in her
true element, for this kind of work offered ample gratification to both the passionate and the calculating side of her
character. Nothing suited her better than the intricate game
of diplomacy, with its ever-present element of risk that stimulated her audacity; or its incalculable and kaleidoscopic permu-
tations that appealed to her speculative faculties, while the
world-wide repercussions coupled with a continually growing
fame were of the utmost satisfaction to her boundless vanity.

In directing and often personally conducting Russia's foreign
relations, Catherine displayed her undoubted genius at its best.
From the very start of her diplomatic activities she had to contend with a number of formidable opponents, among whom
France was for many years the most active one. Russia had
emerged after the Seven Years' War as the strongest power in
Europe—a fact that was profoundly resented by the Court of

Versailles. While 'the Bourbons' could not do very much in effectively fighting the young Russian Empire, which they considered as an upstart and an intruder, the brilliant foreign policy of the Duc de Choiseul created a great deal of extremely unpleasant embarrassment for Catherine. In Poland, in Sweden, and in Turkey, France used her declining influence most effectively against Russia. Together with Prussia, France can be said to have been responsible for precipitating or indeed inspiring the first Russo-Turkish War (1768–1774). Throughout that period, but especially during the thirteen years' interval between the first and the second Turkish Wars (1787–1792), Catherine's diplomatic talents were put to a very severe test, and she came out of it with flying colors. Not only did the peace treaties on both occasions give her exactly what she wanted, but during the whole of her long reign she dealt with all the great powers, as well as the minor nations of Europe, in a truly masterly way. Diplomacy was a field in which, undoubtedly, she shone.

While she never attained the standards she had set herself, both as a legislator and as an administrator Catherine must be considered an able and successful monarch, whose very character and qualities fitted her for the particular task she had to accomplish. The essential problem with which she was faced was not that of breaking virgin ground and initiating a number of fundamental processes, as had been the case of Peter the Great, but rather that of completing those which had already reached a considerable degree of development, and giving the right shape to the new form of class monarchy resulting from Russia's rapid political, social, and economic evolution. It was left to her to reap the harvest sown by her predecessors, of whom Peter the Great was by far the most outstanding, and within the narrow framework of that particular task she achieved a greatness that entitled her to consider herself the inheritor of Peter's task. He it was who extended the territory of his empire to the shores of the Baltic.

Catherine, for her part, established Russia's rule over the whole northern shore of the Black Sea and further added a large part of Poland to her dominion.

In her boundless ambition she would have liked to create new trends and new epoch-making factors. That she never did; but she proved herself exceptionally capable of taking the fullest possible advantage of existing ones and, triumphing over all obstacles, brought them to their logical conclusion. Moreover, she had it in her to give her work a quality of glamour that could not fail to impress both contemporaries and historians, and after having succeeded in completing and consolidating Russia's new social order she knew how to give her empire of privileged nobles and exploited serfs an outward brilliance both dazzling and unique. Her success in this task was due not only to the situation in which she found herself, not only to her undoubted gifts, but also to a certain extent to her very faults and shortcomings. She was in every way a typical representative of her epoch. So were most of her collaborators, and it is to her credit that she knew how to surround herself with so many able and competent men.

In foreign policy for twenty years her closest adviser was Count Nikita Panin, one of the most erudite, intelligent, honest, and lazy people of his day. For some reason he never held the position of chancellor, but in practice he acted in that capacity. Bezborodko, Vorontsov, Repnin, Dimitri Galitsin were also prominent in helping her with the direction of her complicated, and on the whole remarkably successful, foreign policy. Among her generals, under whose command the Russian Army covered itself with glory in every corner of Europe and repeatedly triumphed over such superior enemies as the Prussians, Swedes, and Turks, Field Marshal Souvorov deserves the first place. He, of course, ranks with Hannibal, Prince Eugène of Savoy, Napoleon and Wellington as one of the greatest captains history has ever known. But Field Marshal Roumiantsev, Peter Panin, Alexander Galitsin, Bibikov, were outstanding generals and contributed much to Russia's military success. Many more 'Catherinian Eagles' as they were called at the time, distinguished themselves in various walks of public life.

The outstanding figure of her reign, however, was Potemkin. He combined in his striking personality all the qualities displayed by the others, and in most cases excelled them. Potemkin may not have been the military genius that Souvorov was, but in certain respects he possessed more knowledge and was unquestionably a great soldier. As lover, statesman, proconsul, administrator, diplomat, builder, and colonizer, he had no equal. No one ever enjoyed Catherine's confidence in the same degree. And on no other among her many favorites did she bestow the unique honor of a union cemented by a proper religious ceremony. Not the least interesting thing about Potemkin, who had so much in common with the Empress, and who like herself was a typical representative of his age—with all its faults and all its virtues—is the fact that he was Catherine's husband.

2

YOUTH AND EARLY BEGINNINGS

POTEMKIN'S family is supposed to have been of Polish
origin, but it became completely Russified several centuries ago. Of his many kinsmen the outstanding one is
Peter Ivanovitch Potemkin—soldier, court official, and ambassador of Peter the Great's father, Tsar Alexei Michailo-
vitch. This picturesque ancestor is best known for his stubborn-
ness and his eccentricities. Born in 1617, he pursued a successful
military career and was a leading court official when in 1667,
the Tsar decided to send him as Russia's first ambassador to
Spain, and also to France. On various later occasions he was
sent on special missions to western Europe, as, for instance, to
Vienna, London, Copenhagen, and again to Spain and to
France.

On his first visit to Madrid, Peter Ivanovitch Potemkin
insisted that the young Spanish King Charles II should uncover
himself when inquiring after the Tsar's health, and remove his
hat every time the Tsar's name was mentioned. On his way to
Paris he quarreled violently with the customs' collector at
Bayonne, refusing to pay duty on his jewel-embroidered clothes
and jewel-bedecked icons, for all of which he claimed diplomatic immunity. When this was of no avail he called the customs' collector a 'dirty infidel' and 'cursed dog', and threw the
money demanded of him on the floor. But he was pleased when
two miles outside Paris there was a royal carriage awaiting him,

sent by Louis XIV for the ambassador's personal use, together with a mounted escort of twenty men and seven court carriages for the members of Potemkin's mission. The 'Roi-Soleil' met the Russian ambassador and his staff in the most friendly way, treated them with the utmost deference, and not only reimbursed the duty wrongly collected at Bayonne, but presented the Russians with very handsome gifts. Yet, when Potemkin returned to Versailles, he refused to accept the French King's message, and broke off negotiations because a mistake had been made about the Tsar's titles. In Copenhagen, Peter Ivanovitch had to be received by King Christian V in the royal bedchamber, the King lying ill in bed. Thereupon the Tsar's ambassador demanded that another bed should be brought in for him, since he wished to negotiate with the King on terms of absolute equality. This was duly done, and reclining on a bed placed opposite that of the King, Peter Ivanovitch Potemkin conducted his diplomatic conversations. He came to London on November 21, 1681, and had an audience with King Charles II three days later. He stayed in England, however, till February 15, 1682, when he returned to Moscow. He died in 1700, at the age of eighty-three, obstinate, arrogant, and eccentric to the last.

Various other kinsmen and ancestors held minor court positions under different Tsars, but most of them served in the Army. So did Potemkin's father, Alexander Vassilievitch (1675–1746), who retired with the rank of a colonel, and settled down on his small estate of Tchishovo in the province of Smolensk, in western Russia. He was as yet a young man when, together with a neighbor, he built a modest wooden church in the village, a fact that is interesting in view of the strange religious complex of his son.

One day, while traveling, the colonel met an attractive young widow, Daria Vassilievna Skouratova, *née* Kondireva (1704–1780), who was staying with the family of her late husband in the Kiev district. Potemkin immediately married this childless

and penniless widow of the old squire Skouratov, but concealed
from her that he already had a wife. He was fifty at the time,
and his young bride barely twenty years of age. She did not discover that her husband was a bigamist till some months later,
when she was already expecting a baby. Overwrought with pain
and grief, she embarked upon a very extraordinary course: she
went to see Colonel Potemkin's first wife, and throwing herself at her feet asked for help and guidance. She found in her a
kind and sympathetic soul; indeed, this elderly woman, whose
life with Potemkin had been most unhappy, was so moved by
the whole episode, that she decided to retire to a convent, thus
providing an unexpected solution of the difficult and painful
situation.

The firstborn of the union which had started in such tragic
circumstances was a daughter, Maria or Martha, who later
married a nobleman of Baltic origin, by the name of Engelhardt. Then came another daughter called Helena, who became
the wife of a Russian nobleman and court official, Samoilov.
During all this time Colonel Potemkin treated his young wife
in a disgraceful manner, bullying her and torturing her with his
jealousy. The birth of a son only made things worse.

Grigory Alexandrovitch Potemkin was born in the village
steam bathhouse of Tchishovo on September 13, 1739. For
some reason his father conceived the idea that the boy was not
by him, and that Daria Vassilievna had been unfaithful. He
even started divorce proceedings against her, but later withdrew his petition, and in the years that followed three more
daughters were born of this unhappy union: Pelageya, Daria,
and Nadeshda. Potemkin's mother, to whom he bore a great
physical resemblance, appears to have been a clever, handsome
and vivacious woman, who was much admired by her neighbors. The whole district sought her advice with regard to
clothes, food, house parties, and even holy matrimony. But her
own married life was far from happy, and she must have sighed
with relief when the petty and jealous old colonel died in 1746.

· During his father's lifetime little Grigory had a difficult
· childhood. Not only were there the constant disputes between
his parents, but Alexander Vassilievitch was too poor to engage
for his children special tutors and governesses—usually foreign
—and private teachers, as was the custom of the richer Russian
nobility. Grigory's early education was placed in the hands of
old Timothy Krasnopievtsev, deacon at the little church built
by Alexander Vassilievitch. It must be borne in mind that in
olden days in Russia the functions of a deacon, especially in
the village churches, were much nearer those of a beadle than
those of an assistant priest; he also had to chant at divine
service, of course. Deacon Krasnopievtsev was a very ignorant,
but kind, old man. He took a great liking to his little pupil, a
moody and precocious boy, full of mischief. One day, four-
year-old Grisha caught the deacon unawares, and cut off his
small tress of hair, which is the traditional attribute of that
rank of Russian clergy. But the old man did not give the boy
away, and this saved him from a paternal thrashing. Krasnopievtsev possessed a sure means, however, of making his pupil
take notice or even behave himself. The old deacon had a lovely
voice, and he soon discovered the boy's love for music. When
the dull alphabet and grammar lessons were over, the deacon
would sing to Grisha, who listened as if bewitched; and the
threat that there would be no songs stopped many a practical
joke or produced more than usual zeal in the lad's studies.

Many years later, Krasnopievtsev lost his voice and his post
on account of advanced old age, and on hearing that Potemkin
was now a prince and the all-powerful favorite of the mighty
Empress, decided to appeal to Grisha for assistance. He soon
discovered that his former pupil had not forgotten him. The
poor old man walked many hundreds of miles all the way from
Smolensk to St. Petersburg, and there, after endless obstacles,
including the threat of arrest and deportation, he had the good
luck to attract the attention of one of Potemkin's A.D.C.s.
The latter conveyed to Potemkin the long petition composed

by the deacon and written by a regimental scribe, with the unexpected result that the next day a court carriage was sent to
bring Krasnopievtsev to the palace. Potemkin was delighted to
see his old master again, but was much distressed to hear that
the voice he used to love was gone; they talked about his childhood in Tchishovo and his various escapades, the episode of the
deacon's tress being duly remembered. Finally Potemkin invited Krasnopievtsev to stay as his guest at the palace. He gave
instructions that the old man be given a room and food and
clothes, and two days later he sent for him. The deacon, who
had arrived in the capital looking a regular ragamuffin after his
long walk, was now quite clean and even smart; his little ecclesiastical tress well oiled and neatly trimmed. Potemkin
asked the old man what kind of post he would like. Nothing
that required singing, said Krasnopievtsev, explaining once
more that his voice was gone. For a while Potemkin was deep
in thought, and then suddenly remembering something, said:
'Have you seen the monument to Peter the Great that has just
been put up in the Senate Square? We will make you its first
keeper; a room, clothes, and your pay to come out of my personal budget. Are you happy?' The old man was speechless with
joy, and to the end of his days kept that job, blessing Grisha's
name.

Potemkin was five years of age when his father's cousin ·
and the boy's godfather, Grigory Matveyevitch Kislovsky—an
important civil servant in Moscow—took charge of him. From ·
then onwards young 'Grig', as his family called him, lived in
Moscow, and a year later, when his father died, his mother and
five sisters also moved to Moscow. Together with Kislovsky's
son Serge, 'Grig' was sent to the school of one Littken in the
German quarter of the town. The study of languages fascinated ·
him. He learned Greek and Latin, French and German, was
particularly keen on history, literature, and philosophy; but
it was theology that attracted him most. He made friends with ·
some local priest who instructed him in all the details of the

church services. At that time he was not quite sure whether he would go in for a military or an ecclesiastical career, both of which appealed to him. But of one thing he was quite certain: he wanted to be able to command. 'If I become a general,' he would say to the other boys, 'I shall have soldiers under my orders; if I become a bishop, it will be monks.' He also told his schoolmates that he wanted to build some huge houses, and that perhaps one day he would even rise to be a minister of state. Both his ambition and his thirst for knowledge were enormous, for so young a lad. While staying with relations who happened to have a good library, he could scarcely be dragged out of it, and was wont to sleep on the billiard table in the middle of that room with a book under his head instead of a pillow. Nothing pleased him more than a good argument about some scholarly or scientific question, and here again his predilections went towards theology. To take part in, or just listen to, a heated discussion of some abstruse ecclesiastical problem was to him the height of joy, and he was ever more seriously contemplating the church as his career and vocation. He became a student of the recently founded University of Moscow, while still in his early teens, and shone by his brilliance and versatile knowledge. In 1756 he was even awarded the gold medal and the next year was selected as one of the twelve best scholars to visit St. Petersburg and to be presented to the Empress Elizabeth. What followed is typical of the man and his exasperating moodiness. Having just achieved the highest distinction for his academic merits, no sooner was he back in Moscow than he gave up work altogether and neglected his studies to such an extent that finally in 1760 he was expelled from the University—together with Ivan Novikov (who later became a leading freemason and a prominent educationalist)—for 'laziness and truancy'.

Meanwhile, he had already embarked upon a military career, as was customary for young noblemen in those days, having joined in May 1755, a regiment of Horse Guards as a private.

In 1757, he was promoted a corporal, the following year a sergeant major, and in 1759 a *capitaine d'armes*. His promotion as a corporal he owed to Ivan Ivanovitch Shouvalov, the first curator of Moscow University, who recommended him because of his excellent knowledge of Greek, Latin, and theology—a strange ground for advancement in the army. But his military career was more nominal than actual, and even though he began at the bottom of the ladder, he does not appear to have done much active service. From a note written by Potemkin himself it can be seen that in those days his wealth consisted of 430 peasants (or 'souls' as the technical expression then was) living mainly in the Smolensk and the Moscow districts. Thus he must be classed as a member of the poorer category of landed gentry, the possessions of the wealthy landlords extending to many thousands of 'souls' or serfs. His short visit to St. Petersburg with its glimpse of court life had made a strong impression on him. It had fired his imagination, and he was longing to return there for good. But he was practically penniless, and visiting St. Petersburg required cash. He finally borrowed 500 rubles from his friend the Archbishop Ambrosius of Moscow—in later years he often spoke of this loan, but never returned it —and set out to seek his luck in the dazzling imperial capital.

Before long he succeeded in getting the position of orderly to Prince George of Holstein, holding the rank of a subaltern officer with the title of quartermaster. In St. Petersburg he was able to lead the life that was customary for young noblemen serving in the army. Drinking, gambling, and promiscuous love-making took up most of their time, and Potemkin appears to have plunged into this dissolute life with special and boundless zest. Being a poor man, however, and not wishing to be in any way behind his more prosperous friends, he soon piled up very considerable debts. But he moved 'in the best of circles', enjoying great popularity, among the *jeunesse dorée* of the town. Among the leaders of this clique of wild young men, whose very presence made life in St. Petersburg somewhat un-

safe for the respectable citizen, were the five brothers Orlov,
real giants by stature all of them, strikingly handsome, and
wholly lacking in self-control. The Orlovs were the center of a
daring political intrigue which aimed at the deposition of the
unpopular Tsar Peter III from the throne he had only just
ascended and the proclamation of Catherine, his wife, as re-
gent during the minority of the Tsarevitch Paul. This was in
1762, and only the previous year Grigory Grigorievitch Orlov—
the second of the five brothers—had become Catherine's lover,
a position he was to hold for eleven years. The Orlov's plan of a
palace revolution appealed to Potemkin's vivid imagination and
he eagerly joined their conspiracy. On the night preceding the
actual *coup d'état* he took an active part in agitating on Catherine's behalf among the regiments of the Horse Guards at their
various barracks. What he did on the fatal day itself is not
quite clear. Catherine herself, in a famous letter to Stanislas
Poniatowsky, her former lover whom she later made King of
Poland, has described the revolution of June 28, 1762, which
elevated her to her unique position: 'In the Horse Guards,' she
writes, 'an officer named Chitroff aged twenty-two, and a
subaltern of seventeen called Potemkin, directed everything
with discernment, courage, and activity.' There are, however,
so many inexactitudes in this document—Potemkin's age, for
instance, was not seventeen but twenty-three—that Catherine's
own statement, though written scarcely a month after the event,
is not very reliable. Moreover, it contains no details as to what
Potemkin actually did. The generally accepted story, which in
later years Potemkin used to tell himself, is that during the
review of the troops at the Winter Palace in St. Petersburg,
after Catherine's proclamation and prior to her historic march
to Peterhof, he perceived that there was no proper sword knot
on her sword—she was in masculine attire—and promptly
riding up to the Empress, offered her his own. Only with difficulty, apparently, could he force his horse to leave the Empress' side and resume his old place. This little episode would

naturally attract Catherine's attention, and thus bring Potemkin to her notice for the first time.

Writing many years later, Potemkin's nephew Samoilov denied this story, and argued that the sword knot worn by his uncle could not have suited the Empress, being only that of a subaltern and not of a full-fledged officer. It is clear, however, that Potemkin did perform some service or other, and on the day after the revolution he was one of those entrusted with the confidential task of escorting the carriage of the unfortunate 'ex-Emperor' from Oranienbaum to Peterhof. Though he was at Ropsha on July 6, when Peter was murdered by the Orlovs, he does not seem to have been present at the ghastly scene.

Catherine herself drew up the list of rewards to those who carried out the *coup d'état* and put her on the throne. She distributed over a million rubles and many thousands of peasant serfs. Three of the Orlovs head the list, her favorite being endowed with wealth and honors on a particularly lavish scale. There follow a score of others, and Potemkin comes at the very end of the list. It says: 'Quartermaster Potemkin two ranks in his regiment and [something with many noughts is here erased] 10,000 rubles.'

Thus he was indebted to the Empress personally for the gift of a substantial sum of cash and jumping two ranks in the Army. Later, through the same influence, he jumped over the heads of the whole of Russia and a large part of Europe.

There is yet another list, also in Catherine's own hand, with thirty-six names on it. Grigory Orlov comes first and 'Quartermaster Potemkin' last but one. At the coronation he got as one of the closest 'helpers' a silver table set and four hundred 'souls' in the Moscow district. The same year he was sent as a special courier to Stockholm to announce to the Russian minister there the change on the Russian throne. On his return to St. Petersburg he was given the rank of 'Kammerjunker' (a kind of supplementary groom in waiting) and thus officially admitted to court.

Grigory Alexandrovitch Potemkin was then in his twenty-third year. He was exceptionally tall, slim, and brown-haired, with striking features glowing with virility and intelligence. A real Alcibiades, a contemporary called him. He was educated, smart, and daring. His admission to court was mainly due to the fact that the Orlovs appreciated in their former fellow reveler a brilliant conversationalist, who, moreover, possessed the rare gift of giving perfect impersonations of other people, and whose histrionic and musical propensities definitely made him an asset to any society.

Potemkin was presented to the Empress at an intimate *soirée*, and Catherine promptly questioned him as to his 'impersonations'. Could he show her how he did it, she asked. Whereupon Potemkin, without a moment's hesitation, answered her in her own voice, giving an almost uncanny imitation of her idiom, and her strong German accent. Catherine, always fond of a joke, laughed to tears and thoroughly enjoyed Potemkin's impertinence, which might have ended very badly for him. But on this occasion as on many subsequent ones, he showed himself a daring tactician who staked everything on one chance, blindly trusting his own intuition. He thought the Empress would be amused by such unprecedented insolence, and that after that she would not be likely to forget him, and he proved right.

Potemkin was now admitted to Catherine's intimate circle. He was frequently invited to her 'little receptions' at the Hermitage—there were also the 'big', i.e. gala, and 'middle' ones—to which seldom more than twenty people were asked, and at which all ceremony and formalities were banned. Thus the guests were not allowed to stand up in her presence if they happened to be seated when she came in, or if she chose to remain on her feet while talking to somebody who was sitting. The Empress had herself established a code of behavior at these parties and insisted that it should be strictly observed. In the first instance her guests were to be in good spirits;

secondly, they were not allowed to speak badly of anybody, all unpleasant thoughts were to be deposited with the hats and swords in the cloakroom. Even lying or boasting was prohibited. If a guest or she herself happened to break these rules, a fine of ten kopecks had to be paid, and the proceeds thus collected were given to the poor.

After listening to chamber music or some recitation of poetry, it was customary to play parlor games, Catherine herself leading on her guests and infecting them with her gaiety and cheerfulness. The fines imposed on the merry losers included such things as swallowing down a glass of water in one gulp, or reciting an excessively boring poem without yawning, or just sitting down on the floor—not a very convenient performance for a lady of Catherine's corpulence, for instance, but one to which the Empress herself submitted gladly.

In this free and pleasant atmosphere it was possible for young Potemkin to display all his most attractive qualities. He was witty, cultured, artistic, and musical, and Catherine could not help noticing so engaging a personality. On the other hand, he must have been completely dazzled by the Empress. She was infinitely simple and kind, an enchanting hostess; yet the majestic authority of her rank and her brilliant intellect were awe-inspiring. She was so graceful and feminine, yet there was so much of a man in her outlook on things. Her knowledge and her versatility were astounding, and her wealth of ideas could not but impress anyone who came into contact with her, but especially a man of Potemkin's fiery imagination.

Catherine would not have been the woman that she was if she had not soon noticed the fascination she exercised over Potemkin. Besides, he did little to conceal it.

But others at court had noticed it too; and they began to talk. They were whispering a story—whether true or mere gossip, no one could say—that having by chance met the Empress in one of the palace's endless corridors he had fallen to her feet and kissed her hand, stammering words of admiration and devotion, without being reprimanded by Her Majesty for so unusual an effusion.

The Orlovs too, began to take notice. They had heard of all the talk, and they did not like it. Not that Grigory Grigorie-vitch Orlov was jealous. He felt completely secure in his position as the Empress' favorite. After all, had he not placed her on the throne and done away with her impossible husband? Was he not the father of her children, and were not a thousand and one ties binding them for life? She had given him and his brothers great wealth and genuine power. Every morning all those who wished to approach the Empress waited on him in his anteroom. Decisions of the utmost importance to the state rested with him. The only confirmation of his almost unlimited power over Catherine and over Russia which was still lacking was marriage. Again and again he had tried to persuade the Empress to crown their union by a religious ceremony, but she had always postponed her final decision on this rather delicate subject. There was nothing to worry about, however, and Grigory was hopeful of eventually breaking down even Catherine's resistance to holy matrimony.

No, Orlov of whom the Empress had once remarked that he possessed all the virtues of a real Roman, was not jealous. But this Potemkin business was irritating him. The young man was going a bit too fast, and it was time he was taught a lesson. One day, Potemkin was sent for by Grigory Grigorie-vitch, and on entering the favorite's rooms—immediately underneath those of the Empress—he was faced by two of the Orlovs, Grigory and his elder brother, the supergiant Alexis, who began to rate him for his slovenly unsoldierlike demeanor, declaring that life at court had had a rotten effect on him. They would see to it that his military spirit was soon refreshed. Potemkin, realizing the provocation, said nothing. But Grigory Orlov became so abusive that finally Potemkin could not restrain himself, and answered back. A violent altercation followed, and as a climax, the two Orlov's threw themselves on

Potemkin, who resisted as best he could. Chairs and tables were hurled about the room, and mirrors smashed, and only after much pommeling did the Orlov's allow their bleeding victim to withdraw. It was afterwards rumored that this fight was responsible for Potemkin's loss of an eye. He did actually lose one eye about that time, but a far more credible story is that this was due to the wrong treatment by a quack during a subsequent illness, when, having despaired of his medical advisers, Potemkin sent for some village witch doctor who applied most damaging fomentations.

This mishap seems to have upset Potemkin to such an extent that he withdrew from the court, locked himself up, and would see nobody.

For eighteen months' he lived a hermit's life, giving all his time to reading and meditation. While theology once again formed the main subject of his studies, there is little doubt that during this period he greatly added to his general stock of knowledge. The Empress, of course, soon heard about the accident and the moral suffering his physical disfigurement was causing Potemkin. To show her sympathy she canceled several of her 'little' receptions and openly inquired on several occasions about his health, thus deliberately emphasizing her interest in him. This solicitude was promptly reported to Potemkin on whom it had a most soothing and comforting effect. What is most significant, however, is that it was the Empress who took the initiative of bringing Potemkin back to court. And she selected Grigory Orlov of all people to see to it that Potemkin returned to her circle.

3

PREPARATION

CATHERINE'S interest in Potemkin even at this early
stage appeared in the fact that in appointing him at the
close of 1763, as assistant to the Chief Procurator of the
Holy Synod [the supreme body for dealing with church matters
in Tsarist Russia], she wrote out personal instructions for him
with regard to his future work. In her orders to the Synod she
stressed the fact that the cause of this appointment was her
desire that 'by listening to, reading, and personally drawing
up current resolutions . . . he should become trained in being
well versed and skilled in that kind of work'. At the same time
she gave him special promotion in his military career, which he
was continuing to follow simultaneously with his duties of a
civil servant. For a while he was an army paymaster, and then
was put in charge of a tailoring department that made new uniforms for the soldiers. But in 1766, he was given command of a
regular detachment, and in the following year sent to Moscow
as commander of two detachments of his Horse Guards regiment. Catherine's famous 'Grand Commission', which was going to work out a complete legal and social reorganization of the
Russian Empire—it never accomplished anything like it—was
sitting in Moscow at the time, and Potemkin was soon ordered
to take part in its deliberations. In September 1768, he was ap-

pointed a court chamberlain with the title of Excellency, and
detached from the Horse Guards by special command of the
Empress, who required his services at the court. No doubt,
they saw a great deal of each other when he was in St. Petersburg.

At the Grand Commission he now filled the double function
of Trustee or Protector of the Tartars and other alien races belonging to the Russian Empire, being a member of the Civil
and Religious Commission as well. It is highly significant that at
this early stage of his administrative career he was thus given the
chance of working on two of his principal hobbies: religious
matters and oriental aliens.

He seemed to have a special love of, and understanding for
the Asiatic and other non-Russian elements of the empire.
In later days, when he reached supreme power and had something resembling a court of his own, his entourage was very
largely composed of exotic aliens of all kinds. As a disgruntled
contemporary wrote, it was 'enough to have an Asiatic snout
and wear odd clothes and some incredible headgear to pass one-
self off as belonging to the staff of His Serene Highness'.

As to religion, his early love for ecclesiastical controversy
had, if anything, increased. He never missed a chance of discussing the oddest points of religious dogma, and was fond
of inviting representatives of various creeds to fight such problems out in his presence. Russian high church dignitaries and
little country parsons; monks; representatives of the various
sects, like, for instance, the Old Believers; Roman Catholic
prelates and Jewish wonder-rabbis were always welcome as his
guests, and he delighted in both arguing with, and listening to
them. He could not pass a church without going inside it, and
lighting, wherever possible, a candle to his patron saint,
Grigory, or to St. Catherine. With remarkable knowledge of
church matters and genuine, deep, religious fervor, he combined the most childish superstitions. But like so many people,
especially those of prerevolutionary Russia, Potemkin did not

allow this religiousness in any way to interfere with indulgence in all the pleasures of the flesh.

His work at the Grand Commission, and his functions at court, whatever they may have been at the time, do not seem to have given him much satisfaction. The first Turkish War had just begun, and he immediately volunteered for active service. This was in January 1769, and having obtained Catherine's permission to relinquish his duties and join up, he left for the Army. He first served under Prince Galitsin, and then under Count Roumiantsev, to whom the Empress gave him a special introduction.

Roumiantsev, recognizing his obvious ability, and mindful of his high connections, made Potemkin his A.D.C.—a position which offered the ambitious young officer little opportunity for military distinction, but enabled him to keep in close touch with the court and the Empress. He was longing, however, to show Catherine what he could do in the field of battle, and on May 24 he wrote to her from General Prosorovsky's headquarters on the River Dniestr in the following strain: 'Almighty Empress! The unrivaled cares of Your Majesty for our common good have rendered our fatherland dearly beloved to us. The duty of a faithful subject demanded from each of us that we should carry out Your desires, and in that respect I can say that I have behaved exactly in accordance with Your Majesty's wishes. I have looked with gratitude upon Your Majesty's favors to me, entered into the spirit of Your wise decisions and endeavored to be a good citizen. But the high favors with which I have been specially honored, fill me with particular zeal towards the person of Your Majesty. I must serve my Empress and benefactress, and my gratitude will only then find its full expression when I have succeeded in giving my blood for Your Majesty's glory; this opportunity offered itself to me in the present war, and I did not remain idle. Now allow me, Almighty Empress, to place myself at Your feet and beg of You to appoint me to an active post in Prince Prosorovsky's corps in whatever capacity it may please Your Majesty—without placing me forever on the army list but only for the duration of the war. I, Almighty Empress, have always tried to be of use in Your service; my inclination goes towards cavalry, of which I can claim to have a most thorough knowledge; at any rate, as far as the art of war is concerned, I have best learned the rule that zealous service for one's Sovereign and disregard for one's life are the best means of securing success. That, Almighty Empress, is what I have been taught by the study of tactics and by the general to serve under whose orders I am requesting Your Imperial Command. You will venture to see that my zeal in Your service will make up for my lack of aptitude and You will not have to regret Your choice. Almighty Empress, I am Your Majesty's most dutiful slave, Grigory Potemkin.'

This request was duly granted, and before long Potemkin could take part in active fighting. There followed a series of successes. For his bravery at the battle of Khotin he was raised to the rank of major general. He fought gallantly, and won a number of important engagements. These, however, cannot be classed among the really great victories of Roumiantsev's wonderful army during the campaign of 1767–1774, which place that general in the very front rank of Russia's famous war lords. But Potemkin did help Roumiantsev and when Prince Repnin's troops took Ismail, it was Potemkin who entered the burning suburb of Kylia first. For his gallantry he was given the Orders of St. Anne and St. George, and on September 9, 1770, Roumiantsev, who later, on various occasions, was one of his bitterest opponents, was reporting to Catherine:—

'In the descriptions of the past engagements Your Majesty could see to what extent Major General Potemkin took part in them by his zealous deeds. Not knowing what it was to be prompted to action, he himself of his own free will sought every opportunity of participating in the fighting.' This report was read out at the Empress' Council, and made a strong impression on her. Potemkin was also to be dispatched at his own request to St. Petersburg after the ending of hostilities, the report continued, to inform the Empress of the Army's position and general conditions in the front district. There is little reason to doubt the sincerity of Roumiantsev's praise. Potemkin really appears to have been an excellent leader of cavalry in those days, for his other chief, Prince Galitsin, was also reporting that, 'At no time has Russian cavalry acted with such cohesion and bravery as under Major General Potemkin.'

While in St. Petersburg, Potemkin was received in private audience by Catherine, and gossip had it that he had resumed that fervent love-making upon which the Empress had previously looked with strange condescension. She gave him the permission to write personal letters to her, and in the beginning used to send oral replies through her librarian, Petrov, and other confidential members of her staff. But when he left for the Army again, she soon began herself to answer his numerous and ardently devoted letters, and there developed a regular correspondence. 'In the campaign of 1769–1774, the intelligence and advice of Prince Grigory Alexandrovitch Potemkin was of great help. He is infinitely devoted . . .' she subsequently told her private secretary, Chrapovitsky. Among other things, as a farewell instruction, she asked Potemkin to buy her a Turkish horse, and Roumiantsev duly reported that this was done. Back at the front, Potemkin most successfully fought the Turks in one battle after another, and got further promotion from the Empress, who seemed to follow his activities with the greatest of interest. She even mentioned his exploits in one of her regular letters to Voltaire, taking obvious pride in the fact that her troops had crossed the Danube and had 'dispatched the major part of 20,000 Moslems into a better world'.

Potemkin was now besieging, or as Catherine said in a letter, 'exercising himself in throwing bombs into,' the town of Silistria. While he was still engaged in that somewhat arduous pastime, and showing commendable courage and assiduity (in the second Turkish War he was reproached with a lack of both!) he received, from Catherine, the following letter, which was destined soon to open a new era in both their lives. 'Mr. Lieutenant General and Chevalier,' wrote the Empress, 'You are probably so absorbed by gazing at Silistria that you have no time to read letters, and though I do not as yet know whether your bombardment was successful, I am nevertheless convinced that everything you are yourself undertaking must not be ascribed to anything else but your devotion, to me personally and to the beloved fatherland in general, serving which you like. But since on my part I am most anxious to preserve zealous, courageous, intelligent, and skillful people, I beg of you not to expose yourself to danger. After reading this letter you will perhaps ask: for what purpose is it written? To this I will reply: for the purpose that you should have the confirmation of my ideas about you, for I am always your most well-wishing Catherine, December 4, 1773.'

Potemkin did not hesitate in the interpretation to be put on this letter. He saw in it the much longed-for *Invitation à la Valse*, and within a month he was in St. Petersburg.

4

ALCOVE REVOLUTIONS

THE POSITION Potemkin found in the capital was rather peculiar. Catherine's relations with Grigory Orlov had been becoming increasingly strained. Her attempts to train this man, who had many good qualities, to take a really active part in the affairs of state had proved of no avail. Grigory Grigorievitch was hopelessly indolent and undisciplined; moreover, he was not very intelligent, and lacked the ambition of his more impetuous and clever brother Alexis, whose presence invariably acted on him as a temporary stimulant. His position at court had gone to his head, and he had gradually lost all sense of measure and reticence. He had alienated the sympathy of some of the Empress' closest collaborators, and his relations with Panin—the actual, if not the titular, head of the government—were frankly bad. It was Panin who had prevented Catherine's intended marriage with Orlov in 1763, first by threatening resignation, and then—noting Orlov's persistence—vowing that if ever such a thing took place he would immediately set up the Tsarevitch Paul on the throne. For that, needless to say, Orlov had never forgiven Panin. Now that the idea of marriage was definitely out of the question, Orlov began to treat the Empress with less and less respect. Rumors also reached her of his many infidelities, and a number of notorious women were named.

58

Orlov was the father of three of Catherine's children; they had had many happy moments together. Catherine's loyalty, gratitude, and perhaps even fear, still bound her to Grigory Grigorievitch, but her irritation was scarcely concealed. Orlov could not help noticing it; he felt that he was losing ground, yet he could not or would not change his mode of living. Something drastic had to be done if he wished to retain his position. A favorable opportunity soon offered itself. The plague had broken out in Moscow in 1770, and for nearly two years it caused havoc and devastation in the city and surrounding district. The terrified population was getting out of hand, and in a fit of blind rage, the mob had murdered Archbishop Ambrosius (whose loan of 500 rubles had originally enabled young Potemkin to go to St. Petersburg), foolishly attributing to that prelate some share of responsibility for the plague. Assisted at first by his elder brother Alexis, Orlov fought the epidemic, proving both fearless and efficient. In the long run he succeeded in freeing Moscow of this mortal disease, and on his return to St. Petersburg he was duly rewarded by Catherine with new honors and most munificent gifts. On July 5, 1770, Alexis Orlov, who, after a while had left Grigory to fight the plague in Moscow alone, and had taken command of the Russian fleet, won a smashing victory over the Turks at Chesme, in the Ægean Sea. Thus for a time it seemed as if the authority and prestige of the Orlovs were re-established. Grigory Orlov was appointed by the Empress as her Chief Plenipotentiary to negotiate a peace treaty with the Turks. But on the very day of his departure to the Congress of Focsani, early in September 1772, she discovered his liaison with the Princess Galitsin. This was fatal; Catherine's romance with Grigory Orlov was finished.

It did not require much eloquence on the part of her old adviser and principal minister, Count Panin, to persuade the Empress that the young and handsome Guards officer, Alexander Wassiltchikov, would be a most satisfactory successor to the unfaithful Orlov. Within a fortnight of Orlov's departure, Wassiltchikov was installed as Catherine's favorite.

When Grigory Orlov heard what had happened, he was so overwrought with rage, that completely forgetting the Congress and his great responsibilities, he immediately ordered his carriage, and started on a race to St. Petersburg. The suddenness with which he left Focsani and his agitated state of mind, undoubtedly contributed to the failure of this peace conference.

Catherine herself was not less agitated. She was scared of what the Orlovs might do, and sent a messenger to meet Grigory Grigorievitch before he reached St. Petersburg. The ex-favorite, traveling day and night, had covered several thousand miles in no time. He was almost at the gates of the capital when the Empress' messenger met him and delivered formal instructions to the infuriated Orlov to proceed to the neighboring summer palace of Gatchina. There he was to await further orders. The pretext for this unprecedented disgrace was that, like all travelers from the South, he should spend some time in quarantine before entering St. Petersburg.

Meanwhile, all the locks on the doors of Catherine's private apartments, as well as those of the favorite's official quarters below, were being hastily altered, and military guards were posted in the streets of St. Petersburg. Furthermore, Orlov was called upon to resign from his various official high positions. The treatment meted out by Catherine to her former lover was not exactly tender or even considerate.

Grigory Orlov was in a state of rage. He would listen to no one, demanded permission to proceed to St. Petersburg, and claimed a personal interview with the Empress. The court was shaking with fear lest some violent climax to this conflict between two such passionate and peremptory personalities should bring about major complications. A liaison of so many years' duration is not easily broken, even between more humble and less temperamental people. But in the case of Catherine and Orlov there was no knowing what they might do. During a fancy dress ball at the Hermitage, the rumor suddenly spread that Orlov had somehow found his way into the crowd of masked guests. Terrified, Catherine fled to the private apartments of Count Panin, who in his capacity of the Tsarevitch's tutor had rooms in the palace, and hid there until the alarm (false or genuine, no one could say) was over.

She wrote to Orlov demanding the return of the diamond bedecked medallion with her portrait, which she gave him as a special honor, to wear on his heart. He returned the diamonds, but kept her picture. The Empress ordered him to proceed abroad in order to improve his health. Orlov replied that he had never felt better. She tried to placate him a little by making an official announcement that at her request the Austrian Emperor had created Orlov a Prince of the Holy Roman Empire; the papers from Vienna had just arrived. Orlov seized the favorable occasion, and now really did turn up in St. Petersburg. He behaved at court as if nothing of any importance had happened. He spoke freely of his misfortune, and even made jokes about it. To his successor he showed the utmost friendliness and courtesy; in fact, he was pointedly self-possessed and well-behaved. St. Petersburg was all agog with amazement. Courtiers and foreign diplomats went out of their way to win his good graces, since the future course of developments appeared to them to be by no means as certain as they first thought. Would Grigory Orlov regain Catherine's favor? Could he keep his position of influential minister and close adviser even if the basis of his old relationship with the Empress was lost for ever? A precedent was quoted, that of Count Rasoumovsky, the Empress Elizabeth's favorite and presumed morganatic consort, who remained on the best of terms with his royal mistress when their romance was over.

If Grigory Grigorievitch was himself hoping for that sort of solution, he made a great mistake. His match had now arrived upon the field, and before long was to take complete command of it. Following the call of his Empress, Potemkin had exchanged the Army for St. Petersburg. He soon put the puppet that was Wassiltchikov in a corner, and himself in his place.

Thus the years 1772 and 1774, acquire a special significance in the reign of Catherine. In that period the Empress twice changed her favorite. But the implications of what might superficially appear to have been a very private affair were of the utmost political importance. The dismissal of Orlov who was replaced by Wassiltchikov, only to get himself superseded two years later by Potemkin, must be considered as true alcove revolutions, reflecting certain turning points in the struggle for power between the various parties and cliques around Catherine. The change of favorite was on those two occasions eqivalent to a change of Cabinet.

The foreign diplomats at Catherine's court were deeply aware of the significance of all these developments. They dealt with it very fully in their reports to their respective governments. But there is a most curious divergence of opinion between the British and the French official dispatches, both on Catherine's relations with her ex-favorite Orlov, and his successor Wassiltchikov.

In a long dispatch to the Earl of Suffolk, Foreign Secretary, giving a vivid description of the situation, the British minister in St. Petersburg, Robert Gunning, writes:—'The disgrace of Count Orlov, I have great reason to believe, is an essential loss to us. He and his brothers have of late been as anti-Prussian as they were anti-Gallican, and thoroughly devoted to England. And though the abilities of the favorite were not of the first class, he might, from the situation he was placed in, under proper direction, have been made of great use to us, and it is much to be lamented that in the course of the last four years more was not attempted through this channel. [Great Britain at the time was seeking an alliance with Russia, a matter to which we shall return later on.] He and his brothers certainly deserved every mark of the Empress' bounty, as to them she was solely indebted for the crown she wears. The successor that has been given him is perhaps the strongest instance of weakness and the greatest blot on the character of Her Imperial Majesty, and will lessen the high opinion that was generally and in a great measure deservedly entertained of her. When I first came to the knowledge of this resolution, which was very soon after it was formed, I could scarcely give credit to it; neither the person of the man nor his abilities giving the least appearance of probability to the report. The intention at that time was not to have brought him forward, but the opportunity it afforded of overturning the Orlovs was too favorable not to be made use of. Mr. Panin seized it . . . It is said she has already shown some degree of remorse and that her affection for him [Orlov] has returned, which added to the fear of placing too unlimited power in the hands of Panin, gives her an uneasiness that is apparent.'

On the other hand, writing almost at the same date, i.e. in October 1772, the French envoy, Sabatier de Cabre, was reporting to the Court of Versailles: 'The Empress is constantly writing to Wassiltchikov the most passionate letters; she continuously and without limit makes presents to him; and she holds forth about the infidelities, the neglect, and the outrages she has had to suffer from Orlov.'

A few months later Gunning was reporting to Lord Suffolk: 'Several of my late letters will have informed your Lordship of the very great fermentation that has for some time subsisted here, occasioned by the return of Prince Orlov and the intrigues which were the consequence of it. The Empress had scarcely taken the resolution to give him a successor in her favor (which she was over prevailed upon to do by the artful insinuations of his enemies, to which his indiscretion and imprudence greatly contributed) before she repented of the step she had taken, and determined to recall him; the motives to which arose as much perhaps from policy as affection; he and his connections being, in fact, the only people in her empire upon whom she can safely rely. But in executing the plan she had formed, innumerable difficulties presented themselves. Strong declarations of Panin as well as some expressions which fell from the grand duke [Tsarevitch] and his friends, made it require all her address to accomplish this point with safety, which she now thinks she has effected, and that she shall be able in a little time to reconcile (to a certain degree) the grand duke to the Orlov family; which, if she does, will ensure at least for some time both her own and her son's safety. The only victim on this occasion (if there is one), will probably be Panin.'

The French report, written by the observant Chargé d'Affaires Durand, stated practically the opposite. 'The Empress has said to a confidante: "I have obligations towards the Orlov family; I have lavished rewards and honors on them; I will always protect them, and they can be useful to me; but my mind is made up. I have suffered for eleven years, I now wish to live according to my fancy and in complete independence. As to the prince [Orlov] he can do what is agreeable to him; he can travel or stay in the empire, drink, hunt, have mistresses; he can return to his palaces; he is entirely free to use them again. If he behaves well, he will do honor to himself; if he behaves badly, he will cover himself with shame." "He will cover himself with shame," added the person who had just reported to me these words of the Empress. Nature has only made a Russian peasant of him, and that he will remain to the end. He loves as he eats, and is as much satisfied by a Kalmuck or a Finnish woman as by the loveliest lady at court. That is the sort of mariner he is, but he has a natural mind, and is not a bad fellow.'

As far as Catherine herself was concerned, her break with Grigory Orlov had occurred at a crucial political moment. That very year of 1772, her son, the Tsarevitch Paul, came of age, and thus the question of her own position was being automatically raised. Had she any right to remain on the throne, which she had after all usurped? Was not her son the legitimate heir? Paul's accession had always been a nightmare to her. He was twenty-one now. She knew full well that a powerful clique at court desired to seize the occasion to take action on his behalf. No less a person than Count Panin, her chief political adviser and the Tsarevitch's tutor, was at the head of this group. It was of the utmost importance to Catherine that any sort of demonstration by Panin and his followers should be avoided. She therefore had to find a way of relieving the tension that existed between herself and the Tsarevitch's adherents. Her breach with the Orlovs offered her the opportunity of solving this overwhelming political and personal difficulty; the new favorite was taken on Panin's recommendation, and belonged to the opposition clan.

Young Wassiltchikov was a handsome fellow, yet utterly insignificant. He had a pleasant disposition, but he was a hopeless bore. Catherine never had any regard for him and treated him just as a pretty doll. He served the double purpose of helping her to forget her *chagrin d'amour* over Orlov's unfaithfulness, while at the same time the bestowal on him of her favor was a sop to Panin, whose hopes it fired. The insignificance of Wassiltchikov, together with the decline of the Orlovs, whom he had always so hated, seemed likely to put the old statesman in absolute control and sole charge. But his hope was never realized. Catherine had not the slightest intention of surrendering her power, especially to Panin, whom she neither liked nor trusted, and whom she had never forgiven for his plain language when he interfered with her alleged matrimonial intentions. Moreover, Wassiltchikov was too insipid to be of any use even as a mere instrument in Panin's hands, and his reign as favorite was clearly not to be a long one.

Catherine felt a growing vacuum around her. Yet she was faced with a number of difficulties that were assuming dangerous proportions. The peace negotiations with Turkey, which Orlov had so badly conducted and finally dropped at Focsani, had failed. The war was dragging on. At the same time, Pougatchev's Revolt, about which she had at first written so many witty epigrams to her foreign friends, was snowballing itself into a regular 'Jacquerie'. Everywhere peasants were rising in response to the appeal of this Cossack bandit who had had the impudence to proclaim himself Peter III, Emperor of all the Russians, miraculously saved from his would-be assassins.

The Ural mountains and the Volga seemed to be in his hands, and he was rapidly moving from one district to another, causing Catherine and her government the greatest embarrassment.

With all this and so many other problems on her hands, she felt the need of a strong and reliable man who would give her good advice, and would help her to shoulder her heavy responsibilities. She wanted somebody to whom she could entrust both her heart and the well-being of the Russian Empire.

Orlov, who on his return from Focsani had made such a pathetic effort to regain his old position, was no good for that sort of thing. But she knew somebody else who was.

At first he had attracted her curiosity, then her interest, and finally her admiration. Moreover, she was by now herself deeply in love with this one-eyed giant—'Cyclops' they called him at court—who had distinguished himself in practically everything he had done. A gallant soldier, a wise counselor, a devoted subject, and an ardent suitor, who had had the courage not to conceal his feelings for her—where else could she find such a rare combination of the very qualities she wanted? It was clear to Catherine that no one possessed in a higher degree the gifts that make both a first-rate statesman and a fascinating lover than General Grigory Alexandrovitch Potemkin.

5

FAVORITE PRESUMPTIVE

WHEN NEWS of Orlov's fall had reached Potemkin, he, too, had felt that his hour was approaching. But when the Empress summoned him to St. Petersburg—first in spontaneously expressing her appreciation, and then actually inviting him to the capital—and he found on his arrival the ridiculous Wassiltchikov firmly entrenched in the favorite's apartments, he was rather annoyed. But on thinking it over he rightly interpreted this rapid appointment of a successor to Orlov, whose position during all these years had appeared impregnable, not merely as a political move on the Empress' part, but also as an indication that the deserted Catherine was not prepared to wear a 'widow's veil' any length of time. There was obviously scope for other possibilities.

When Potemkin arrived in St. Petersburg, where he put up at the house of his brother-in-law, Samoilov, the Empress happened to be at Tsarskoe Selo. It was January 1774. For a while, Potemkin studied the position and collected what information and what gossip he could. Then he asked for a private audience, which the Empress was pleased to grant. He journeyed to Tsarskoe Selo, which is twenty miles from St. Petersburg, and had a long talk with Catherine. In that conversation they must have agreed on their future course of action, for the subsequent developments scarcely look like an improvisation. Indeed, the comedy enacted by Catherine and Potemkin during the weeks that followed shows to what an extraordinary degree the two matched each other. With finesse and patience they played their little game, the result of which must have been a foregone conclusion from the start. Potemkin was now something like the 'heir presumptive' to the favorite's position. He continually appeared at court, seemed in a radiant mood, and dazzled everybody with his wit and interesting conversation. He made the Empress laugh to tears, and again and again Catherine writes to her various correspondents—Russian and foreign—that no one amuses her so much as General Potemkin, who only recently returned from the Army.

The court saw in Potemkin the coming man. One day he met Grigory Orlov descending the palace staircase just as he was about to go up. 'Any news at court?' asked Potemkin, and Orlov answered in a frigid tone: 'Nothing in particular, except that you are going up and I am coming down.'

It was impossible for young Wassiltchikov to compete with so entertaining a person as Potemkin, whose stock of stories of every kind and knowledge of matters military, religious, and governmental, appeared quite inexhaustible. Moreover, he was a poet, and the Empress, who was herself a prolific author, but quite incapable of writing verse, was most impressed by the sonorous rhymes he composed in her honor.

Yet for a while Wassiltchikov remained favorite. Catherine was apprehensive lest too rapid a change of lover should make a bad impression at St. Petersburg, and at foreign courts. She was afraid of upsetting Panin and his clique by dropping their man, but most of all she was, as ever, mindful of foreign opinion. Throughout her reign she was always concerned about what people abroad, but especially the foreign rulers and courts, would think of her, and she frequently acted solely with that consideration in mind.

Suddenly, Potemkin altered his tactics. Was that also prearranged, or did he feel genuinely depressed by Catherine's procrastination since his arrival? Certain it is that he now became dull and almost monosyllabic, hardly ever came to court, and finally disappeared altogether. Catherine, who was missing him, inquired the cause of this strange behavior, and got the surprising reply that General Potemkin was suffering from a very strong, and most unhappy love-sickness, because his love for a certain lady was not reciprocated. He was in absolute despair, and contemplated shortly retiring to a monastery. He was almost insane with grief and jealousy, but still had understanding enough to realize that he must avoid at any price ever seeing again the object of his unrequited passion. Catherine knew exactly what all this meant. 'I do not understand,' she said, 'what has reduced him to such despair since I have never said anything unfavorable about him. Indeed, I thought my friendliness must have made him realize that his fervor was not displeasing to me.' These words were naturally reported to Potemkin, together with the assurance that Wassiltchikov's favor was rapidly coming to an end.

But now that Grigory Alexandrovitch was finally certain of his triumph, he indulged in one of his typical eccentricities. He did not reappear at court on hearing such favorable news. On the contrary, this time he really withdrew to the Monastery of St. Alexander Nevsky, on the outskirts of St. Petersburg. Visitors found him in a state of such melancholy, alternating with wild excitement, that genuine fears were entertained that he had lost his reason.

This, too, of course, was reported to Catherine. But she could see through the game completely, this game in which love and power were the stakes, and which was not merely a good entertainment, but also deadly serious. Things had taken such a shape that a final decision was now necessary. Panin, too, could see through the situation, and fully understood the seriousness of what was going on. The eventuality of a change of favorite was too close at hand, and its importance both for the court and the whole empire too obvious to allow any further suspense.

The old minister asked Her Majesty for an audience. This being granted, he told her point-blank that the merits and capabilities of General Potemkin were recognized by everybody. But ample rewards had been lavished on him: rapid promotion in the Army, the orders of St. George and St. Anne, the Empress's own benevolent attitude at court. In other words, nothing was due to the gentleman in question; he had had more than his share. But in case further advancement were contemplated, it would be necessary to bear in mind certain aspects of General Potemkin's character. On this point, said Panin, with much emphasis, opinion varied a very great deal. 'The state and Yourself, Madam,' he went on, 'will soon be made to feel the ambition, the pride, and the eccentricities of this man. I fear that Your choice will cause You much unpleasantness and is not likely to meet with the approval either of Your subjects or of Europe.'

Catherine's reply to her old adviser was that the raising of this issue was premature. Besides, General Potemkin's capabilities were such that he could be usefully employed both as a soldier and a diplomat. Clever, educated, and able men were, after all, not so numerous in Russia that she could afford to allow this one to bury himself in a monastery. She, for one, would therefore do her utmost to prevent General Potemkin from taking Holy Orders, and would endeavor to place him once again in a position to serve herself and the state. She refrained from telling Panin that with all her heart, with all the passion that was now consuming her brain and her body, she was longing for this strange man, the only one who had dared to woo her (all the others, both before and after him, she 'distinguished' herself), and who, just as she was ready for him, seemed to seek an escape, or else had the infernal impudence to play-act.

This monastery business had certainly not been prearranged in their momentous talk in Tsarskoe Selo. And although Potemkin was admittedly a first-rate comedian, his almost abnormal penchant towards religion was also well known to the Empress. She could take no risks. Perhaps he really did mean to become a monk. Something had to be done about it. She dispatched her most confidential lady in waiting, the Countess Bruce, to the St. Alexander Nevsky Monastery to see Potemkin and explain to him that he could rely on the Empress' greatest favors if he chose to come back. Greatest favors— surely Potemkin would be shrewd enough to understand what that meant.

But the task of Countess Bruce was not made easy by Potemkin, who did not even receive her straight away. On her arrival at the monastery, he sent a message asking her to wait, since for the moment he was engaged in prayer. In monastic garb he walked in the traditional procession with the monks, and took part in divine service; then he remained for a long time prostrated before the holy icon of St. Catherine, murmuring prayers with much fervor. Finally he got up, made several times the sign of the cross, and went to hear Catherine's envoy.

The message Countess Bruce conveyed to him sounded convincing. Moreover, the fact that it was she whom Catherine had selected for this delicate negotiation showed that the Empress meant business.

For the faithful Countess Bruce, like her successor, Mademoiselle Protassov, filled a number of remarkable functions, not the least of which was the intimate and highly confidential task of 'trying out' the prospective favorite. This 'trying out' ultimately cost the Countess her position, for one day, having found one of Catherine's later favorites much to her satisfaction, she ventured to repeat the 'test'. Unhappily she was discovered *in flagrante delicto* by the irate Empress, who dismissed her on the spot. The 'test' was only allowed before a favorite was chosen, and not after.

The two ladies in waiting, Countess Bruce and Mademoiselle Protassov, are described under the joint name of 'Turfana' in the famous parody on Catherine the Great's court written by the Italian poet Giambattista Casti, and called 'Il Poema Tartaro'. He dubs the collective 'Turfana' 'amazzone di Venere e d'Amore', and after devoting some very pointed lines to an interview between 'Turfana' and Tomaso, a candidate for the position of favorite to the almighty 'Toleicona' (i.e. Catherine), he makes 'Turfana' say: 'I usually first test the candidate for the favor in order to find out whether he combines with his appearance also general merit. And no one gets this position unless he has been beforehand tried and approved by me.'

Byron, in his *Don Juan*, actually names Mademoiselle Protassov, and refers to her by the term Catherine's court had invented for her and her predecessor's functions: 'L'éprouveuse.' He calls it a 'mystic office'.

It is not likely that Countess Bruce had to 'try out' Potemkin. But her visit to the monastery was in itself a sufficient indication of the character of her mission. Grigory Alexandrovitch allowed himself to be persuaded. He shed his monastic clothes, shaved off the beard he had grown, and returned to St. Petersburg with the triumphant Countess. His next move was by obvious pre-arrangement with the Empress. He wrote to Catherine the following letter: 'Almighty Empress! I have determined my life to be spent in Your service and have not spared it wherever there has been a chance of glorifying Your name. This I considered my plain duty, never thinking of my own station, and if I saw that my zeal corresponded to Your Majesty's wishes I deemed myself already rewarded. Finding myself, almost from the time I joined the Army, at the head of troops detached from the main forces and close to the enemy, I did not fail to cause the latter every possible damage: this can be warranted by the commander in chief and by the Turks themselves. I am by no means actuated by envy of those who younger than myself have yet received more signs of the imperial favor, but the only thing that worries me is whether in Your Majesty's thoughts I am not considered as less worthy than the others? Being tortured by this, I have taken the liberty of begging Your Majesty, placing myself at Your Majesty's holy feet, to relieve me of my doubts through appointing me—in case my services are considered worthy of Your pleasure and Your imperial favor towards me is undiminished—as a personal adjutant general of Your Imperial Majesty. This cannot offend anybody, but I will consider it the height of my happiness, all the more so since being under Your Majesty's special protection, I will have the honor of receiving Your wise orders and in studying them shall become more capable of serving Your Imperial Majesty and the fatherland.'

As he wrote this he smiled, and could not help thinking of an Italian author he had read in the time of his long seclusion that followed the loss of his eye. Machiavelli was the man's name, and Potemkin had been much struck by the book even then. And now he himself had written: 'This cannot offend anybody.' The mere thought of how Panin and Wassiltchikov and the Orlovs and all the others at court would take his appointment made him laugh with malicious joy. The rank of personal adjutant general was the outward sign and official status of Catherine's favorites. And he knew that not only would his strange application for so high a distinction now be granted, but also how strongly the whole court would resent it.

Potemkin's letter was dated February 27, 1774. The Empress's reply came the very next day—an amazing effort in the general atmosphere of dilatoriness which reigned at the court and in government circles. This is what Catherine answered:—

'Mr. Lieutenant General: Your letter was handed to me this morning by Mr. Strekalov, and I found your request so moderate in the exposition of your services, rendered both to myself and to the fatherland, that I have ordered a deed to be prepared appointing you an adjutant general. I confess that I am particularly pleased that your confidence in me is such that you addressed your request in a direct letter to me and did not seek indirect ways. I am your ever well-wishing Catherine.'

Everything now proceeded with astounding speed. On March 1, Catherine was writing to General Bibikov that she had appointed Potemkin her personal adjutant general, 'and as he thinks that you being fond of him will rejoice at this news I am letting you know. Moreover, it seems to me that considering his devotion and services to me I have not done much for him, but his joy it is hard to describe; and I, looking at him, feel glad that I see near me at least one person who is entirely happy.'

A few days later she wrote to the same correspondent: 'Everybody in town is backing your friend Potemkin for a lieutenant colonelcy of the Preobrashensky regiment [she herself was colonel of it]. The whole town often lies, but this time I will not leave them as liars, and probably it will be true.' It *was* true; in fact, Potemkin was made a lieutenant colonel of her regiment immediately. Other honors were soon to follow.

Sir Robert Gunning, as he now was, had been promptly informed, and within three days of the change at the palace, i.e. on March 4, 1774, he reported to the Earl of Suffolk:—

'A new scene has just opened here, which in my opinion is likely to merit more attention than any that has presented itself since the beginning of this reign. Mr. Wassiltchikov, the favorite, whose understanding was too limited to admit of his having any influence in affairs, or sharing his mistress's confidence, is now succeeded by a man who bids fair to possessing them both, in the most supreme degree. When I acquaint Your Lordship that the Empress' choice is equally disapproved of by the great duke's party and the Orlovs, who both appeared satisfied with the state in which things had for some time been, you will not wonder that it should occasion, as it has done, a very general surprise, and even consternation, and if I did not myself know this country, by reasoning from causes to the effects, I should apprehend the most fatal consequences from it, but as any conclusion drawn from so recent an event may be fallacious, and perhaps appear presumptuous, I shall confine myself, for the present, to acquainting Your Lordship with the name and the character of the person who has been thus precipitately drawn forth and placed in the conspicuous light he now appears in; this is General Potemkin who arrived here about a month ago from the Army, where he has been during the whole course of the war and where I am told he was universally detested. His figure is gigantic and disproportioned, and his countenance very far from engaging. From the character I have had of him he appears to have a great knowledge of mankind, and more of the discriminating faculty than his countrymen in general possess, and as much address for intrigue and suppleness in his station as any of them; and though the profligacy of his manner is notorious, he is the only one who has formed connections with the clergy. With these qualifications, and from the known inactivity of those with whom he may have to contend, he may naturally flatter himself with the hopes of rising to that height which his boundless ambition aspires to.' The last few lines are a reference to Panin, whose statecraft was much impaired by his hatred of the least effort. 'Wait and see' would have been his slogan if the expression had existed at the time.

It is to the credit of the British envoy at the Court of Russia that he grasped at so early a stage the full significance of the alcove revolution of March 1774. From then onward reference to Potemkin is made in practically every dispatch of importance sent by Sir Robert Gunning to the Foreign Office, and not only by him, but by all his successors during the next seventeen years, i.e. up to the time of Potemkin's death.

Having appointed her new adjutant general, Catherine hastened to dismiss the boring Wassiltchikov, generously endowing the young man with money and other gifts and favors. Potemkin was in official attendance on Her Majesty on the very day after his nomination, and showed such zeal that both Russians and foreigners in St. Petersburg were completely flabbergasted. They could talk of nothing else, and their correspondence was full of it. On March 7, Panin's brother, the veteran generalissimo Peter Ivanovitch Panin, wrote to a friend: 'I fancy that this new actor will perform his part with great vitality, and cause many changes, if only he establishes himself firmly.' Madame Sievers, wife of the Governor of Novgorod (he later became one of Potemkin's fiercest enemies), wrote to her husband from St. Petersburg: 'The new adjutant general is in constant attendance and takes the place of all the others . . . they say he is very modest and pleasant.' Potemkin's old fellow-student at Moscow University, the brilliant satirist Von-Visin, who was not only a great playwright but also an adroit opportunistic civil servant, wrote to a friend in Budapest: 'The only thing of interest at the court here is that Mr. Chamberlain Wassiltchikov has been expelled from the palace and Lieutenant General Potemkin has been made adjutant general and lieutenant colonel of the Probrashensky Regiment. *Sapienti sat.*' And Madame Roumiantsev, wife of the field marshal, wrote to her husband: 'Wassiltchikov moved out of the palace yesterday; the thing to do now, my sweet, is to address yourself to Potemkin.'

The question of what Potemkin was actually going to do, how he was going to use the power he had now acquired, and what his relations with the various parties and cliques at the court, and especially with people like Panin or the Orlovs, would be, was naturally exercising everybody's mind.

On March 7, barely a week after Potemkin's appointment, Gunning reported to the Earl of Suffolk: 'There is no forming any judgment with respect to what effects the late change may be attended with, or what influence it may have upon affairs. The new favorite, conscious, I suppose, that the situation cannot be agreeable to the Orlovs, seems to pay his court most assiduously to Panin, hoping by that means to render the great duke less averse to his advancement, since which period the Empress, it is said, has doubled her attention to His Imperial Highness and shows unusual marks of distinction to Mr. Panin, who seems perfectly well pleased with the whole of this transaction, as is natural for him to be with everything that contributes to diminish the power of the Orlovs. I question whether Count Zachary Tchernichev [until then supreme master of the College of War, an influential soldier and courtier] will be equally satisfied at seeing a person so much his superior in art and address placed in such a station.'

Nearly a month elapsed, however, before Potemkin took up residence at the favorite's official quarters situated immediately below the private rooms of the Empress, and connected with them by a winding staircase. True to the pattern of Versailles, this was covered with a green carpet, like the staircase leading from the apartments of Louis XV to those of La Dubarry. When Potemkin was not in attendance or dashing about the streets of the capital in a carriage drawn by six horses, he was staying at the house of one of Catherine's most devoted court officials, Senator Elaghin. Meanwhile, artists and decorators were busy preparing his future residence. But on April 10, Madame Sievers could write to her husband: 'The new adjutant general's rooms are ready and he has moved in; they say that his quarters are magnificent.'

6

THE LOVERS

CATHERINE was forty-four years of age when Potemkin became her lover. He was ten years younger than the Empress. Both had had ample experience, and both were anything but *blasé*. It is true that neither Catherine's digestion nor her circulation were as good as formerly, and she was ever more inclining towards that plumpness which in later years became so prominent. But her zest for life, her mental and physical alertness, her capacity for continually renewing herself were still quite astounding. Many a young girl might have envied not only the freshness of her complexion, but also her sentimental romanticism and her fiery temperament.

From the very outset Potemkin could see that his passion for this woman, which had now lasted for a good many years, was not only reciprocated completely, but that Catherine's love for him was as stormy in character as his own feeling for her. Having achieved his desire, he might have settled down to the comfortable and luxurious life of the Empress's favorite and merely sought to accumulate what benefits such a position offered. But if to the ordinary lover possession means the end of romance, to a superior one it means only the beginning of it, and all the preliminaries merely appear as so much time wasted. Moreover, this ambitious man had not waited for twelve long years, to become just a glorified playboy ministering to the very private pleasures of Her Majesty of all the Russias. His hopes and longings had been for a life full of action and responsibility, in the service of Russia and of the woman whom he had not only loved, but who also personified to him his beloved country. To work for her was to work for Russia, her glory was Russia's glory. To dominate Catherine meant to dominate the whole Russian Empire.

Potemkin was determined to serve and to dominate. Insatiable as he was, and never knowing measure in anything, the mere fact of becoming Catherine's lover was not in itself a realization of his dreams and ambitions. He felt that he had only reached a useful steppingstone; that was all. Physical possession was not enough; dauntlessly he set out on the further conquest of his Empress, and through her of that vast and complicated body called Russia, over which hitherto God and she had alone exercised any real power.

To achieve this object two things were essential: first, a mental or spiritual ascendancy over Catherine, in addition to the physical sway already won; secondly, the elimination of his innumerable rivals both in the political and personal sphere.

In the art of winning complete domination over his mistress, he excelled beyond measure from the very first day. He was not merely passionate, but witty, courteous, and entertaining. His stories and even his practical jokes amused her intensely. When the gigantic 'Cyclops' proceeded to appropriate for his own use the little woolen bedcover she was knitting for 'Thomas', her inseparable lapdog, she laughed so much that she almost had a fit. In a letter to Grimm she says: 'I have parted from a certain excellent but very boring citizen [Wassiltchikov], who was immediately replaced, I do not myself quite know how, by one of the greatest, most bizarre, and most entertaining eccentrics of this iron age.' Potemkin completely captivated her imagination. She could scarcely think, or speak, or write of anything else. She even mentions in a letter that General Potemkin has introduced in her apartment a particularly comfortable large

Turkish divan on which twelve people could easily go through the craziest contortions without interfering with each other, and recommends it to a friend. And again she writes to Grimm about Potemkin: 'Oh, what a marvelous head this man has got! he has taken a greater part than anybody in this peace (Kuchuk-Kainardje, ending the Turkish War) and this good head is as amusing as the very devil.'

His versatility appealed to her so; this 'bizarre and entertaining' man, this shrewd adviser with a 'marvelous head', was not only an ardent lover, but a romantic one at that. Though herself utterly devoid of any musical sense, Catherine simply adored Potemkin's way of singing to her. And he had made some progress since those early days when Deacon Krasnopievtsev was his first music master in the ancestral village of Tchishovo. She liked him to recite his poems, too, and was invariably moved when he sang to her some sentimental verses he had written when he first fell in love with her. The Russian text begins with the words: 'Kak skoro ya tebya vidal,' and translated into English it is something like this: 'As soon as I beheld thee, I thought of thee alone; thy lovely eyes captivated me, yet I trembled to say I loved. To thee love subjects every heart, and enchains them with the same flowers. But, oh Heavens! what torment to love one to whom I dare not declare it! One who can never be mine! Cruel gods! Why have you given her such charms? or why did you exalt her so high? Why did you destine me to love her, and her alone? her whose sacred name will never pass my lips, whose charming image will never quit my heart!' There follows more in a similar strain, and it gave Catherine much pleasure.

She was quite bewitched by Potemkin, and genuinely thought him not only the greatest genius but also the handsomest man she had ever met. Love completely blinded her to his obvious physical defects, and he had many, quite apart from the facial disfigurement caused by the loss of his left eye.

At the age of thirty-four, Potemkin was by no means the 'Alcibiades' he may have been when he first came to St. Petersburg. He had put on a lot of weight, and his enormous body, once so slim and upright, was now quite shapeless. His unlovely habit of biting his nails had by now become an obsession, making his fingers a revolting sight. He had a delicate, sensitive, and sensual mouth, with marvelously white teeth, but the large and bumpy nose was rather ugly. The empty cavity of the left eye gave the face of this 'Cyclops' a strange expression. Moreover, his head was somewhat pear-shaped, being narrower at the top than at the bottom. Few impartial observers would have disagreed with Gunning's statement that Potemkin was now 'gigantic and disproportioned, and his countenance very far from engaging'.

With all that, it is significant that not only the Empress, but later the various other women who loved him, were invariably fascinated by his physique, and again and again stressed the attraction of his good looks.

Potemkin was not an easy lover, and much though Catherine was enjoying her association with him, there was a stormy side to it, which she found definitely painful. He was madly jealous of her past. Indeed, there was something to be jealous about. Apart from the husband who had been forced on her and whom she rightly loathed, she had had four lovers before Potemkin came on the scene. The Grand Duke Peter Theodorovitch, whom she married at the tender age of sixteen, was a sadistic half-wit, and her life with this degenerate German prince whom only a chance had made heir to the throne of his aunt, the Empress Elizabeth of Russia, was most miserable. After eight years of conjugal unhappiness she finally took a lover, an insignificant young courtier, named Serge Saltykov. He was exceedingly handsome, an accustomed 'lady-killer', and a snob to whom the principal attraction of his new affair was the royal quality of Catherine; after all, a grand duchess and heiress to the throne is not an ordinary adventure. Apart from awaking her sensuality and initiating her in the art of love, Serge Salty-kov cannot be said to have left a very strong impression on Catherine. Whether he was the father of the Tsarevitch Paul is not quite certain, since both physically and mentally Paul bore a striking resemblance to Peter III.

Her second lover was of a very different kind. Stanislas Poniatowsky, a young Polish nobleman, came to Russia as private secretary to the British ambassador, Hanbury Williams. He was delicate, cultured, distinguished-looking, with exquisite manners and a pleasant disposition. In Paris he had moved in the best literary salons, and himself had pronounced artistic inclinations. He was no trivial seducer, like his predecessor, and Catherine was actually the first woman in his life. His love for her was deep and genuine. On her side it was a real explosion of passion. She adored Poniatowsky and was heartbroken when in 1758, he had to leave Russia. She remained infinitely attached to this tender lover who had taught her the more noble side of romance, and six years later, when an opportunity presented itself, she made him King of Poland. There followed the long liaison with Grigory Orlov, about which Gunning had written, among other things: 'Most people believe that a private marriage took place before the coronation, and that it was a public declaration of that and not a new ceremony she solicited Mr. Panin to agree to.'

Finally, there came young Wassiltchikov, who was merely the equivalent of a 'kept woman' as he himself put it, and cannot be said to have affected Catherine in any way.

This long list of predecessors enraged Potemkin, who accused the Empress of having had no less than fifteen lovers. She tried to placate him by drawing up for his benefit a most peculiar document, entitled 'A sincere confession'. In this document she admits her four lovers, and endeavors to explain each one. Then she describes how he, Potemkin, whom throughout the 'sincere confession' she calls her 'Hero' with a capital 'H') came and eclipsed everybody else. 'Well, Mr.

Hero,' she continues, 'after this confession may I hope for your forgiveness of my sins? You must see that it was not fifteen but one-third of that. The first one out of compulsion, and the fourth out of despair, as I do not think you can put them down to levity. And the three others, if you really go into it, God knows, [were] not due to any debauchery for which I have no inclination. If in my youth I had been given a husband whom I could love I would have remained eternally faithful to him. The trouble is only that my heart cannot be content even for an hour without love.' She does not know, she adds, whether this is a vice or a virtue, but to emphasize her monogamous inclinations she states that as far as she is concerned Orlov would have remained with her forever if he had not himself thrown her over.

Catherine's 'Confession', however, had little effect on Potemkin, and his jealousy remained quite insane. Not only did the past torture him and send him into fits of rage or depression, but even now when he possessed and dominated this woman completely, he took umbrage at her smallest attention to anybody else. One night at the theater, when she ventured to address a few friendly remarks to Orlov, he got up and demonstratively left the imperial box. Hardly a day passed without a scene, and it is significant that it was usually Potemkin who did the quarreling and the sulking, whereas it was the Empress who invariably had to take the first step towards reconciliation.

He sometimes doubted the durability of her feelings, and worried her and himself with questions and reproaches. She had to soothe, flatter, cajole him like a little child. 'No, my little Grisha,' she writes, 'it is impossible for me to change as far as you are concerned. You must be fair to yourself: can one love anybody after having known you? I think there is not a man in the world who could equal you. All the more so, since my heart is constant by nature and I will say even more: generally speaking, I do not like change. When you know me better you will respect me, for I assure you I am respectable. I am most truthful, I love truth, I hate changes, I suffered horribly during two years, I burned my fingers, I will not return to that, I am perfectly all right; my heart, my spirit, my vanity are equally pleased with you, what is there better that I could wish? I am perfectly pleased. If you continue to let your spirit be alarmed by this kind of gossip, do you know what I will do? I will lock myself up in my room and I will see none but you: I know when it is necessary to take extreme decisions: and I love you beyond myself.'

Not only his jealousy of Catherine's rich amorous past or his general moodiness, but also his extraordinary sensitiveness as to his position, gave the lovers ample cause for quarreling. He was quite incapable of being treated merely as the Empress's apanage, and the merest suspicion of any such attitude on her or on anybody else's part never failed to infuriate him. A document relating to one of these early quarrels deserves special attention, for it is a kind of contract drawn up between the two lovers. It is written by Potemkin, with Catherine's replies point by point penned by her in the margin.

In Potemkin's Hand.	*In Catherine's Hand.*
Allow me, dear Soul, that I should tell you in the last resort how I think that our quarrel will end. Do not be surprised that	The sooner the better.
I should feel worried about our love. Apart from the innumerable benefactions you have lavished on me, you have also	Do not worry. One hand washes the other.
placed me in your heart. I want to remain there alone and above all those who have preceded me, because not one of them has	Firmly and solidly. There he is and there he will remain.
loved you as I love you, and since I am what you have made me, I	I see it and I believe it.

also wish that my soul's rest should be arranged for by you, that you should enjoy doing me good, that you should apply yourself to making me happy and that you should find in it a pleasant distraction from the serious work your high position impresses on you. Amen.

I rejoice about that in my very soul.
That is my very first joy.
That will come by itself.

Please allow calmness to re-enter the thoughts, so that the sentiments may regain their liberty. They are tender and will themselves find the best way. End of the quarrel. Amen.

Catherine, infinitely loving, tender, and patient, certainly did 'apply herself' to making him happy, and nothing caused her greater joy than seeing Potemkin pleased and satisfied. Whenever he was in that happy state, he was perfectly enchanting. But this seldom lasted very long, and his restless soul was never wholly content. Catherine was by far the steadier of the two.

Temperamental and passionate though she was, she had not been born a German princess for nothing. She had an orderly mind, and great will power which enabled her to exercise considerable control over both brain and body. Potemkin, on the other hand, was a typical specimen of the temperamental, unbalanced Russian. His moods alternated, and he swung like a pendulum, from exuberant activity to introspective melancholia, which made him incapable of the smallest effort. After bouts of energy and long periods of almost unbelievably hard work he would relapse into days, in later years even weeks and months, of gloom and apathy. Reclining on a sofa, clad only in an old dressing gown with nothing underneath, occasionally nibbling at a bit of radish or a crust of black bread which was all he would have for a meal when in that state, he seemed completely oblivious of everything around him. But these periods of meditation, when he was also furiously biting his nails, were never sterile. Indeed, it is on these occasions that he did some of his best thinking, and whenever he returned to activity after such an interruption he was invariably full of ideas or had found the solution of some difficult problem concerning the state and Russia's vital interests. Not only did he pass for no apparent reason, from creative work to complete inactivity; but equally without notice or provocation he could turn from being an enchanter into an insufferable, petty, tiresome, and even rude individual. He was possessed by that Russian nostalgia or moodiness, which has its attractions, but makes any intercourse excessively trying for people with more balanced temperaments.

From the very beginning of their romance Catherine tried to instill some equilibrium into her lover and friend. She cannot be said to have been very successful, but to his death she never gave up preaching self-control and moderation to Potemkin, or encouraging and comforting him when he was depressed, or toning him down when he was overboisterous. It is for him that, half in seriousness and half in fun, she had written in paragraph three of her famous regulations for the guests' behavior at the Hermitage receptions: 'You are requested to be gay, without, however, destroying, breaking, or biting anything.' But he was quite irrepressible and, especially in those early days of their close association was more intent on both active work and romance than on melancholy and meditation.

Catherine's intuition about Potemkin had not deceived her. With his installation as her favorite there begins that unique period in her life when the man at her side could give her all she wanted. Both as a lover and as collaborator —it pleased her vanity to describe him as her political disciple —he surpassed all her expectations. Despite the amorous quarrels, despite the inevitable occasional clash of two such strong wills, despite his moodiness, it would be hard to find a more perfect example of mental as well as physical communion between two people.

The stormy aspect of their love only added to its quality. They came together as if they had been both love- and brain-starved in the past, and seemed almost afraid of losing even a minute in catching up. They had so much to say to each other —subjects for discussion between them were quite inexhaustible. To their own surprise they were now discovering more and more how much their perception of most of the fundamental things in life was identical; to what an extent their minds were working on parallel lines. Not only were they going to remodel the whole of Russia: that went without saying. But they were going to kick the Turks out of Europe and replace the Christian cross on the ancient St. Sophia in Constantinople whence it had been removed by the infidels a good many centuries before. They even quite seriously discussed the conquest of China. No ambition was too high, no flight of imagination too daring, no plan too adventurous. At such moments, when every fiber of them was blended in unison, both Catherine and Potemkin felt inspired by genius.

'She is crazy about him,' said Senator Elaghin to the French chargé d'affaires, Durand. 'They may well love each other, for they are absolutely alike.'

Their intimacy established itself at once to such an extent that Potemkin had no compunction in frequently coming up to her room in the morning with nothing but a dressing gown over his naked body, despite the fact that the Empress' levée was invariably attended by various visitors and court officials. But he did not seem to mind a bit, especially if he wished to continue some important conversation which had been interrupted by Catherine's being obliged to leave his apartments below and return to her own quarters a few hours before. And the Empress, who, despite her own mode of living, was in many ways a prude and very particular about court etiquette, put up even with the dressing gown.

Potemkin appears to have had a peculiar predilection for that garment, wearing little or nothing underneath it. He often received visitors, or even traveled that way, throwing a fur coat over his shoulders if it happened to be winter time. Quite apart from the scandalous disregard of morals and manners, this seems a particularly odd habit in view of the Russian climate. Perhaps it was the cause of his frequent colds from which he always suffered so much. The green-carpeted staircase in St. Petersburg, or the hall at Tsarskoe Selo, which separated him from the Empress, and which he often crossed several times a day or night—must have had a very irregular temperature.

Potemkin and Catherine were now seeing as much of each other as was humanly possible. When they were not together —Potemkin, as will be shown in the next chapter, plunged into the affairs of state almost at once—from their different ends of the palace they wrote little notes to each other, not infrequently several times a day. These notes have been rightly described as an equivalent of present day telephone calls. And indeed they were the continuation of their endless conversations and covered a range of subjects that is quite kaleidoscopic. Conveying protestations of love and ardent terms of endearment, reproaches and explanations, the fighting out of a quarrel, important state affairs and court gossip, details about some reception or their food, information about the state of their health, their visits to the steam bath, sometimes just a question and sometimes just a series of cryptic signs the meaning of which no one can guess—these notes are an astounding illustration of the true character of the mutual relations of the two lovers. One can almost hear them talk.

French is mingled with Russian, the more informal Russian 'thou' with the stiffer 'you', and sometimes the same note contains all these features alternating every few sentences. Catherine's vocabulary of terms of endearment is quite inexhaustible. The Russian language is particularly rich in them; but not satisfied with that, she makes up the most loving, tender, almost childish names for her beloved. Some of them sound particularly strange in their application to a man of Potemkin's dimensions. She calls him 'My golden pheasant', 'Dearest pigeon', 'Kitten', 'Little dog', (*Toutou* in French), 'Dear little heart', 'Twin Soul', 'Papa', 'Little parrot', 'Daddy', and, of course, endless variations of his name—'Grisha', 'Grishenok', 'Grishenka', even 'Grisshifishenka'. Indeed, her repertoire is as rich as it is varied, for she often addresses him—especially when she is lovingly remonstrating about something—as 'Cossack', 'Muscovite', 'Lion in the Jungle', 'Tiger', 'Giaour', and sometimes ironically 'My good Sir', 'Monseigneur', or 'Prince', or 'Your Excellency', or 'Your Serene Highness', or just 'General'. Potemkin's form of address was always more ceremonious. He, too, was ardent and tender, yet when he wrote to Catherine he deliberately emphasized the difference in station. He usually called her 'Mother', or 'Ma'am', and unlike some of her subsequent and completely insignificant lovers, never allowed himself to call her 'Catisha' or any frivolous terms of endearment. That he too could write that way we shall see from his love letters to other women.

With characteristic inconsequence, he did not mind the scandal and the gossip he was creating by his general demeanor, but did feel very strongly on this particular detail of his correspondence with the Empress, whether it was of a private or official character. And he always insisted that the messenger who brought him her letters should kneel down and remain in that position until allowed to withdraw.

It enraged Catherine that he used to carry her little *billets-doux* and other messages in his pocket like a packet of bank notes, occasionally getting out this ever-growing bundle and rereading them. She was afraid lest they might fall into indiscreet hands, and while abandoning herself completely to Potemkin she still had some illusions about keeping up certain appearances. She invariably destroyed at once the messages she received from him, and therefore only a few notes written by Potemkin have been found. The contents of the others, however, can often be judged by the nature of her reply. Whereas thanks to that habit of his, which she disliked so, of always carrying her letters and notes with him, several hundreds of Catherine's messages to Potemkin have been preserved for posterity.

Here are extracts from an early effusion sent a few days after they had come together:

'Darling, I think you really fancied I would not write to you today. I woke up at five, and it is seven now, I will write to you . . . I have given a formal order to the whole of my body, up to the smallest hair, not to show you the least sign of love. I have locked up my love in my heart under ten locks [this is an allusion to a Russian folk song], it is suffocating there, it is not comfortable there, and I feel it might explode. Just think of it, you, a reasonable man, can one express so much folly in a few lines? A whole stream of absurd words flows from my head, I do not understand how you can bear a woman with such incoherent ideas. Oh, Mr. Potemkin, what a damned miracle you have performed in thus upsetting a head, which heretofore was reputed in the world as being one of the best in Europe. It is time, high time, for me to become reasonable. What a shame! What a sin! Catherine II, to be a victim of this mad passion.—You will disgust him with your folly,—I am saying to myself. I will often repeat these last words. They alone can bring me back to reason, and that is yet one more proof of your supreme power over me. Enough! Enough! I have already scribbled such sentimental metaphysics that they can only make you laugh. Well, crazy letter, go to those happy parts where my hero is dwelling. I hope, however, you will not find him there and that they will bring you back: and then I will throw you into the fire. My little Grisha will never read these lines, full of madness and yet with so much love in them. Goodby, Giaour, Muscovite, Cossack, I do not love you.'

For a message penned at seven in the morning by a lady

of forty-four with Catherine's experience—not to mention
her rank—this is a surprising document. Yet there are scores
and scores written by her to Potemkin in a similar strain. And
here is a typical short message, of which there are also innumerable specimens: 'My pigeon, good morning. My dearest
darling, I wish to know whether you slept well and whether
you love me as much as I love you.' Or else, playfully: 'General
do you love me? Me love General very much' (Général,
m'aimez-vous? Moi, aimer Général beaucoup). Or again,
'Night, darling, I am going to bed.'

After a scene with the jealous Potemkin she writes: 'Good
morning, my heart. How are you? Darling, what a shame to
have said what you said: "He who will take my place will
not survive me." What is the point of trying to keep a heart
enslaved through fear? This ugly way is not worthy of you,
nor of your way of thinking . . . Don't worry: some day
I will probably bore you much more than you will ever bore
me. Anyway, I am always open hearted and I am of stable disposition: friendship and habit merely consolidate love. You
are not doing yourself justice though you are a *bonbon* by
profession. You are extremely courteous, I confess that in
your very fears I guess much tenderness, but I assure you
that you have not the least cause for worrying. There is not
in the whole world a man who could equal you. I properly
burned my fingers with that fool Wassiltchikov. Chief of all
I was afraid that force of habit would make me unhappy
for all my life or should shorten my days. If that fool had
stayed one more year with me and you had not come—or
else if I had not found you such as I desired to—it is highly
probable that I would have grown accustomed to him and
that habit would have triumphed. Now you can read in my
soul and in my heart. I open them to you frankly and in every
way. If you do not feel it and do not see it, then you are
really not worthy of the great passion with which you inspire
me. My love for you is boundless. Please understand it well!

But I ask you to pay me back in similar currency: otherwise it will be difficult to avoid streams of tears and torrents of misery. As far as I am concerned, when I love, I become cruelly tender. You need but satisfy my tenderness with your own and by no other means. Here is a letter which is not very short. Will it please you as much to read it as it pleased me to write it? I do not know.'

Frequently she sends him short business notes but cannot refrain from expressing her feelings, all the same. Here is an example: 'Darling, I hope that Zavadovsky has told you what I had ordered with regard to the Sapojevsky business. I could not answer your note, which was so sweet, because the grand duke was with me, and now I just want you to know that you are my beloved soul, and that I love you as such.'

He had a peculiar effect on her: under his influence she becomes quite poetical. One morning she sends Potemkin the following *billet-doux:* 'Good morning, darling. A strange thing has happened to me. I have become a somnambulist.' And she goes on describing how she dreamed of a wonderful walk through the gardens, which brought her to a strange palace where she met the most fascinating of men; they have a long talk and he is enchanting. 'Then I leave him,' Catherine's letter continues, 'and am suddenly awake again. Now I am looking everywhere for this man of my dreams, but can find him nowhere. His picture will always remain engraved on my memory. How I treasure him, more so than the whole world! If you could see him you would never take your eyes off him. Darling, when you meet him, give him a kiss for me. He really deserves it. It is very probable that you will meet him. All you have to do when you get out of bed is to turn your head to the right and glance at the mirror on the wall opposite.' But side by side with this fragrant, poetical letter, she could write in a very different strain: 'My dear General in Chief and Knight of several Orders; I find that this week has been too rich in idiots. If your silly ill temper has departed from you, kindly let me know, for it seems to persist. As I have given you no cause for such tenacious anger, the time seems to me really much too long. Unfortunately, it is only I who find it too long, for you are a nasty Tartar.'

But such letters were comparatively rare, and real outbursts like the following one, quite exceptional: 'Fool! I am not ordering you to do anything! Not deserving this coldness from you, I attribute it to my deadly enemy, your spleen. You are placarding, it seems to me, this coldness, and both this display and the coldness are two beasts together. However, if this display is only meant to make me say tender things I want you to know that this is a futile effort for I have sworn not to show you any tenderness unless you show me some too. I seek the sweetness and most perfect of tenderness: but stupid coldness and idiotic spleen will result in nothing but spitefulness and anger. It was difficult, I suppose, to say: "my dove" or "my soul". Does your heart still keep silent? Mine is not as silent as that.'

Then again she would go on raving about him, not like the mature woman that she was, but like a young girl in love for the first time. 'Good morning, Mr. Lieutenant Colonel. How are you feeling after your bath? I am well and feel very merry thanks to you. As soon as you left, do you know of what we talked? It is easy to guess, seeing how intelligent you are: of you, my darling! Nice things were said about you, you were found beyond comparison. Goodby. Will you look after the regiment, and the officers all day. As to me, I know what I am going to do. I will think—of whom? Of him. It is true that the thought of Grisha does not ever leave me. I do not love him but there is something extraordinary between us that cannot be expressed in words. The alphabet is too short, the letters are not numerous enough.'

This reference to the bath, which means the old-fashioned Russian steam bath, is interesting because it occurs many times. Their intimacy was such that they often used to go there together. One day, she sends him the following note: 'I keep on forgetting to tell you what you should know: please note to what an extent your presence makes me lose my head. This is what it is about: Today Alexis Orlov asked me laughingly: "Yes or no?" I said, "Yes." After which, still laughingly, he asked: "And you meet at the steam bath?" I then asked, "Why do you think that?" "Because," he replied, "For the last four nights lights could be seen there." Then he added: "It was easy to notice last night that you had also made an appointment with him, since you pretended to be detached merely to put others off the track, which by the way is quite a good method of proceeding." ' In the same note she refers to another subject, which was also on her mind, and that she had forgotten to mention before. 'Tell Panin that he should send Wassiltchikov away to take a cure somewhere. His presence upsets me a great deal, and at the same time he complains about pains in the chest. After his cure we will send him as ambassador somewhere, where there is not much work to do. He is a nuisance and a bore.'

Orlov remonstrating with her about the bath, and her desire to get rid for good of the boring Wassiltchikov—what a glimpse of real life at court we get, thanks to this short note.

Here is another picturesque message: 'My pigeon, if you want to eat some meat, please note that everything has been prepared at the bath. But I beg of you not to remove it from there: otherwise everybody will know that cooking is being done there.'

More about the bath in connection with the following *billet* from Potemkin: 'My dear Mother, I have just arrived, but am frozen to such an extent that I cannot even get my teeth warm. First of all, I want to know how you are feeling. I thank you for the three garments and I kiss your feet.' To which Catherine replies: 'I rejoice that you are back, my dear. I am well. To get warm: go to the bath; it has been heated today.' One note begins: 'My beauty, my darling, whom nothing resembles, I am full of kindness and tenderness for you and you will have my protection as long as I live. You must be, I suppose, even more handsome than ever after the bath.' She is simply bubbling over with love and admiration for him.

They were in the habit of telling each other a great deal about their health, his affliction being chiefly colds and hers indigestion. She writes: 'I do not advise you to come to me, my beloved, you could easily catch cold. But I am very glad you are feeling better after the bath, because I love you.' Or, 'My pigeon, I am most upset that you should be sick. Please do me the favor of sending for Kelchen, he will examine you. I am worried because I know how negligent you are in looking after your illnesses. My dear friend, I pray to God that you should feel better tomorrow.' He could be tiresome even when sick; hence the following unusual note from Catherine: 'Really, it is time to settle down to the right order of things. Be quiet and let me be quiet too. I tell you sincerely that I am sorry you are ill, but I will not spoil you by words of tenderness.' Now it is his turn to have an attack of indigestion, and the loving Catherine writes: 'My beloved soul, precious and unique, I can find no words to express my love for you. Do not be upset because of your diarrhœa—it will clean up the bowels well. But do be careful, my beloved, my adored one.' They happen to be sick both of them at the same time, and she writes: 'If really you must see me, send somebody to tell me; since six o'clock in the morning I have the most atrocious diarrhœa; I am afraid, that passing through the nonheated corridor, and especially with this bad weather, would only make my pains worse, which are bad enough as it is. I am so sorry you are ill. Try to be quiet, my friend, that is the best remedy.'

During a quarrel, Potemkin tells her that he does not feel tender towards her at all. Catherine replies: 'Although you have told me that you have no tenderness for me and I, for my part, have many reasons not to feel any towards you, and say that to you as well, if this suited my purpose, I would consider as an act of cowardice lying to you that way, because there is not one cell of my body that is not drawn towards you, O Giaour.' She knows he hates getting long and sentimental messages from her and that they irritate him. She promises again and again to be brief and to the point. But she cannot help relapsing into her endless effusions, always apologizing at the end and trying to explain her long-windedness by saying that she enjoyed writing at such length and rereading her own message. No doubt she did; in fact, she probably enjoyed even the quarrels—within limits, of course. One day, she pretends not to have read a message of his, and goes on: 'Was there something written on that sheet? Certainly reproaches, for Your Excellency has sulked yesterday all the evening, and I, broken hearted, sought your caresses in vain and failed to get them. What has happened? Oh, God, my ruse put right what my frankness had spoiled. The quarrel took place the day before yesterday, when I tried, in all sincerity, to have it out with you about my plans which cannot harm anybody but in my opinion could be very useful to you. Last night, I confess, it was on purpose that I sent no one to you, awaiting all the time that you should come. But when you had not arrived by nine o'clock I sent for news about your health. Then you did come, with a sulky face. I pretended not to notice your ill-humor, which ended in completely upsetting you. Now you can reproach me with this: instead of the tender letter from me you asked for, here is the repetition of our quarrel. Wait, darling, let my wounded heart heal again. Tenderness will return as soon as we grant each other an audience. I have actually too much of it for you. It is an obsession and it drives me always towards you. And when it sees the impossibility of being expressed frankly it covers itself with a ruse. You must understand how strong my tenderness is: It is capable of masquerading as anything only to get to you. It receives a blow with a fist and leaps back only to return at once as close as possible to the friend of my heart. Who is this beloved friend?

They call him little Grisha. My tenderness overcomes his fits of anger: it forgives his wrong interpretation of my words: it knows how to diminish the wickedness of his reproaches: it pretends to ignore his rudeness, it forgets his unjust words. In a word, my tenderness is our love, frank and extraordinary love. Try to manage that I should stop loving you if you can find the means of achieving that. But I assure you there is much to be gained from being sincere.'

Either to punish her for pretending not to have read his note, or just to annoy her, Potemkin sends her a blank sheet of paper, and this is the reply he gets: 'This is not the first of April to send me a blank sheet. Probably this is the result of your last night's dream, or else you have done it not to spoil me too much. But as I do not as yet know what you are up to I do not guess the meaning of your silence either. Yet I am full of tenderness for you, Giaour, Muscovite, Pougatchev, golden cockerel, peacock, cat, pheasant, golden tiger, lion in the jungle!'

Like a capricious *prima donna*, he constantly reproaches her that she does not pay enough attention to him. She writes: 'Allow me to tell you, my beloved friend, that I never forget you. As soon as I finished listening to the reports, which took three hours, I wanted to send somebody to you, especially as it was not yet ten o'clock and I was afraid of waking you up before. As you see, your anger has no foundation, but I know there do exist some people who instead of thanking for a delicate attention are looking for a chance to remonstrate. Darling, I love you like my soul.'

She went out of her way to please, to honor, to glorify him. She lavished distinction after distinction on him. And all the time, she was the loving, humble, tender woman, trembling at every whim of the moody and fascinating 'Cyclops', convinced that no one could be as handsome and as clever. Almost like a little seamstress writing a fan letter to her film favorite she says in one note that she is not in the least bit surprised to hear no woman can resist him: 'I think there is not another man in the whole world who knows how to get them as well as you do.' She also writes: 'In all my work I seek but one reward: your tenderness. I only try to see you as a god full of indulgence and not at all as an angry Pluto. Having said everything, I only add this: If you find that difficult, I shall yield to your will which I always put above all my little caprices you sometimes dislike so.'

Potemkin was like a bottomless pit. He devoured everything: money, honors, and her love; and the more he got, the less happy he felt. He was as yet the dazzling, enchanting, tender lover of her dreams, her mate in every sense of the word, and her best adviser. But she could see he was not happy. Something was torturing him. 'Calmness is for you a state that your soul cannot bear,' she said in one note. And yet, when he was in the right mood everything was so wonderful. 'With you, anything becomes easy. That is what it means really to love!'

She liked to call him in the morning, but often she was afraid of disturbing his sleep or his work, and sent him tender little messages instead. At times it seemed to her he was drawing away from her: 'I must scold you,' she writes one day while at Tsarskoe Selo. 'I came to you to wake you up, and instead of finding you in bed I see you are out. Now I understand that this sleep of yours was but a pretext to get rid of me. In town you spent hours with me, sometimes before lunch, sometimes in the evening, whereas here I only see you for short moments. Giaour, Cossack, Muscovite, you are always trying to leave me! Take care! you could that way make me lose the habit of seeking your company. I will be cold then. You can laugh about me, but I do not laugh when I see you bored in my presence. You wish to be far, anywhere, but away from me . . .'

She is always missing him, yet she rejoices that he should work hard, and encourages him in every way when he attends to the affairs of state, despite the frequent absences that this may necessitate.

On one such occasion she just sends this line: 'Go, my pigeon, and be happy.' He returns and writes: 'Mother, we are back, now it is time for supper,' and she, enthusiastically: 'Good God! who might have thought you would return?' Is that not indeed the nearest approach to a telephone conversation? Or else the following little note, which gives their relations in cameo: 'How much longer will you forget in my rooms things that belong to you! Please do not throw your handkerchiefs all over the place as is your Turkish fashion. Many thanks for your visit, and I love you a lot, a lot.'

Every time he is nice to her she thanks him profusely; she finds his tenderness unbelievably touching and marvelous. And invariably after that she assures him of her own love and devotion in particularly glowing terms: 'My dear pigeon, my precious friend, I must write to you to keep my promise. Please know that I love you, and this should not surprise anybody. For you, one would do the impossible, and hence I will be either your humble maid or your humble servant, or both at once.' Sometimes he treated her exactly as if she were one. There are dozens of little notes in which she complains that she could not come to his rooms because he had locked the door, or that when she did get there, he happened to be out. This contrasted markedly with her own tender care, for if for some reason she had to put him off or close the door, she invariably informed him—to save him an unnecessary effort. 'Darling, I am going to bed and the door will be closed. If, contrary to all expectation, you do come, and cannot enter, I will weep hot tears to-morrow. I beg you, therefore, to stay in and to believe that it is impossible to love more than I love you, my little soul.'

One long note of hers relates to an episode where Potemkin's behavior must have been particularly humiliating to her. 'Thanks for your visit, but I fail to understand what kept you back. Is it possible that my words were the cause of this? I said I wanted to sleep solely to make the others go away, and you did not return fearing to find me in bed. But you may be sure I am perspicacious enough. I went to bed to drive the others away, but as soon as they were gone I got up, dressed, and went to the library in order to catch you there. I remained there in vain for over two hours, exposing myself to the drafts: after which—towards eleven o'clock—quite sadly I returned to my rooms, where thanks to you I had spent four nights without shutting an eye. I spent last night the same way, seeking in vain the cause of your changed disposition towards me, which however had seemed to me most sincere.'

This sounds quite unbelievable. Here is Potemkin, Catherine's ardent lover, who at the height of their romance makes her spend over two hours in a cold, drafty, dark room without bothering to turn up or to apologize, and Catherine not only accepts this sort of treatment, but, as will be seen from the continuation of this very long letter, does not let it interfere with certain plans she and Potemkin were discussing. It must be interjected here that naturally the court and especially the Orlovs, who had watched the development of Catherine's affair with Potemkin with unconcealed alarm, were most anxious to get rid of him. Intrigue followed intrigue, and from time to time various friends and advisers who could speak to Catherine freely, gave vent to their feelings. And none spoke more bluntly than Alexis Orlov—nicknamed by Potemkin 'the Apothecary'—who was in a sense in a privileged position. He had done more than anybody, even more than his brother Grigory Grigorievitch, to put Catherine on the throne. Since then he had served her gallantly and faithfully. Finally, not having been her lover, like Grigory, Alexis Orlov could speak to her without being suspected of jealousy and without all the memories of a long and only recently terminated liaison standing between them. He had already drawn her attention to the fact that her nocturnal expeditions with Potemkin to the steam bath were not exactly a secret at court. But that was a comparatively innocent amusement. What was worrying the Orlovs and all the others was the unprecedented speed with which Potemkin had climbed to power, and the intimidating firmness of his complete domination over Catherine.

In her letter to Potemkin after the library episode, the Empress continues: 'I must see you at any price and talk to you, for this is necessary. The one whom you call the Apothecary has been to see me, and spoke to me at some length, but he did not succeed in making me cry. He tried to make me see the madness of my behavior towards you and finally said that, for my happiness, he would persuade you to leave for the army: to which I agreed. They are all of them at least trying, so it seems, to lecture me, whereas in real truth you do not disgust them more than Prince Orlov. I did not reply yes or no to any of the Apothecary's words to avoid in the future the reproach of having lied. In short, I have masses of things to tell you and particularly on the subject we spoke about yesterday between noon and two o'clock: but I do not know whether you are in the same mood as yesterday, and I do not know either whether your words correspond always to your acts, since you promised me several times you would come and you did not come. Do not be annoyed by my reproaches, which are justified. Goodby, and may God protect you! Despite everything, I am thinking of you all the time. Oh! la! la! what a long letter I have written to you. Excuse me. I always forget you don't like it. I will never do it again.'

The plans they were discussing were of a most far-reaching nature. His boundless ambition, seconded, perhaps, by his deep religious feelings, made Potemkin most anxious to legalize their union. Religion and debauchery had always oddly accommodated themselves in his restless soul, where they seemed to occupy watertight compartments. Yet he could not help feeling very strongly about the immoral aspect of his as-

sociation with Catherine. He certainly raised the question
fairly soon after the beginning of their romance. And just as in
a moment of weakness Catherine had once promised Orlov to
marry him, now she made the same promise to Potemkin. Only
this time neither he nor she would allow it to be frustrated by
outside interference.

Surreptitiously, with the utmost care and after much preliminary discussion, they made the necessary preparations.
Nobody was to know. But they had to have witnesses if it
was to be a proper religious ceremony and of course they had
to have a church and a priest. Towards the close of the year
1774, only a few months after he had become her favorite, the
former Princess Sophia Augusta Frederica of Anhalt-Zerbst,
now Her Imperial Majesty the Empress Catherine II of all the
Russias, widow of his late Imperial Majesty Tsar Peter III, was
of her own free will married to Grigory Alexandrovitch Potemkin.

According to Professor Barskov, a distinguished Soviet historian, the wedding took place at the Saint-Sampsonievsky
Church in a part of St. Petersburg far removed from the
fashionable quarter, and the Empress arrived accompanied
only by her faithful and inseparable attendant Maria Savishna
Perekousikhina. The two male witnesses or 'grooms' were Potemkin's nephew Count Alexander Nicolaievitch Samoilov and
the chamberlain Evgraf Alexandrovitch Tchertkov. One of the
two copies of the marriage certificate was entrusted to Samoilov
and the other to Perekousikhina. Professor Barskov quotes a
witness, Samoilov's nephew Count Bobrinskoy, who asserted
that this marriage certificate was placed in his uncle's coffin
when he died in 1814, the other certificate having been eventually handed down to the Volkonsky family.

Quite apart from these statements, however, there is other
evidence that Potemkin and Catherine were married. In a dispatch sent by the French ambassador, the Comte de Ségur, on
December 21, 1787, occurs the following striking passage, after

a description of the unusual position enjoyed by Potemkin: 'The strange basis of his rights is a great mystery which is known only to four people in Russia: a happy chance has enabled me to discover it, and when I have fully ascertained it, I will inform the King by the first opportunity that presents itself.' What is significant in this dispatch is in the first place the number of people to whom the 'mystery' is known: there were four of them. Were they not the priest, Perekousikhina, Samoilov, and Tchertkov? Moreover, why was the French ambassador going to inform the King personally and not his Foreign Minister? Was it not because this secret royal wedding was a matter of direct concern to Louis XVI? Again the following conversation has been recorded between the Emperor Joseph II of Austria and the British ambassador, Sir Robert Murray Keith. On a summer's day in 1782, the Emperor and the ambassador were having a walk and a friendly chat in the Augarten Park. Certain rumors had reached Keith, and he asked Joseph II, who was particularly well informed of everything going on in Russia (to which he had only recently paid a personal visit), 'Does it appear, Sir, that Prince Potemkin's weight and influence is diminished?' 'Not at all,' was Joseph's answer, 'but in politics they have never been what the world imagined. The Empress of Russia does not wish to part with him, and from a thousand reasons, and as many connections of every sort, she could not easily get rid of him, even if she harbored the wish of doing so.' The Austrian Emperor did not go on to explain his words. But why, one may ask, did he think it would be difficult or even impossible for Catherine to get rid of Potemkin if she wanted to? After all, she did part even from Orlov, who, together with his brothers, had put her on the throne, and murdered her husband—thus having a firmer hold over her than anybody else, and this in addition to being the father of her children and her lover for eleven years. What were then the 'thousand reasons' and 'as many connections' alleged by Joseph to constitute such an indissoluble tie between the Empress and

Potemkin? What, indeed, if not marriage? But while the meaning of Ségur's dispatch or Joseph's words can only be guessed
at—even though such an interpretation seems convincing
enough—there is yet another body of evidence which can
leave no doubt as to the marriage.

In a large number of her daily private messages to Potemkin, Catherine addresses him as 'dear husband', 'tender spouse',
signs 'your devoted wife' and in various other ways emphasizes
the fact that their union has been legalized. She never called
any of her other lovers, either before or after Potemkin, 'husband,' nor herself a 'wife', nor did she make solemn declarations to them like those in the following note for instance: 'My
master and tender spouse, I begin by replying to what touched
me most. Why do you want to cry? Why do you prefer to believe your unhealthy imagination rather than the real facts, all
of which confirm the words of your wife? Was she attached
to you two years ago by holy ties? Have I since changed my
attitude towards you? Is it possible that you should no longer
be loved by me? Have confidence in my words. I love you and
I am bound to you by all possible ties. Just compare, were my
acts more useful two years ago than they are now?' This note
alone is eloquent enough, and there are many others written
in a similar strain.

It is significant that two years after their wedding Potemkin
was as full of melancholy and doubt as in the early days of their
romance. Yet for some time immediately after the marriage he
appears to have been in an exuberant mood. 'Darling, what
stories you have told me yesterday! I cannot stop laughing
when I think of them. What happy moments I am spending
with you! We stay together for four hours without a shadow
of trouble and I always leave you reluctantly. My darling
little pigeon, I love you greatly, you are handsome, clever, amusing. I forget the whole world when I am with you. I have never
been so happy as I am now. I often try to conceal my feelings,
but my heart betrays my passion. Of course it is too full, it over-

flows. I did not write to you earlier this morning for I got up late and I know you are on duty today [as a chamberlain]. Goodby, my friend, behave well in front of other people, so that no one could suspect what is going on between us. It amuses me greatly to fool people.'

They were expert at bluffing other people, both of them. In the early days of her liaison with Orlov, Catherine had even succeeded in fooling the observant French ambassador to such an extent that she actually persuaded him Orlov was only a silly young officer who did not mean anything to her. When she summoned Potemkin to St. Petersburg they both played the comedy for a while until Wassiltchikov was finally removed, and Potemkin officially installed. It will be seen that later she and Potemkin gave the court and the shrewd foreign diplomats the impression that they had parted company, whereas in point of fact their relations were still as tender and as intimate as could be.

The following letter appears to have been written a day or two after the wedding: 'I thank you for the dinner you gave me yesterday, and although I felt a little embarrassed, all the same I remember your tenderness. I was thinking of it going to bed last night and getting up this morning. Will you be nice and tell me what our nephew Engelhardt told you when you remained alone. I think that our madness must have seemed strange to him. . . . Goodby, little Grisha! I think that if really you are obliged to stand behind my chair I will be red like a lobster. I hope it will be cold in the gallery. When I get up from the table I will say "Ouf, ouf!" Only don't forget that you too must dine. I will dispense with you as soon as the dinner is over just as you did for Alexander Samoilov last night.'

Vassily (Basil) Vassilievitch Engelhardt was Potemkin's nephew, the son of his sister Maria Alexandrovra, who married Vassily Andreyevitch Engelhardt, a nobleman of Baltic extraction. Why does Catherine refer to 'our' nephew and not to 'your' nephew unless she now considers herself a member of the family? And why did she all of a sudden feel so uneasy about Potemkin's having to stand behind her chair, when as chamberlain on duty he had done it on innumerable occasions since he became her lover? Is it not their new secret that made her so self-conscious?

She wanted to know what Engelhardt thought of their 'madness', and it appears that somehow or other one or two people did find out or had guessed the truth. Potemkin was upset by this, and she wrote: 'What can we do, darling? These things happen often. Peter the Great in cases like that used to send out people to the market who used to bring back information he alone thought was secret; sometimes people guess by combination. Goodby my soul. I am selecting your apartments on the plan of the palace of Moscow.'

They were living very happy days at the time, and Catherine writes: 'How nice you are! And how happy you made me, my soul, my tender friend.' Or again: 'Darling, I am not at all angry and see no reason to be. My darling Grisha, the day of yesterday was one of the happiest of my life because it ended so well. If only all the days finished like that one! I will be always ready to give in, my soul, but you too must be indulgent, my beauty. Goodby, my jewel, my heart, my beloved husband.' Or again: 'Dearest soul, your Cossacks are very beautiful: they made me crazy. I am sending you the drawings, my beloved husband.' Or again: 'Belovedest, can I come to you, and when? I am dying of the desire to see my little Grisha, the one who belongs to me.' She was always afraid he might be annoyed by something. 'My darling friend, I fear you might be angry with me. If not, all the better. To prove it, come quickly to my bedroom. My soul is longing for your presence.' Or else: 'My pigeon, eight o'clock. I came as far as your door, but there I found your valet, and did not dare to enter. I am writing this to explain why I had to interrupt our usual order of things which is so precious to me. Goodby, my golden pheasant. I love you a lot, a lot.'

Their little ailments were still frequently interfering with their accustomed meetings and pleasures. 'I am very sorry to hear,' writes Catherine, 'that you are sick. It is a good lesson for you: don't you go barefooted into staircases! If you want to get rid of your cold as soon as possible, take a little tobacco and you will feel better at once. Goodby, my love, my heart, my dear husband, the sweetest, the nicest. You are all that imagination can conceive of niceness, pleasantness and intelligence! My beloved, my angel, if your health depended on my love for you, you would be the healthiest man in the world. Oh my darling, my precious soul!'

'Darling, I am sorry you did not sleep well. I, on the other hand, had a good sleep, but my legs still feel very tired. Rogerson [her Scottish doctor] says my pulse is not good. I do not know whether I should go out today. What do you think?' Then she gets a cold too, and promptly she writes: 'My dearest husband, I will not come to you because I perspired all night and all my bones are aching like yesterday, and above all it is very cold, my soul. However, I have slept well and love you with all my soul.' Finally: 'My soul, my darling pigeon, my most precious possession, I have a slight diarrhœa today, but apart from that I am well, my beloved, my dear husband.'

Both the tone and the volume of this correspondence leaves little doubt as to the question of marriage. Moreover, that would at last explain the otherwise almost incomprehensible problem of their relations with each other when their actual liaison came to an end. Contemporaries and students of the period have invariably been baffled by the unique authority enjoyed by Potemkin, by his position at court, and by Catherine's devoted affection, even after he had deliberately brought their physical association to a close. Yet if we look upon him as her secret husband, the situation becomes clear at once. This, however, did not begin to develop till two years after their marriage, that is till 1776. But both throughout the period of their romance and later, Catherine's attitude to the restless Potemkin is best characterized by the following little note: 'My husband has said to me: where shall I go? Where shall I find my proper place? My dear and beloved husband, come to me, you will be received with open arms.'

7

CONSOLIDATION

SIMULTANEOUSLY with the process of winning complete domination over Catherine, Potemkin was also engaged in building up an impressive façade so far as the outside world was concerned. His appointment as personal adjutant general to the Empress and as lieutenant colonel of the Preobrashensky Regiment had been the two first outward signs of his rise to power. There followed an almost unending stream of new honors and privileges. Whether Catherine had originally intended to lavish quite so much on Potemkin; whether it came from her desire to please and assuage her moody and insatiable lover; or whether he actually suggested, not infrequently perhaps, even demanded it himself, his career was now developing at an unprecedented tempo.

On May 6, 1774, not more than two months after Potemkin's installation as favorite, Gunning was reporting to the Earl of Suffolk: 'Though favorites have risen nowhere so quickly as in this country, yet there has been no instance, even here, of so rapid a progress as the present one makes. It was to the surprise of most of the members that General Potemkin was yesterday admitted to a seat in the Privy Council.' And a month later the British chargé d'affaires, Richard Oakes, was writing to William Eden, the undersecretary: 'Approaching changes are talked of in several departments here: one promotion of great

consequence has just taken place; and which must prove a great
blow to the power of Count Zachary Tchernishev, which is that
General Potemkin was on Saturday last appointed to the office
of vice president of the College of War, with the rank of general in chief.' This rank, peculiar to the Russian Army of those
days, was something between that of a lieutenant general and a
field marshal. As to Count Zachary Tchernishev, who until
then had ruled alone over the College of War, he could scarcely
be expected to like the appointment of anybody else, but least
of all of Potemkin, whose knowledge of military matters, combined with the authority he now exercised, was bound to make
things unpleasant and difficult.

Yet another month later, on July 10, the title of Count
of the Russian Empire was bestowed on Potemkin in connection with the peace of Kuchuk-Kainardje just concluded
with the Turks: 'for assistance towards it with good advice'.
Moreover, his 'bravery and untiring efforts' were rewarded
with a diamond-bedecked sword and he was also given, as
a special 'sign of the Monarch's satisfaction', a portrait of the
Empress set in diamonds to be worn on his heart. Only Orlov
before him and Zoubov after him were ever deemed worthy of
this latter distinction. There must have been some hitch over
the portrait, for at the end of the year Catherine was informing
her 'dear husband' in a private letter that 'to avoid misunder-
standings' she would actually hand the portrait to him later,
during the peace celebrations to be organized in Moscow early
in 1775, and of which he was in charge, displaying for the first
time his talents of showmanship on a really large scale.

One by one he now gets all the Russian orders and decorations or else is promoted to the highest grades of those—like
the Cross of St. George—which he already had before. After
bestowing on him the rare honor of the Order of St. Andrew,
on Christmas Day, 1774, the loving Catherine sends a little
note across: 'My love, good morning. Please let me know how
the Knight of St. Andrew slept last night since I am worried

lest His Excellency might have been troubled by his extraordinary exploits. If he is, as I suppose he must be, that will cause me much pain; for I love very much that Knight.' And she drafts in her own hand, a long letter by which she wishes Potemkin to inform Prince Henry of Prussia—Frederick the Great's brother—that the prophecy he made during his recent visit to Russia has come true, and that he, Potemkin, has now joined the distinguished clan of Knights of St. Andrew, the highest order in the whole empire.

She also takes steps to secure the principal foreign decorations for him, and herself conducts a voluminous correspondence for that purpose. The response in most cases is satisfactory. Prussia sends Potemkin the Black Eagle, Poland the White Eagle and St. Stanislas. From Denmark comes the White Elephant and from Sweden the Holy Seraphim; the latter is secured only with difficulty and through French diplomatic intervention. But France herself refuses to give Potemkin the Holy Ghost on the ground that this can be granted only to members of the Roman Catholic faith. Austria declines to make him a Knight of the Golden Fleece for the same reason, but now Catherine's—or Potemkin's—ambitions go even higher and Catherine writes a long secret letter to the Russian ambassador in Vienna instructing him to use every means in his power, and even to approach the Emperor Joseph II in her own name, with a view to obtaining for Potemkin the title of Prince of the Holy Roman Empire. She says that this is 'a matter of great personal interest' to her, that she will be grateful to the Austrian Emperor if he gratifies her wish, and she orders her ambassador to address all his correspondence on this subject to her personally. Not without a struggle with his mother and coregent, the Empress Maria Theresa, who loathed and despised Catherine—'this woman' as she usually called her— Joseph II does bestow the title of Prince of the Holy Roman Empire on Potemkin, the necessary documents arriving in March 1776. Henceforward Potemkin is known throughout

Russia as 'His Serene Highness', 'Serenissimus' or just 'the Prince'. This foreign title was much more coveted and appreciated in Russia than any national distinction, and so far had only been bestowed on Grigory Orlov, who was also frequently referred to as 'the Prince'. An attempt was made a few years later to get Potemkin the Garter. The new British ambassador to Russia, James Harris, whose instructions were to win, at any price, Russia's friendship or even alliance, for Great Britain, warmly recommended the bestowal of such a signal honor on Potemkin. George III, however, was adamant, and as the Russian ambassador in London, Count Vorontsov wrote to his brother: 'The king has not only refused, but was greatly shocked, and ordered that Harris should be severely reprimanded.'

Various Russian individuals and institutions were now seeking to honor Potemkin. Poets and writers like Soumarokov and Dershavin glorify him in their works and praise in him a patron of the arts. Innumerable court officials, state and church dignitaries, leading generals, and young subalterns write to him to express their admiration and to seek his benevolent interest. Even Alexis Orlov—perhaps his bitterest enemy—sends most flattering epistles from Pisa. The very University of Moscow that had thrown him out for laziness, presented him with an honorary diploma written in Latin verse and addressed to 'Illustrissimo Comiti Grigorio Alexandridi de Potemkin hoc grati animi sui documentum offert Academia Moscuensis'. Soon after that he met Professor Barsov, one of his former teachers who took a particularly active part in getting him dismissed from the university. 'Well,' Potemkin said, 'do you remember how you got me kicked out?' and the old professor replied: 'You deserved it at the time, Your Serene Highness.' This frank answer pleased Potemkin, for the chorus of adulation with which he was now met wherever he went, was beginning to irritate him. But characteristically enough an honor that caused him particular joy was the dedication to him of a 'Church

Dictionary' specially composed for the purpose by the Arch-priest Alexius.

In all of this Catherine took a most active interest and not only used her influence to obtain honors for Potemkin, but as a loving wife actually used her hands to embellish her difficult hero. She writes: 'Good morning, my darling, with the White Eagle, with its red ribbon and ends of striped tissue which I have made myself together with all these new decorations of which you are worthy on account of your courage and the great services you have rendered the state. I beg of you not to humiliate me any more and to keep quiet about all my faults and vices instead of telling them to the others. In the first place this is not very pleasant for me and in the second place it is not very nice even if it were anybody else, but least of all towards one's wife. Here is a good reprimand for you! but of the most tender kind. I woke up very gay this morning which can be attributed to last evening, to your good cheer and your pleasure: I love so much to see you in high spirits! I suppose that today you will stop a long time in front of your mirror trying on your decorations. Goodby, my precious jewel, you often have no common sense but you are always most pleasant. You have not written me nor even told me anything about Reinsdorf.' From this note, where, as usual, business—the last sentence—is mixed up with sentimental effusions and loving reprimands, it appears that even at the time the greatest honors were being showered upon him, Potemkin could be publicly unpleasant to the Empress and had no compunction in discussing her defects with various people. And all she does is to beg him not to humiliate his 'wife' in the presence of others, and then goes on raving about him in her accustomed style!

Senator Elaghin, at whose house he stayed for about a month before he moved into the Winter Palace and who was devoted to both Potemkin and Catherine, described to Durand the scene that led to Potemkin's appointment to the Privy Council. It must have been a typical example of his sulking fits.

'When he arrived here,' said Elaghin, to the French chargé d'affaires, 'he spoke to me at once about state matters with a frankness that amused me. He blamed everything. I took the opportunity . . . to tell him what we had agreed on. He listened to me with interest and then replied: "What can I do? I have not even been made a member of the Council yet." "And why don't you join it?" "I am not wanted to: but I will press matters to a head!" He was resolved to renew his requests. They must have met with a refusal, for on Sunday I happened to be seated at table next to him and the Empress and I saw that not only would he not speak to her, but he did not even answer her questions. She was quite beside herself and we were utterly upset. The silence was only interrupted by the occasional monosyllables of the Master of the Horse [Leo Narishkin, a regular jester and the acknowledged court buffoon] who simply could not start a conversation. Upon getting up from the table, the Empress retired alone, and when she returned her eyes were red and she looked worried. On Monday she was more cheerful and he entered the Council the same day.'

Before long he was also appointed governor general of the Southern Provinces, and to celebrate this occasion she blessed and presented him with a valuable old icon covered with jewels. At the same time she took steps to provide Potemkin with an income. Thus he was the first favorite to draw a regular allowance amounting to no less than 12,000 rubles a month. In addition to this, he was constantly getting the most generous monetary presents, usually of 100,000 rubles at a time. His own or Catherine's birthday, christening day, and other festive occasions were used as an excuse for this. When, in connection with one such celebration, the Empress sent him a valuable present worth 30,000 rubles, instead of the usual cash, he sulked and showed his discontent so pointedly that she hastened to send him the customary 100,000 in addition to that. But he cannot be said to have been mercenary or mean in any way, and he in turn was continually sending Catherine the choicest and most expensive of presents, always trying to find something original that would appeal to her fancy. Moreover, he frequently used his own money for state purposes, instead of asking for, or ordering, the necessary grant to be made; he simply could not be bothered with such red tape.

The Empress's munificence, however, was not limited to cash alone. She liked to send him fur coats, jewels, elegant luggage, furniture, and all sorts of other valuable things. When she ordered a most expensive porcelain table set for him she pretended it was for herself, 'to make sure it would really be of superior quality,' and she sent it to him with a note: 'to the greatest nail-biter in Russia.' His food and wine were charged to her personal expenses and cost her well over a hundred thousand rubles a year. She also granted him the privilege of having a private staff of his own, and in his capacity of governor general of the South, and commander in chief of the cavalry regiments stationed there, the expenses were to be defrayed by the Southern Provinces. But since, despite all this, he was often in debt, she more than once settled the very considerable financial obligations of her over-generous and extravagant husband. And whenever she had any lands or serfs to distribute, he now got the lion's share and soon became one of the largest landowners in Russia.

It seemed to grieve both Catherine and Potemkin that one who had risen so high and was such an important person in the realm had no aristocratic ancestors to boast about. The picturesque and stubborn Ambassador Peter Ivanovitch Potemkin, who about a century earlier had made such a firm stand for his own and his Tsar's honor in all the foreign capitals he had visited, was therefore rescued from the oblivion into which he had fallen and his portrait put up in a prominent place at the Hermitage.

Potemkin's mother, as well as his five pretty nieces, the daughters of his elder and widowed sister Maria Engelhardt, were brought to St. Petersburg and all of them given court rank.

Catherine was full of attention to her mother-in-law. Here is a little note to Potemkin: 'I have noticed that your mother was most elegant but that she has no watch. Here is one which I ask you to give her.' Or again: 'To please your mother I ask you to give the title of lady in waiting to all those of your Engelhardt nieces that you wish.' He gave it to all the five: Alexandra, Varvara, Nadeshda, Ekaterina, and Tatiana. With three of them, and especially with Alexandra, Catherine's relations soon became particularly close and remained so to the end. 'Our nephew Engelhardt,' as Catherine once described these girls' brother, was made Potemkin's personal A.D.C. and various other members of the family were also brought to court.

Potemkin's male relations and kinsmen, especially the two brothers Michael and Paul Potemkin, who were distant cousins of his, owed much of their career to him. These two brothers distinguished themselves as civil servants, as courtiers, and as soldiers. They belonged to their omnipotent kinsman's most intimate circle, and Paul Potemkin, who achieved greatness as a soldier and administrator, was a particularly close collaborator of his cousin.

It is hardly surprising that this rapid rise to power, fraught as it was with the many considerable changes that the advent of Potemkin and his adherents was bound to effect at court, created much jealousy and discontent. Potemkin was shrewd enough to realize that his future depended very largely not only on his romance with Catherine, but also on his positive achievements once he settled down to work, and on his capacity to undermine the power of the various court cliques opposing him.

No sooner had his relations with the Empress placed him in a position to exercise his influence in affairs of state, than he plunged into work with tremendous zeal and with the obvious determination of showing his power at once. That was precisely what the people around Catherine had feared, foreseen, and unsuccessfully tried to avert. They had had the

perspicacity to recognize in Potemkin from the very beginning, a man of great gifts and dauntless energy; they had noted
the boundlessness of his ambition; they had realized at once
that he would be neither a puppet like Wassiltchikov nor a
charming, easygoing, and indolent fellow like Grigory Orlov.
The court, therefore, soon became divided into two groups: ·
those who accepted the advent of a new master and tried to ingratiate themselves with him; and those who felt insulted or
threatened by Potemkin's rise to power and were determined to
oppose him or even, if possible, to oust him from Catherine's
favor. As to the foreign diplomats—all of whom at this time ·
were bidding for Russia's friendship and support—they felt
uneasy, and while realizing the importance of keeping in
with the ruling party they were not quite certain which side
to back.

Foremost among all these interested personages was old
Count Panin, in whose experienced but lazy hands rested
the infinitely complicated direction of Russia's foreign relations. He was known to be opposed to Potemkin's advancement. But his hatred of the Orlovs was notoriously even greater
than his dislike of the ambitious newcomer, and he was likely
to welcome anything that would diminish the Orlovs' authority. As to the Orlovs themselves and their friends or political ·
associates, like the Counts Ivan and Zachary Tchernishev, they
represented a group so powerful and with such important
vested interests that it seemed almost unbelievable that their
influence could ever be reduced or altogether destroyed. ·
Characteristically enough, nobody was concerned about young
Wassiltchikov, who for his part seemed quite content with the
farewell gift he had received of 3,000 peasants, 50,000 rubles
in cash, and a silver tea set worth 25,000 rubles. This young
man cherished no further ambitions.

It is significant that both the British Minister, Sir Robert ·
Gunning, and the Swedish envoy, Baron Nolcken, impressed
though they were by Potemkin's spectacular career, still

thought that Grigory Grigorievitch Orlov had chances of re-
gaining his lost favor. But they mistook certain outward signs
for deeper processes of which they were not aware. It is true that
after the violent animosity provoked by the alcove revolution
of 1772, when Catherine so unceremoniously dropped Grigory
Orlov and replaced him by the insignificant Wassiltchikov, had
subsided, the Orlovs had reappeared at court, and that they
were still, or once again, allowed to play a conspicuous part in
court life. Grigory Grigorievitch, as Nolcken remarks, kept
up his accustomed *ton de maître*, behaving as if he were still
in the privileged position he had enjoyed for so long. He even
continued to pay nightly visits to the ladies in waiting, and
since these were prepared to accept his love-making it was
obvious that Orlov was still a man of great influence. He
snubbed Potemkin and provoked him at every possible opportunity. Nolcken narrates how on one occasion he even
beckoned to Potemkin, as if Potemkin were his underling, and
to everybody's surprise the 'Cyclops' made no scene but came
up and asked Orlov what he wanted. The truth of the matter is
that Catherine so much dreaded any sort of row between the
two that she was constantly imploring Potemkin not to take
umbrage at Orlov's behavior and for her sake to avoid quarreling with Grigory Grigorievitch or his brother and friends.
While Potemkin appears to have been curiously full of consideration for that request in public, privately he must have
given vent to his feelings more than once. For again and again
Catherine writes to him begging him not to run down the
Orlovs, and to make this request less annoying to Potemkin
she invariably adds flattery and protestations of love on a particularly generous scale. Here is one of her typical long effusions. After telling him how unique, incomparable, superior
he is, she goes on: 'The only thing I beg of you not to do is to
seek to prejudice my mind against the Orlovs, for I would consider this as great ingratitude on your part. There is nobody
else in the world of whom the prince [Grigory Orlov] used to

tell me so much good, or whom he used to love so well, as yourself. If the prince has his faults, it is not for you or me to
criticize them and to draw the attention of others to them. He
used to love you and as far as I am concerned he and his
brother [Alexis] are both my good friends and I will never
abandon them. Here is a moral for you! If you are intelligent
you will accept it. It would not be intelligent for you to contradict me on this subject for it is the pure truth. How strange it is!
Everything I have laughed about all my life has happened:
so much so that my love for you dazzles me. Sentiments, which
I used to consider as idiotic, exaggerated and not very natural,
I feel them now. I can not tear away my stupid look from you;
I forget everything my reason tells me and I feel I become
quite stupid when I am in your presence. I must, when an occasion presents itself, avoid seeing you for at least three days
in order to bring myself back to reason and establish my
balance: otherwise you will soon be bored in my company,
which would anyway be very natural. I am very angry with myself today; I have scolded myself well; I have made every possible effort to render myself more reasonable and to find the
necessary firmness and force of character—features that distinguish you. I have such a good example before me; you are
intelligent, firm, unshakable in all your decisions. The last proof
of it is what you told me yourself and others have confirmed:
during how many years did you seek the way leading towards
me? Which I did not even notice myself. Goodby, darling.
We will only be able to see each other during the next three
days, since after that we will have the first week of the Great
Fast which is destined to prayers, fasting, and during which—
apart from the fact that I must prepare for the sacrament—it
would be a great sin for us to meet. Oh! the mere thought of
this separation makes me sad, drives me to tears in advance.
Goodby, Monsieur. Please write to me how you feel today.
Have you slept well or not? Do you still have any fever? Mr.
Panin used to repeat: Take some quinine, Sir, nothing but

quinine! I would like so much to be with you, to chat with you. If we loved each other less, we would be far more intelligent, even far happier. I am gay and amusing when my head, and especially my heart, are free. You will not believe me, my soul, how indispensable it is for an intellectual conversation to be less possessed by love. Please tell me whether you have had a good laugh reading this letter, for I had fits of laughter rereading it. What absurdities I have written! It is really the ravings of somebody with delirium. It does not matter, let it go! Probably it will amuse you.'

That kind of letter could scarcely 'amuse' Potemkin, nor is it likely that Catherine herself found it as funny as she pretends. But what she says about the Orlovs is significant. She must, however, have been a quite unusual comedian or else the people at court must have been astonishingly unobservant if they mistook her loyalty to, or fear of, the Orlovs for love towards Grigory Grigorievitch. Her passion for Potemkin, to whom she could write: 'If we loved each other less we would be far more intelligent, even far happier', was supreme, and even if Grigory Orlov had not behaved as foolishly as he apparently did, he could not have regained his place. The fact that he was allowed to be in attendance on Her Majesty for a few days—one of his normal duties as a court official and personal adjutant general—was completely misinterpreted by most people, not the least among them being the otherwise well-informed Gunning and Nolcken. Both were as yet rather prejudiced against Potemkin, and on the other hand overestimated the Empress's attachment to her former lover. There is a curious similarity in their reports that Catherine's tender feelings for Orlov are not completely changed, that there is no one else in the empire she can so fully trust and rely on, and that the prestige of the Orlov family is still very great.

If only Grigory Grigorievitch could behave reasonably he would be certain to regain Catherine's favor, they thought. But that was precisely the thing Grigory was incapable of doing, and finally even his own brother Alexis had to reprimand him for his lack of sense and moderation. As to Potemkin, whose jealousy of Orlov used to be quite insane, he seemed to realize quite suddenly that given enough rope Orlov would hang himself. Perhaps that was also one of the reasons why he now so patiently endured his hated predecessor's and alleged rival's offensive behavior. Grigory Orlov was not worth fighting any more; he was rapidly destroying himself without any pressure from outside, and Potemkin had other potential or active · enemies to think about. First and foremost, there was the problem of the 'young court'—the Tsarevitch Paul and his wife, the Grand Duchess Natalie, a former German Princess of Hessen-Darmstadt. Their closest and most powerful friend, and at the same time the unrivaled leader of the government, was the Tsarevitch's tutor, Count Panin. It is to this close association with the heir to the throne that Panin in a large measure owed his influence, and it was in his pedagogic—not his political—capacity that he was able to live at the palace. As he himself remarked on a certain occasion: 'As long as my bed remains in the palace, I shall not lose my influence.'

His position was quite exceptional in that he was the only person who exercised considerable influence on both the Empress and her son. From the outset of his political career Potemkin sought to win the good graces of Panin and the 'young court', and in the case of the former he was fairly successful. The Tsarevitch's relations with his mother, however, were so strained and the 'young court' was so violently opposed to everybody and everything concerning Catherine—who for her part was no less hostile to it—that Potemkin's efforts did not achieve very much. Panin was the principal link between the two factions, and since Potemkin kept off Panin's privileged domain—foreign affairs—so that as yet relations were quite friendly, it can be said that at least indirectly the favorite was thus on better terms with Catherine's son then than at almost any other period.

As Gunning reported to the Earl of Suffolk, 'Mr. Potemkin still continues to live in the greatest intimacy with Mr. Panin and affects to be governed by his opinion in Council, and the day on which that is held in town he separates himself from the rest of the members to form Mr. Panin's party.' What united Potemkin and Panin was their joint hatred of the Orlovs and the brothers Zachary and Ivan Tchernishev. The latter were dangerous and powerful enemies. Members of the Council both of them—Zachary, the field marshal, powerful at the War College of which he was vice-president, and Ivan, the senator and former ambassador to London, equally powerful at the Admiralty—both were past masters of intrigue and wirepulling at court, especially Count Zachary. The reactions of all these formidable rivals, who not unnaturally loathed Potemkin and were scared by his rapid advancement, led to many unpleasant scenes. It was known that Grigory Orlov had had an altercation of unprecedented violence with the Empress, which had moved Catherine a great deal, without, however, inducing her to depart from the established course. Her confidence in Potemkin was supreme, and she was placing ever greater power in his hands.

It is only natural that the foreign diplomats should in the first instance have tried to surmise how the intrigues and changes at court would affect the national interests they happened to represent; moreover, they all had their special friends and enemies at the court, so that the elevation of one or the loss of influence by another was of fundamental importance to them. They saw—some with alarm, others not without satisfaction—how the Orlovs and Tchernishevs, whose power had hitherto seemed unshakable and positions impregnable, were being rapidly ousted out of both; yet they found it hard to believe this was final and were often misled by the fact that in this great reshuffle some of the most prominent people, while losing their influence, managed to conserve their rank. Again, some of them were deliberately maintained in their positions by Catherine for political or personal reasons, yet at the same time deprived of any possibility of performing even the most harmless functions. Thus the direction of the College of War was soon taken out of Count Zachary's hands, instructions being issued that only orders signed by Potemkin should be obeyed, and yet for some time the infuriated and humiliated count was not allowed to resign. When finally, he was able to go, he demonstratively left St. Petersburg and put up a notice on his house: 'To be Sold or Let.' The Orlovs too, having given up the hope of counteracting Potemkin's ever-growing influence and of re-establishing their own, were preparing to withdraw from the court: the two younger ones, Theodore and Vladimir, had already resigned. Alexis was in Italy and Grigory, who had been dangerously ill, was making his final arrangements for a prolonged sojourn abroad. With the Empress's special permission he married a young relation of his, Catherine Zinoviev, and did not return to live in Russia till after her death in Lausanne in 1782. There remained of course many other powerful enemies, as, for instance, Sievers, the Governor of Novgorod, who for some reason simply loathed Potemkin. When he wrote a long letter to Catherine pouring scorn and contempt on Potemkin, the Empress promptly replied: 'Jealousy has dictated your letter, which I have burned,' and she stood up for her 'Hero' then as she always did later against any such criticism from whatever quarter.

But for a while at least it seemed as if the principal obstacles to a more peaceful atmosphere around Potemkin were removed, and as if he would now be able to settle down to the important work awaiting him without wasting time and energy in fighting the various cliques and parties opposing him. 'During the whole of my residence here,' wrote Gunning at the close of 1774, 'I have never known the interior of this court so free from intrigues, as it has been for this month past; not even the restless and turbulent spirit of the Princess Dashkov has been able to interrupt the calm that has prevailed during that time, this therefore may safely be attributed to the absence of Count Zachary Tchernishev, the main dictator and principal mover of them all. Mr. Potemkin gives, if possible, still less attention to foreign affairs than the prince did, and consequently he has not contributed either to diminish or to increase the Prussian influence.'

Gunning does not appear to have realized that Potemkin's whole attention and energy were now concentrated on home affairs, and that the internal situation of Russia was to him and to Catherine a problem of such immediate concern that foreign policy for the time being had receded to the second plane. Moreover, Panin being in charge, and neither the Empress nor Potemkin wanting any complications from that quarter, they were perfectly content to leave things as they were until circumstances would allow them to give these matters their full time and consideration.

8

POTEMKIN TAKES CHARGE

FOR a clever and energetic man there was plenty of scope
in the vast Russian Empire, and Catherine knew full well
what she was doing when she made Potemkin her lover
and principal adviser. He revealed himself a statesman from
the very first moment he came to St. Petersburg, and the
Empress saw that she had at last found the kind of support
she had been seeking so anxiously and so unsuccessfully among
her entourage. She needed that support.

Her position on the throne which she had usurpingly seized
in July 1762, was by no means as safe as appearances seemed
to suggest. There were pretenders, both dead and alive, and
there were other difficulties. Even after the brutal assassination
of her husband, the deposed Tsar Peter III, by the Orlovs,
there remained another legally crowned Tsar whose very
existence was a threat to her. Kept at the fortress of Schlüsselburg as 'Prisoner No. 1, of unknown origin', was the unfortunate Ioann Antonovitch, who in 1740, aged barely five
months, had succeeded to the throne of his great-aunt the
Empress Anna Ioannovna, as Tsar Ioann VI. But exactly a
year after his accession, in December 1741, this infant prince
was removed from the throne by force and thrown into prison
by his other aunt, Elizabeth, who now became Empress of all
the Russias. His parents, belonging to the Brunswick branch

125

of the family, were banished while he remained in the fortress where in August 1764—by now a semi-imbecile—he was strangled by his custodians, during an unsuccessful attempt to liberate him organized by a young officer called Mirovitch. In all probability Catherine, who had had to deal with this abortive plot to place him on the throne, knew of the intended murder and condoned it.

It was not easy to live all this down. People talked, and there were always some who were only too glad to dig up stories like this to prejudice opinion against the Empress. Then, in 1774, there suddenly turned up in Venice, that paradise of adventurers, a strikingly handsome young woman who claimed to be an illegitimate daughter of the late Empress Elizabeth, and styled herself 'Princess Elizabeth II of all the Russias'. She also used various other names, and although it soon became clear that she was neither Russian nor even knew anything about the alleged country of her origin, Catherine found her activities embarrassing. She feared in her an agent of her various foreign enemies, especially France and Turkey. Elizabeth was therefore lured on to a Russian boat whereupon Catherine had her transported to St. Petersburg, where the young adventuress was locked up and soon died in prison, allegedly of consumption.

True, the wretched Ioann Antonovitch and the bogus princess were mere shadows, yet even they had caused Catherine anxiety and unpleasantness. But a third shadow suddenly arose and threatened to grow into a catastrophe. Peter III, Catherine's murdered husband, had risen from the grave and soon became the center of a most dangerous movement. Shortly after the marriage of her son, the Tsarevitch Paul (yet another 'pretender' with a better claim than all the others), had been celebrated with pomp and splendor in St. Petersburg in the autumn of 1773, a rumor reached the capital that a revolt had broken out among the Ural Cossacks and that the peasants of the region were joining them. The leadership of

this movement soon passed into the hands of Emelian Pougatchev, a fellow Cossack, but from the Don district in southern
Russia, who proclaimed himself Tsar Peter III, saved by a
miracle from his would-be assassins.

It is important to note that the early organizers of the
rebellion by no means believed that this man, who did not
bear the slightest resemblance to the late Tsar and was just an
illiterate peasant, could really be Peter III. But they were not
much concerned about that. The idea was a good one and
greatly increased the chances of their movement. There had
always been false Tsars in Russia, the huge distances on the
one hand and the general ignorance of the masses on the
other making it comparatively easy for a clever swindler to play
that game. In the case of Pougatchev, the name he assumed,
and was allowed to bear by his entourage, enabled him to become a magnet attracting all the discontented elements with
which Russia was seething at the time.

Catherine's government at first greatly underestimated the
scope of this revolt, failing to see its overwhelming political
and social implications. But when, within a few months, the
rebellion had snowballed itself into a vast national movement;
when with unusual dexterity Pougatchev attracted into his
camp not only some of the desperate peasants but the various
oriental tribes living in the Ural and Volga regions as well, and
these wild Asiatics—especially the Bashkirs—began something
of a national and a religious crusade against the Russians as
such, people in St. Petersburg got a real shock. Catherine was
still trying to laugh it off, and was ironically reporting to Voltaire on the exploits of the 'Marquis de Pougatchev'; but the
failure of the local government authorities and later of the
regular troops sent out to fight and capture the rebel chief
caused her the greatest alarm.

She dispatched one of her best generals, Bibikov, to take command of the various army units whose lack of co-ordination
had hitherto proved the worst impediment to success. Under

his able leadership much ground was soon recovered from the rebels and they were driven out of most of the small towns and even fortresses they had been able to seize. People in St. Petersburg were already imagining that the mutiny was suppressed and the Pougatchev movement smashed, when General Bibikov died. His successor proved particularly indolent and inefficient. But even Bibikov himself had as yet been very far from final victory. Meanwhile, the rebellion had gathered impetus, and after the storming of Kazan on July 12, 1774, assumed the character of a Russian 'Jacquerie'. Whole estates were being burned down and the noble landlords, unless they escaped in time, hanged by the dozen.

Moreover, Pougatchev now issued a manifesto in which he promised to liberate from serfdom all the peasants who would join him, and ever-growing numbers of them did. This, and the fall of Kazan, an important city which he burned down and sacked (within twenty-four hours of his taking it, out of 2,873 houses there remained only 810), caused a real panic in the imperial capital. People began to fear that before long, carried by the revolutionary movement of which circumstances had all of a sudden made him the chief, Pougatchev might march even on Moscow.

To stave off the danger something drastic had to be done. A man had to be found not only with sufficient military ability, but of such personal authority as to inspire the rebels with fear and the country with confidence. On Potemkin's strong recommendation Catherine, conquering her personal aversion to General Peter Ivanovitch Panin, addressed herself to this distinguished brother of her old adviser and statesman. She did not like the idea of reinforcing Count Panin's influence by placing his brother in so prominent a position, and she could not forgive General Panin—a hero of many wars and famous battles—for his outspoken criticism of her. Yet she fully saw Potemkin's point that no one was better suited for the difficult task of suppressing the Pougatchev rebellion, and Peter Ivano-

vitch Panin was appointed. It is obvious that in supporting this
unpopular candidature Potemkin was anxious to ingratiate
himself further with the Panin clique, including the Tsarevitch; at the same time he saw clearly the importance of the
situation and the necessity of giving the job to the right man,
irrespective of personal considerations. The choice soon proved
a happy one. General Panin fought the rebels very successfully;
moreover his appointment practically coincided with the end
of the Turkish War so that he could use as many troops as he
wanted. But it was some time before Pougatchev, who suddenly lost his nerve and was betrayed by his closest followers,
was captured. He was publicly executed in Moscow on January 10, 1775. The very village where he had been born was
razed to the ground and rebuilt on the other side of the river,
being renamed after Potemkin as a tribute to his services in
quashing this revolt.

While General Panin was as yet fighting the rebels who
were causing havoc and devastation in one district after
another, Potemkin was busy in St. Petersburg. The Empress
had ordered all the state correspondence in connection with
the rebellion to be addressed to him, and he was ceaselessly
occupied in drafting documents, writing letters, and taking
an active part in the general direction of operations. It was
on his initiatve also that an attempt was made to get down
to the deeper cause of the rebellion. He wrote many shrewd
reports on the question of the peasants' discontent; at his suggestion prisoners were minutely cross-examined and not merely
flogged or executed as had been the case before. This reasonable
measure he only obtained after fighting the stubborn opposition of his enemy, Count Zachary Tchernishev. It is true that
Catherine and Potemkin did not draw from the knowledge
thus obtained the logical inference that it was necessary to
remedy the peasants' lot: animosity against the mutineers was
too strong for that, and to loosen the grips of serfdom or abolish
it altogether seemed unthinkable. But the Pougatchev rebel-

lion had also revealed another important aspect of Russia's internal weakness: the chaotic state of local administration in the provinces, the lack of co-ordination between the authorities on the spot and the central government, and the ignorance of St. Petersburg concerning the empire's more distant parts. That was a thing both Catherine and Potemkin took very much to heart. And night after night, in the middle of their amorous delectations, they discussed and prepared a most far-reaching set of administrative reforms, which became law on September 7, 1775, and lasted for nearly a century.

Potemkin did much work in connection with the final stages of the Turkish War, in which he had seen active service for some years before he came to St. Petersburg, and he urged the Empress to give his former chief, Roumiantsev, a free hand. According to Catherine, he was also greatly concerned in the peace of Kuchuk-Kainardje that ended this war. At the same time he was developing an active interest in the administration of the Southern Provinces, of which he was now governor general. This soon brought him into conflict with the 'Zaporoshskaya Setch'—that quaint and picturesque free community of Cossacks living beyond the Dniepr cataracts—and although their fate must have been decided then, he did not as yet take the final step of dissolving their governing body. That happened a year later, when upon his instructions a strong armed detachment suddenly seized these Cossacks' territory, arrested their elected leaders—who were characteristically enough not destroyed but compulsorily placed in a number of monasteries for life—while the 'Setch' or commune was declared nonexistent and its warrior members made into ordinary Russian peasants. There followed a vast redistribution of land formerly in their possession, Potemkin and two fellow generals each getting 100,000 acres, while some of the Cossacks who were unwilling to submit to this wholesale spoliation fled to Turkey. Those who remained were soon incorporated in the regular Russian troops.

The College of War, of which Potemkin now had sole charge, took much of his time and offered him scope for the widest possible range of activities. He had to deal with the various questions, but mostly with military, financial, and administrative problems, and he also had to attend more and more to the general transaction of the nation's affairs. He often expressed his views at the meetings of the Imperial Council, but sometimes he took it upon himself to overrule his colleagues' decisions and to act on his own initiative. In a dispatch written by Gunning at the time it is stated: 'The whole of the favorite's conduct during that day (Saturday last) manifested his most perfect assurance of his standing upon good ground. He has acquired a much greater degree of power in proportion to the time of his being in favor than any of his predecessors, and omits no opportunity of displaying it. He has lately, from his sole authority, and in opposition to the senate, let the brandy farms (the most important object of the revenue) in a manner that is not likely to prove advantageous to the Crown.' To the joy of his enemies this was not a lucky transaction, but then business was never Potemkin's strongest point. When he wrote a long memorandum suggesting the reasons for, and advantages of, leasing to his old friend and protégé the army contractor and merchant Faleyev, the rights of collecting the salt tax, Catherine's reply was short and definite: 'As long as I live no taxes will be leased.' There were also other occasions when she rejected his advice, but they were rare indeed. But when he reorganized the various economic departments and abolished the Colleges of Trade and of Manufactures she found his ideas 'entirely in agreement with her own'. His arguments for closing down the College of Trade included a strong plea for the merchants' private initiative, which should not be curtailed by government interference.

The Empress was now consulting him about everything, from the state affairs of the highest importance to the most trivial court and personal matters. He even had to correct the grammar, spelling, and style of her letters, which she would send over with an accompanying note, like, for instance, the following one: 'If there are no mistakes, please return the letter and I will seal it. If there are some, kindly correct them. Let me know whether I can come to you or not, since I absolutely forbid you to venture out into the cold corridors after the bath. Goodby, my precious.' He often had to revise the documents she was drafting. In connection with one of her innumerable manifestoes on the Pougatchev rebellion there is the following typical note from Catherine: 'Your Excellency, it is already past eleven o'clock and you have not yet returned to me the end of the manifesto; therefore it will be impossible either to copy it or to read it in Council; which will delay by a few days all other business. I beg of you to let me have it at once, if you are satisfied with my ideas; if not, please correct them. I am faithful to you unto death.'

Two more typical notes, illustrating the character of this collaboration: 'I beg of you and implore you to put a little cross like this one opposite each article you approve. If you want to cut out anything, mark it this way. If you want to make any changes, write them out,' and again: 'Either the ukase and the letter are perfectly clear, or else I am stupid today; but having full confidence in your honesty I have signed them and returned them herewith.' She even wanted his opinion on odd matters of art, sending across to him a musical score, a new play, or a poem.

He never dated his letters or documents, much to Catherine's exasperation. But he was one of the few people at her court whose command of the language, heavy and ponderous though it was in those days, was perfect. And Catherine enjoyed reading him, and frequently expressed her admiration of his strong and lucid style.

These manifold activities, developing simultaneously with his absorbing romance and the fight against his enemies, re-

quired time and energy. He knew how to find both. His behavior was a surprise to everybody: 'Grigory Alexandrovitch
now leads a very different kind of life,' Countess Roumiantsev
reported to her husband in a long letter. 'At home in the
evenings he does not play cards, but is always working there,'
and it seemed indeed new and sensational that a nobleman—
the favorite, of all people—should not be spending his nights
gambling but actually doing some work. What amazed the
countess even more was that this strange fellow, 'to whom of
course, nothing is denied, whatever he asks for,' should be personally attending the purchase of horses for the army and even
the fitting of uniforms on the soldiers. He looked into everything, much to the annoyance of the old courtiers, who did not
like his interference, and much to the joy of the loving Catherine, who felt so pleased with this striking proof that the new
favorite was not merely a lover, but a statesman, a consort in
the fullest meaning of the word.

At the same time she suffered from not seeing enough of
him. He was always out, or else he was engaged when she
happened to be calling on him. She tries to complain: 'This is
really too much! Even at nine o'clock I cannot find you alone!
I came to your apartment and found a crowd of people who
were walking about, coughing, and making a lot of noise. Yet
I had come solely to tell you that I love you excessively.' On
another occasion she writes: 'It is a hundred years since I saw
you. I do not care what you do, but please arrange that there
should be nobody with you when I come after the performance.
Otherwise this day will be unbearable. It has been sad enough
as it is. What the devil brought Von-Visin while I was with
you? I fully understand that this man may amuse you much
more than I do, my sweet, but please remember that I love
you, whereas he only loves himself.' This outburst about Potemkin's old schoolfellow and clever playwright sounds truly
pathetic. But even more so is the following short note: 'My

God! I am asking myself whether I shall see you today. Everything is empty and joyless. You can organize the political meeting anywhere you like, so long as I see you.'

Not only in politics, but in everything affecting the court, all the important decisions now rested with Potemkin. Even the drawing up of lists of candidates for honors and decorations was in his hands. Since his advent, life in St. Petersburg had assumed a different and somewhat explosive character, for the old nobles and government officials did not always surrender to his influence without a fight. According to the Swedish minister, Baron Nolcken, Potemkin so much dominated the scene that he had completely changed the aspect of the whole court—'Le Tableau de la Cour' he calls it—and gave the impression 'as if he alone had the honor to rule this empire'.

There was much evidence in support of this latter contention. When the Empress and the court were to take a short trip, for which all the preparations were already made, it was suddenly remembered that this would interfere with Potemkin's name-day, and in order to enable him to receive the congratulations of all the ranks, the nobility, and the common people, Catherine postponed her proposed excursions. In addition to her traditional present of 100,000 rubles, she granted his very special request that a Greek Archbishop should be appointed to his Southern Provinces. Church matters absorbed him as much as ever and he would interrupt an important political consultation, or any kind of work he might be engaged on, to receive a priest or stage one of his favorite theological discussions. Any cleric, whether eminent, or quite unimportant, was always certain to be well received by Potemkin. Representatives of other religions, too, could rely on his sympathetic support and understanding. He did much to alleviate the position of the various dissident sects of the Church of Russia and was anxious to improve Catherine's relations with the Vatican. Contrary to the established tradition, he felt quite

friendly towards Roman Catholicism and had many talks
with Roman prelates, both those residing in Russia and the
Pope's special envoys.

His relations with the foreign diplomats on the other hand,
were peculiar. Most of the time he seemed to avoid them. He
felt that his hour to take an active interest in foreign affairs
had not come as yet—the question of Turkey and Russia's
eastern policy being the only exception—and he wished to remain on good terms with Panin, who would have resented and
opposed any such interference. But at the same time he had
taken the unprecedented course of paying a courtesy call on the
leading diplomats—a fact recorded with amazement by
Nolcken—and when the day of Catherine's accession to the
throne was being celebrated, it was Potemkin who entertained
the Corps Diplomatique at a sumptuous supper in the palace
of Peterhof. Nolcken and his French colleague Durand were
much impressed, and despite their original animosity were now
anxious to establish friendly relations with Potemkin. But
whenever he met them or their colleagues he refused to be
drawn into a discussion on international politics and invariably
changed the subject or just tried to laugh off their overtures and
questions. This prompted Sir Robert Gunning to report that 'as
far as I can judge from the few opportunities I have had of con-
versing with him, he does not appear to me to be possessed of
those talents and abilities which he was generally supposed to
be endowed with, but on the contrary shows a great share of
levity, and a fondness for the most puerile amusements; and
what is no proof of his discernment, he has recalled a worthless ignorant Frenchman who had been for some time his
governor, in order to employ him as his secretary'.

On the question of Potemkin's ability the British representative was soon to revise his opinion, and there came a
time when, as will be seen, Potemkin's diplomatic gifts and
his statesmanship were much appreciated by England. As to
the Frenchman, whose appointment Gunning mentions with

such disapproval, he was one Vaumale de Fages—a defrocked monk, a nobleman, and former officer who had fought at Pondicherry and then had somehow found his way to Russia, where Catherine recommended him to Potemkin as a French master. He remained with Potemkin for twenty-three years and was one of his special French retinue which included an A.D.C.—the noble Chevalier de la Teissonnière, a doctor— Massot, a poet called Destat, and a number of servants, or minor attendants.

Potemkin's predilection for having picturesque foreigners on his private staff was most striking, and in addition to this odd collection of Frenchmen he had a whole army of orientals of all sorts. But his faithful factotum was a Russian, Vassily Stepanovitch Popov—the son of a village priest, who at an early age exchanged the military career on which he had embarked for the civil service, and soon distinguished himself as the efficient and omniscient secretary of Prince Dolgorouky, one of Catherine's best governor generals. Upon Prince Dolgorouky's death, Popov was taken on by Potemkin, to whom he soon became indispensable. He was his secretary, *chef de cabinet*, and confidant, carrying out the most important official and private commissions; in fact, Potemkin used to call on Popov's services at any time of the day or night—sometimes just to have a talk —and could not bear to be without him. Through his master's influence Popov also won the confidence and the favor of the Empress, who bestowed honors and decorations on him, gave him an estate, and corresponded with him about Potemkin when Potemkin himself was too busy or too casual to write.

Another particularly confidential member of Potemkin's staff was Lieutenant Colonel Baur, a Russian officer of German origin, now a principal A.D.C. to 'Serenissimus' who never gave him a moment's peace. When Baur was not in attendance he was always being sent on the most complicated errands either in Russia or abroad, the ostensible purpose being frequently to get some new delicacy for his master's table or a bottle of perfume or a jewel with which Potemkin wanted to present a lady. But in reality there was in most cases a serious political mission behind this screen of frivolous capriciousness. Baur's continuous travels led his friends to compose the following mock epitaph:

> "Ci-gît Baur sous ce rocher
> Fouette, cocher!"

Popov, Baur, the Frenchmen, and the orientals, together with innumerable others, constituted Potemkin's private staff, or 'court' as it was usually called, and Catherine also used to describe it as his 'Basse-Cour', greatly pleased with this pun which could mean either a poultry yard or a low court at choice. He liked to surround himself with interesting people, and his intellectual avidity was as strong as in his young days. He never missed the chance of talking to persons who had traveled a great deal or possessed some special knowledge—no matter how abstruse the subject—and his memory was so phenomenal that he never forgot what he had once heard. His work left him little time for reading, yet he kept up with current literature and took a great interest in the arts as well as in politics and in theology. Most of the receptions and artistic entertainments at court were now directed by him. His gift of showmanship, his love of magnificence found plenty of opportunities to manifest themselves at the Hermitage or at Catherine's various country residences, especially at Peterhof and Tsarskoe Selo. But his first great chance of revealing what he could do in this direction was in Moscow, where the court spent most of the year 1775, the purpose of that long sojourn being the celebration of a double event: the end of the Pougatchev rebellion and the end of the first Russo-Turkish War.

It was Potemkin who had persuaded Catherine to select Moscow—the heart of the empire—for these celebrations rather than stage them in the westernized and cosmopolitan St. Petersburg. Moreover, the Empress herself wanted to make a demonstration of her courage and authority in view of the unending rumors that Pougatchev had escaped from prison and been supplanted on the gallows by another, or that new serious disorders were about to break out, all of which was alleged to embarrass Catherine and her government a great deal. And Moscow, Russia's old and somewhat old-fashioned capital which had always stood in opposition to the Court of St. Petersburg whose ideas and habits it did not like at all, seemed only too willing to accept these unfavorable rumors. Catherine and Potemkin thought that it would be a good thing to counteract this by a series of spectacular displays. Potemkin had to organize it all: triumphal arches, illuminations, parades, a series of brilliant court balls at the ancient Kremlin Palace, and efforts were also made to please the lower ranks and common people. Here is a typical note from Catherine: 'Have you sent some wine to the two regiments who paraded in front of me? And have you received the list of those employed in making the peace fireworks? Excuse me if I importune you, my heart, but I would like that both these things were done, since I fear that trifles like that might be forgotten, and yet it gives pleasure to people and always has been done in the case of the artificers.'

In another note to him she says: 'I forgot to tell you that it does not matter whether the marshal [Roumiantsev] passes in the daytime or at night through the triumphal arch for it is very beautiful in the daytime as well.' It was to Potemkin that Catherine gave all her instructions with regard to honors and presents she lavished on this occasion on the various heroes of Russia's victory over the Turks. Potemkin's old chief, Field Marshal Roumiantsev, was the principal recipient of the Empress's favors, but Potemkin's other old chief Prince Galitsin, as well as Alexis Orlov whose fleet had achieved wonders in the Ægean Sea, and the rebel Pougatchev's captor General Peter Panin also got handsome rewards and new honors. How Potemkin himself was distinguished has already been described in a previous chapter.

In one of her many letters to her foreign confidante Madame Bjelke, Catherine gives a very full account of this Moscow interlude. She says: 'I have been here for four weeks now, and they seem pleased to have me. Twice a week I hold a reception at court, and each time there are not less than four or five hundred ladies. I gave three fancy dress balls to which only the nobility were admitted, and on none of these occasions were there less than six or seven thousand entrance tickets distributed. The other day I received the ratification of the treaty, signed by the Sultan. Thus this great business is finished and all the articles are confirmed word for word. I will give some peace festivals here in July, than which nothing more brilliant has ever been seen. You will say that I am entirely given to cele-· brations. But we also work a great deal and soon we will issue something which shall do infinite good to the internal state of the empire, and this year will not end without being in a sense epoch-making.'

Catherine here refers to the great administrative reform she and Potemkin were preparing, which completely reorganized the system of provincial government. But Potemkin · was also thinking of other urgent reforms, and while acting as the principal master of ceremonies at the Moscow celebrations and transacting the normal daily affairs of state, he was making · the first drafts of his great plan for reorganizing the Army. The actual army reforms, which formed one of the most outstanding achievements of his career did not take place till eight years later, the year 1783 being in that respect a landmark in Russian military history; but even in the summer of 1775 he did much to improve the status and the life of the common soldier with whom he had infinite sympathy.

Yet another idea of Potemkin's was Catherine's pilgrimage · to the ancient monastery of the Holy Trinity near Moscow. ·

The Empress, who had had to renounce the Protestant faith
and join the Church of Russia when she was about to marry
the heir to the Russian throne, had always laid great emphasis
on her devotion to her new religion. She was particularly
anxious to impress the people with the difference that existed
in that respect between her and her husband Peter III, who was
like herself a German prince, and never concealed his contempt either for the Russian people or the religion that he too
had been forced to adopt. After his assassination Catherine had
been very skillful in using to her advantage this difference between herself and the late Tsar, and succeeded in building up a
special kind of popularity for her 'Russianness', which seems
strange in view of her strong accent and poor grammar. The
intricacies of the Russian religion were also something of a
mystery to her, and when Potemkin appeared on the scene she
eagerly sought his advice and explanations. Here he was more
than ever in his element, and accompanying her to church
he loved to point out to her the various peculiarities of divine
service, and it gave her a special thrill to get this instruction
from one so well versed in these matters.

·   But she did not enjoy the pilgrimage to the monastery
of the Holy Trinity, for on their arrival there Potemkin, suddenly responding to an acute mood of religious fervor, or else
indulging in a fit of play acting, turned quite monk-like and
even talked of resigning from all his offices and retiring to a
· monastery for good. This episode has led to a story, repeated
in many books, that his religious fit was only make-believe and
that he was hoping by this means to bluff the Empress into
marrying him, which she refused to do. Since, however, they
were already married by then, and since there is no evidence
of any kind that Potemkin was bluffing (while his religious
mania is an established fact), the whole story may be dismissed
as absurd. But the fact remains that Catherine did not feel
happy and was scared of the long dark corridors with the steps
of sinister-looking bearded monks echoing in them. Had Po-

temkin been friendly, it might have been different. But he was completely aloof, and absorbed in prayer or religious discussion. She sent him a little note: 'I will never go on another pilgrimage. You are so cold with me, and my heart is faint, Giaour, Muscovite, Cossack, mixture of wolf and of bird.'

An interesting illustration of Catherine's publicity methods is the letter in which she described her visit to the monastery to Madame Bjelke. Here the sinister pilgrimage is represented in a very different way. 'My pilgrimage was very pleasant and a real picnic: we had a large and excellent party and not a dull moment: I came back in perfect health.'

This letter, which provides an eloquent counterpart to the little note she sent to Potemkin, was followed by several similar ones, in all of which she describes with enthusiasm her various other pilgrimages to the Moscow monasteries and convents, undertaken by her on Potemkin's suggestion and despite her own strong reluctance.

The same letter to Madame Bjelke also contains an interesting description of some of the celebrations, worth noting because it throws some light on Potemkin's showmanship and is in a sense a prelude to some of his later alleged or actual achievements in this respect. Catherine writes: 'I have had fever and violent diarrhœa, of which I was cured by strong bleeding; this compelled me to postpone the festivities by eight days, so that the people's celebration did not take place until Tuesday of this week, and yesterday, Thursday, it all ended with a fancy dress ball and fireworks. All these entertainments have been most successful; for staging the popular feast a large field two miles from town had been chosen, and called the Black Sea. The two roads leading to it were called: one, the Don and the other Dniepr. On the sides of these were built views of farms, windmills, villages, inns, etc. The sea was covered with boats, on the hills bordering on this field were put up buildings called [all the names that follow are towns in the Black Sea region] Kertch and Yenicalé. These were ballrooms,

Azov was the dining room and Kinburn a vast theater; the bulls, fountains of wine, rope dancers, seesaws and other amusements for the people were placed on the other side of the sea; in Tanganrog we made a fair: a firework was placed beyond the Danube; the rest of the space was adorned with an illumination; finally sixty to a hundred thousand people, perhaps even more, enjoyed themselves as much as possible on Tuesday and Thursday in this delightful spot, the sight of which was in addition to that most splendid. I am sending you a printed plan of this festival, but it is impossible to describe to you the picture represented by such a multitude of people of all ages and ranks gathered together on this space of four square miles or so. Something like four thousand carriages were there: well, despite such a multitude everything happened without the least mishap and to the general delight and merriment.'

On a site of four square miles Potemkin had staged the whole of the Black Sea region with its towns and fortresses, rivers, farms, windmills, a theater, and fountains of wine or other similar diversions. No wonder, some of his contemporaries were so impressed that later they were inclined to look even upon his real achievements as sham and nothing but a collection of scenery and decoration.

Meanwhile, not to miss the chance of spreading the news of all this magnificence abroad, Catherine not only supplied her foreign friends with a printed plan of the Moscow peace celebrations, but had a special etching prepared, which she sent to her press agent in chief, the ever-serviceable Grimm. Here again, however, the favorable picture drawn by her does not wholly agree with the facts, and according to the Swedish minister, Baron Nolcken, the people of Moscow did not show nearly as much enthusiasm as Catherine suggests. He even reports that on several occasions crowds assembled under the windows of the Tsarevitch Paul's apartments and cheered him every time he appeared, which was a deliberate insult to Catherine. Nobody came to her windows, and nobody cheered

her. Nolcken even quotes in his dispatches a private letter of
Catherine, of which he managed to obtain a copy, where the
Empress complains of the hostile atmosphere she found in
Moscow and says that she is surrounded by people 'whose
attachment appears doubtful'.

The observant Swedish diplomat, who disliked both Russia
in general and Potemkin in particular, is full of gossip about
the court's protracted stay in Moscow. He notes with a certain
amount of malicious pleasure, various titbits of society scandal,
such as a row between two influential courtiers ending in a
duel, which was ascribed to Potemkin's Machiavellian machinations; the discontent of those left out of the honors list,
the somewhat sensational elopement of young Countess
Rasoumovsky with young Count Apraxin, who were caught
and severely punished. A more lenient attitude on Catherine's
part was generally expected, but her strong condemnation of
other people's immorality was due to stern prudery which was
not a pose: it was quite genuine, and not visualizing herself
in the same light as others, she never understood the full extent of this paradox.

Despite his hostility, even Nolcken cannot help being impressed by the magnificent dinner offered by Potemkin to
the foreign diplomats at the Kremlin and the tour of inspection on which their host takes them through the ancient
citadel and palace, every detail of which he points out and explains to them. An amusing diversion is procured through the
arrival of a Turkish delegation with 500 musicians, spahis, and
janissaries led by Kerim Effendi, who repeatedly march
through the streets of Moscow, this picturesque procession
naturally attracting much attention.

On the whole, however, despite the festivities and general
merriment, the atmosphere at the court was growing tense.
Potemkin had had a warm altercation with the Tsarevitch
Paul, who, according to Gunning, was rapidly growing more
and more like his half-witted father, his behavior causing

much consternation and apprehension. It also seemed that
Panin had lost all his influence over his former pupil, and in
consequence of that his own position was weaker than it ever
had been.

The old count was even thinking of offering his resignation, and was visibly hurt that his brother's victory over
Pougatchev had not received greater recognition. Moreover,
Potemkin was now venturing more and more into the domain
of foreign affairs so that relations between him and Panin
were getting rather strained. That the Empress had selected
Potemkin for the purpose of entertaining the Corps Diplomatique, both in Peterhof and now in Moscow, was humiliating enough to her old adviser, who for so many years had acted
as Foreign Minister. But what annoyed him even more was
that Potemkin, abandoning his earlier deference at the meetings of the Imperial Council, was getting into the habit of con-
tradicting him and even challenging his opinion. Before long
it came to an open conflict.

A report happened to arrive on disturbances in Persia. Potemkin suggested that it might serve Russia's purpose to fo-
ment these disturbances still further. Whereupon Panin broke
out in a regular diatribe against him saying that he would
never be a party to such a policy. None of the other members
of the Council took any part in the debate, and among general
silence, visibly annoyed, Potemkin broke up the meeting.

All this was promptly reported to London, since the British
minister, who had always followed Russia's affairs with zeal
and in a friendly spirit, was at the time particularly interested
in Catherine's foreign policy and in the respective influence of
her various advisers. A new and unprecedented chapter was
rapidly developing in Russo-British relations, on which
curiously little light has been thrown by the historians in both
countries. For some time past England through her various
envoys had been seeking an alliance with Russia, Gunning's
original instructions and those of his predecessor Lord Cath-

cart being very definite on this subject. Independently of that, the British representatives were also to give Catherine formal assurances that England had no objection whatever to Russia's expansion in the Black Sea region, and the congratulations offered by London in connection with the victory over the Turks were surprisingly profuse. But although relations · were most friendly between the two countries neither of them seemed willing or capable of giving them the final shape of an alliance. Great Britain's insistence in that direction is most · remarkable and at no time were her efforts more energetic than during the five-year embassy of James Harris, who was soon to succeed Gunning. Both these diplomats, who began by being antagonistic to Potemkin, had eventually to seek his support, and Harris gradually learned to like and admire him. In the meantime, however, an issue had arisen, which was altogether outside the wider question of an alliance. King George III found it necessary to approach the Empress of Russia to request the loan of some of her troops to fight the rebellious American colonies. The first instructions on this delicate matter sent to Gunning by the Earl of Suffolk were very carefully worded. The Foreign Secretary wrote: 'The rebellion in a great part of His Majesty's American colonies is of such a nature as to make it prudent at least to look forward to every possible exertion that any unfavorable concurrence of circumstances would call for, and to be prepared with full information thereon; at the same time that the very idea of some of the means which present themselves for inquiry, may, at this moment, seem both exceptionable and romantic or, at least, such as we have no probable reason to apprehend will become necessary. Subject to this explanation, I can venture to mention to you my private wishes that you will endeavor to learn whether, in case it should hereafter be found expedient to make use of foreign troops in North America, his Majesty might rely on the Empress of Russia to furnish him with any considerable corps of her infantry for that purpose. I need not observe to you that

this commission is of the most delicate nature and proper only
to be entrusted to a minister of approved discretion and abilities; its whole propriety indeed depends on its execution; and
in whatever method you introduce the conversation, whether
with Mr. Panin or Count Ostermann [the Vice-Chancellor]
or the Empress herself, you will be very careful to do it unaffectedly, so as to give it quite the air of an idle speculation of
your own and by no means that of a proposition, and you will
avoid on the one hand, an appearance of seriousness in the
business which does not, and I hope never will, exist, and on
the other, the letting empty assurances be set down to our account as solid obligations. If you should find readiness or a disposition in the Russian court to embrace the suggestion, you
must defer your departure for England until you hear from
me again in consequence of your answer to this despatch. I
shall be sorry, in that case, to have deranged the plan which
you had settled for the removal of your family; but I am too
well convinced of your zeal in His Majesty's service, to doubt
your cheerful acquiescence, when the occasion is so important.'

This private and confidential message, dated June 30, 1775,
found Gunning in Moscow, whither he had followed the court
although he had originally thought that the celebrations would
leave no time for business and that his presence would be
merely costly and quite useless. To his surprise, he found
Catherine and her ministers hard at work, despite the festivities, and that there was a great deal to report. But when the
delicate question of borrowing troops from Russia arose, his
task proved arduous indeed. Before long, the British Govern-
· ment became much more explicit. What they wanted was a
Russian army of 20,000 men and they were prepared to shoul-
· der all the expenses of such an unusual expedition. Catherine,
flattered as she was that her soldiers were held in such high
repute by a country like England—no doubt Russia's recent
victories had greatly enhanced her military standing—and
though feeling very sympathetic towards King George III,

could not see her way to grant his request. But endless negotiations took place, poor Gunning using every means in his power to achieve the desired object. Having failed to get any action out of the friendly but ever dilatory Panin, the British envoy finally conquered his prejudice, and in despair sought the support of Potemkin, whom he had previously believed to be obstructing his *démarches*. But Catherine was absolutely adamant, and although first Panin and later Potemkin tried to sponsor England's interests—which led the British envoy on several occasions to the optimistic conclusion that he had obtained what he wanted—the Empress refused Russia's intervention. This refusal is all the more remarkable when one recollects that in those very days the German kings and princes were gladly selling their soldiers to the highest bidder. Even a personal letter from George III, accompanied by a draft for a treaty between Great Britain and Russia, could not move her. She, too, wrote the King a long personal letter and, while wishing him every success and expressing her friendly feelings towards him, explained why the sending of a Russian expeditionary corps to America was impossible. Of the mass of correspondence that developed around this interesting episode, the following dispatch is worth quoting, because it reveals that not only the Russian Army but even her comparatively young Navy was held in high repute by the British envoy. This is what Gunning wrote to the Earl of Suffolk: 'I flatter myself I shall not be disapproved of for suggesting to Your Lordship the means of obtaining, at a very short warning, a considerable body of excellent and experienced seamen; I mean those who have for some time served on board the Russian fleet in the Mediterranean, part of whom have already returned, and the rest soon expected, out of which number, I am assured, nearly four thousand could be selected fit for service.' The British minister thought that Catherine would gladly lend her best sailors, but she would not even hear of it.

In making his suggestion Gunning had overlooked a very

important fact. While all these diplomatic negotiations were going on, Potemkin—as yet in Moscow—was giving much of his time to a special task he had set himself and which he took much to heart throughout his career: the fortification of Russia's southern border through the expansion of the Black Sea fleet, and the construction of new cities in that vast region, of which he was governor general. The earliest and one of the most important steps he took in that direction was the project he submitted to Catherine, and which she promptly approved, of building two new fortresses near the Turkish frontier, with more to follow. The first of these fortresses, to be placed quite near the sea, at a point where the rivers Dniepr and Bug became confluent, was called Kherson and from the very outset Potemkin determined to make it a trading center as well as an important naval base. Within two years of its foundation, Kherson, which Potemkin had endowed with large wharves and a nautical school, saw a host of ships, sailing under the Russian flag and carrying important merchandise, make a rapidly increasing use of this new harbor, while foreign merchants soon began to open offices there. And here was only the beginning of his great work as a builder, a work that was to assume a far wider scope in the years that followed.

But in this, as in everything else, his enemies at the court were continually seeking to minimize his achievement, criticize his methods, discredit his authority. They even tried to steal his ideas, and he had to fight to keep their realization in his own hands. From the following note by Catherine it may be inferred that an attempt was made to get the building of Kherson away from him. 'I kiss you a thousand times, my friend, for your letter of today and you are right: Kherson shall not be built without you. Thank you for not being angry, and a thousand thanks. Be merry and keep in good health.'

Nothing could shake the Empress's firm belief in Potemkin; but attempts to oust him from her confidence were made almost daily. His personality seemed to create enmity among

Catherine's entourage almost at sight. He towered so high above them in intellect, resource, authority, and even physique, that he could not but provoke jealousy and irritation. His own attitude to people—well in conformity with the general display of arrogance towards, and contempt for, their fellow courtiers, so prevalent even among the best men around Catherine—was calculated to give offence. By a perverted sense of humor, or out of genuine goodness of heart, he was always kind and human with those in a humble position and insolent in the extreme with people of rank. The power which he exercised over the Empress infuriated the different court cliques, and he had to wage a constant war against them, sometimes being driven to side with one group and sometimes with another, but always in danger of being betrayed by them, or else of adding to his difficulties through his own lack of balance and ever-increasing moodiness.

9

LOVE ADJUSTED

POTEMKIN'S liaison with the Empress had now lasted over two years. Despite their love, despite their close collaboration which was a joy to both of them, despite even the strong bond of their secret marriage, the stormy aspect of their relationship had not subsided. There were frequent scenes. His spleen, his eccentricities, and his insane jealousy continued to give this passionate association a most explosive character.

He always reproaches her with condoning the incessant intrigues against him or allowing his enemies to remain in her entourage. She, on the other hand, complains of his lack of confidence in her, or that he is not as considerate, loving, cheerful, tender, as she would like him to be. They repeatedly accuse each other of depriving their union of that harmony, for which both of them pretend to be craving, and which neither of them has it in his nature to create.

'Really, it is time to live in perfect harmony,' she writes to him. 'Do not torment me by treating me badly and then you will not see my coldness. But I will no longer answer your rudeness by being tender. I love frankness and feel no difficulty about being frank. I am sorry, my pigeon, that you are ill. Try to give your mind a rest, it needs it. Besides you must rely on the goodness of my heart, which does not like to create or see suffering; I would be glad to see the same disposition in other men towards me.'

In another long letter she says: 'I think you love me, though often, very often, there is not the slightest trace of love in your conversations with me. But do not worry, I am just and understanding: I never judge others by their words when I see that they are speaking them in anger . . . All my acts, darling, have had no other purpose than to bring harmony into our lives.'

He would write to her, putting down his complaints and grievances, asking for her protection against those who he thought were insulting or besmirching him. And here is Catherine's reply to one of these letters: 'Your long letter and the stories you tell me in it: all that is very well, but what is ugly is that it does not contain a single tender word for me. What profit can I derive from learning all the vast lies of other people, lies which you have reported to me in such detail? And to think that in repeating to me all this nonsense you never bothered to remember that there is a woman in this world who loves you and who is entitled to a word of tenderness from you. Fool, Tartar, Cossack, Giaour, Muscovite, demon!' Then they would make it up again and love each other so ardently that she feels constrained to write to him imploring him to leave her earlier, since staying up so late is bad for her health. One day they even draw up a new 'contract'—a letter written by both of them on the same sheet—just as the one that settled one of their early quarrels. Here it is:—

In Potemkin's Hand.	*In Catherine's Hand.*
My beloved soul.	I know.
You know I belong to you.	I am aware of it.
I only have you in this world.	It is true.
I am faithful to you unto death.	Undoubtedly.
Therefore your interests are very dear to me.	I believe you.
The thing that pleases me	Proved a long time ago.

most is to serve you and to be
used by you.

Having done anything for me   What exactly?
You will never regret it, you   I am willing to do it, but tell
will see what benefit you will de- me what it is you want, for I am
rive from it.   stupid.

Potemkin sends her a note: 'I was prevented, dear Mother,
and Empress mine, from congratulating you personally in
connection with the Holy Communion. God grant you a long
life and perpetual success. As to me, I only seek your approval,'
and she writes back: 'I thank you very much; am going to bed,
for I am very tired.' Then he has a fit of anger again and she
hastens to send him the following *billet:* 'If you have a grain of
pity for me, please come to me and get your fury off your
chest. I assure you that I am innocent.'

Sometimes his behavior completely exasperates her, and
even she, who is normally so tender and forgiving, so humble
in making the first approaches for a reconciliation, indulges
in an outburst of considerable violence: 'I must expect such
fury from Your Serene Highness, since you seem to be anxious
to prove to the public, and to me, how boundless is your lack
of self-control, and of course this will be a clear proof of your
ingratitude to me and how little attached to me you are. For
this fury is contrary both to my desire and the difference in our
affairs and stations. The Court of Vienna, too, will now be
able to judge how reliable I am in recommending people for
their highest honors; that is how you care for my glory.' But
her anger never lasts long, and when Potemkin goes on sulking
for days and she does not see him, she feels quite miserable.
She then mixes her reprimands with protestations of love,
makes pathetic attempts to be funny or detached, and ends
up by producing one of those long effusions which she knows
irritate him so. 'If you find any pleasure in a permanent quarrel
with me,' she writes to him one day, 'if you no longer have the
least spark of love for me, I beg of you to put a curb on your ill-

temper and to listen to my words without immediately showing
me your annoyance. Since Friday up to this day I find myself in
a state of incessant anxiety. If my peace of mind is dear to
you, have the kindness to stop your sulking. Make room for
the good sentiments, which, together with rest and tranquillity,
will be much pleasanter for both of us than our present state. I
really love tender words but I equally like to see a friendly face
in front of me. Awaiting the result of this letter I am full of
hope, without which I could not live—just like all other humans, by the way.'

But the following two letters explain better than anything
else the nature of their quarrels and the state of their minds
as they were approaching a crucial point in their stormy romance.

'Your tender conduct towards me,' writes Catherine to
Potemkin, 'shines everywhere, but your foolish acts remain
the same: at the very moment when I feel safest a mountain
drops on me. At the present moment, when the least word
from me causes you annoyance, will you please compare your
own words and acts to mine? Just now, when you are preaching
to me that we should live in perfect harmony and have no
secrets, you are aiming at nothing else than causing both of us
to be worried—since to you peace is an unbearable state of
mind. The gratitude I owe you has not disappeared, for there
is not a single instant when I do not give you proofs of it. But
it is equally true that having given me the means of being an
Empress you take all my force away from me by tormenting
me all the time with your insufferable and continually recurring caprices. Thus my situation is most unpleasant; please tell
me whether I should be grateful to you for that? Until now I
had always thought that good health and a quiet life represented a certain value; but I would like to know how this is
possible when one is linked up with you?'

The second of these letters, written almost entirely in
French, is a very full statement on the subject of their eternal

conflicts, and their growing discord. This is how the Empress puts it:

'The way you sometimes talk, one might say that I am a monster! which has all the faults, and especially that of being stupid. I am horribly dissimulating; when I am in pain, when I cry, this is not owing to sensibility but for some other entirely different reason, and therefore you must despise all that and treat me with contempt, which is bound to score over my mind; yet this mind, wicked and horrible though it may be, knows no other way of loving than making happy whomsoever it loves, and for this reason it finds it impossible to bear even for a moment a breach with him whom it loves, without—to its despair—being loved in return. It is even more impossible for that mind to be constantly occupied with reproaching, at all moments of the day, him whom it loves with this or that. On the contrary, my mind is busy trying to find some virtues, some merits, in the object of its love. I like to see in you all the marvels. Just tell me, how would you be if continuously I were reproaching you with the faults of all your acquaintances, of all those whom you respect or whose services you use most, if I made you responsible for the silly things they do, would you be patient or impatient? If, seeing your impatience, I became angry, got up, ran away slamming the doors behind me, if after that I were chilling with you (*sic*) and refused to look at you and even pretended to be more cold than I really was, and added threats to all that? You might settle that question. If I gave myself airs with you, finally if, after all that, your head were hot and your blood were boiling, would it be surprising if both of us proved lacking in common sense, or that we should fail to agree or that we should both talk at the same time. For God's sake, please do all that is in your power to avoid our quarreling, for the causes of all our quarrels are always insignificant. The essence of our disagreement is always the question of power and never that of love. This is the truth. I know what you will answer me, but do not give your-

self the trouble of doing so. Leave this without an answer
since I have decided not to worry about all this. Do you want
to make me happy? Talk to me about yourself and I will never
be angry.'

Catherine was quite right; it was the question of power ·
that was incessantly worrying Potemkin and causing most of
the trouble between him and the Empress. Yet what more
could she give him, when she had already gratified every wish
of his, raised him to unprecedented heights, and even
cemented this union by formal marriage? He was the first ·
man in the realm, he dominated both Russia and the woman
through whom he had achieved this vertiginous ascension to
power, yet he was neither happy nor satisfied. A duchy or ·
even a throne could have been his for the asking—Catherine's
influence in a number of vassal states was strong enough for
that. He did not want any of these things. But his restless soul
knew no peace and the idea of trying to find it in the service
of God rather than that of the state never abandoned him.
Yet even a monastery offered no real solution, for Potemkin's
moody and tempestuous nature, his keen intellect, could not
have been lastingly subdued by religious fervor, deep and
genuine though it was. His relations with Catherine were
weighing heavily on him. He had been in love with her almost
since the first moment he saw her. But now, after two years ·
of the closest proximity, of a mental and physical intimacy
beyond which it was impossible to go, he found that their passion was wearing them out and that they were tempera-
mentally quite unsuited for carrying on much further with any
measure of success, the existing relationship.

Despite the invaluable services he had rendered, his power
rested entirely on the monarch's favor; he was fully aware of
that. But he saw with equal clarity that if their uninterrupted
love quarrels, which neither of them seemed able to avoid or
prevent, were allowed to continue and assume ever-growing
vehemence, there was a serious danger that one day Catherine

the Empress might triumph over Catherine the woman and dismiss him altogether. He would then be reduced—marriage or no marriage—to the hateful status of his many predecessors whom he despised so much. Potemkin was not prepared to suffer that humiliation. He was not ready to go yet. There was a great deal of work to be done; his head was simply seething with ideas and plans of the utmost importance for the good of his beloved fatherland, for the glory of his adored Empress. Who else was capable of doing it all? He was not going to shirk his duty or miss his chance.

He realized that a moment was approaching when he would have to make the choice between love and work, between power and romance. Potemkin decided in favor of power. A subtle psychologist, he foresaw the development things were bound to assume and began to make his preparations. With the same dexterity and intuition, with the same resolve that had originally won him his position, he now gradually withdrew from it. And he managed it so skillfully that not only did his power suffer no diminution but that, on the contrary, he found new and practically unlimited scope for its application.

To assure the full success of this maneuver three things were essential. In the first place he must keep Catherine's absolute confidence at any price, even without sharing her bed. Secondly, when selecting a successor for that particular function he would have to make sure that the new favorite, or *mignon* as the foreign diplomats used to describe it, was a man personally devoted to him and of sufficient insignificance to be entirely dominated by him. Finally, the whole change must be brought about in such a way that Catherine should feel convinced she was acting on her own initiative. Under no circumstances was she to realize that he desired a change in their relationship; he remembered only too well to what an extent Catherine the Empress had resented Orlov's disregard of her female susceptibilities, and he was not going to risk provoking her that way. In carrying through his plan

he therefore behaved throughout in such a manner as to give
Catherine and the outside world the impression that it was he
who was losing ground, and that it was the Empress who was
gradually bringing their notoriously stormy liaison to a close.

Both the court and the foreign diplomats were taken in
completely. 'If I may credit the information I have lately received,' reported Gunning early in 1776 from St. Petersburg,
whither the court had finally returned from Moscow, 'the
Empress begins to see the liberties of her favorite in a different
manner from what she had hitherto done. Count Alexis Orlov
resigning all his posts hurt her so much, as to have brought on
an illness and first taught her the general report that prevails.
It is already whispered that a person who has been placed about
her by Mr. Roumiantsev, bids fair to gain her entire confidence. This will ensure the marshal's credit; he is by no means
French, but altogether devoted to the Prussian Majesty.'

What Gunning, who was, as ever, concerned with the diplomatic consequences of the possible change, did not know, was,
that the whole episode of Alexis Orlov's resignation had been
fully discussed between Catherine and Potemkin, who drafted
all the documents and correspondence relating to it, so that
there was really no surprise and no shock of any kind. As to the
question of a possible new favorite, Potemkin himself was
secretly looking for a suitable candidate. It was not easy to find
one to comply with his own and the Empress's requirements.
There were many presentable young men at the court, but
Catherine was so much in love with Potemkin and so faithful
that she had not even bothered to glance at one of them. Perhaps there was just one solitary exception. Of the two clever
young private secretaries she had recently appointed, Bezborodko and Zavadovsky, the latter was particularly good-
looking and pleasant. He wrote well, possessed some rudi-
ments of history and philosophy, and knew a little Latin; quite
an erudite young man. That Catherine liked him had not
escaped Potemkin's notice. Nor had he failed to perceive

that this young secretary was a modest, moderately capable, and easily manageable person. The fact that he was the son of a prominent priest from the Ukraine was yet another asset in Potemkin's eyes.

Young Zavadovsky's record was good. He had served in the Turkish War, where he had even earned the St. George's Cross, had then entered the civil service in Moscow, and was finally recommended to the Empress, together with Bezborodko, for secretarial work by his former chief, Roumiantsev. It was left to Bezborodko to achieve by far the greater career of the two, and in later years by mere hard work and ability he raised himself to the position of one of Catherine's principal ministers. But as yet he and his young colleague were running in double harness, and whatever distinctions, presents, and rewards Catherine saw fit to bestow on her private secretaries were divided with absolute equality. The mere suspicion of any special favors for Zavadovsky would have roused the insanely jealous Potemkin, with whom the promise to kill any possible successor was by no means an idle threat, to such fury that Catherine would never have dared to show her tender feelings, even if she had any.

Now, however, the question became very different. Having once made up his mind to provide the Empress with a suitable playmate, and having selected his candidate without either of these two people even suspecting anything about it, Potemkin, step by step, proceeded to put his plan into operation. Pretending to be affected by ill-health, he was withdrawing more and more from the exacting presence of the loving Catherine. Even during the Moscow celebrations hard work or indisposition had repeatedly compelled him to stay away from some of the very festivities he had himself organized. Back in St. Petersburg his growing inattention to the Empress or his frequent absence from court functions soon became the talk of the town. It was obvious that relations between the lovers were strained, and Potemkin seemed to be riding for a fall.

Yet there was something very paradoxical in the whole situation, which neither the foreign diplomats nor the Russian courtiers, who were watching these developments with ever-growing suspense, could understand. Whether the cause of Potemkin's strange behavior was a breach with the Empress, or ill-health—he was reported to be suffering from serious in-digestion—or just one of his recurring fits of melancholia—with the monk's hood always in the offing—the bewildering thing was that, instead of diminishing, his power seemed to increase. All the principal posts previously held by Grigory Orlov now devolved on him. An intrigue in which Potemkin was believed to be actively concerned, aiming at the removal of old Count Panin from office, seemed to be on the verge of realization, and according to rumor it was Potemkin's inten-tion to take the direction of Russia's foreign affairs into his own hands. Thus Richard Oakes, who, on Sir Robert Gun-ning's departure, had become British chargé d'affaires, was justified in reporting to Mr. William Eden, the under-secre-tary, that Potemkin's influence 'is certainly in its meridian without the least signs of a diminution'. Yet the apparent rift between Catherine and her lover seemed to be growing, and the atmosphere in the palace resembled a lull before the storm. The Orlovs re-emerged at court and it was even rumored that they would soon return to power. Alexis, who had only just arrived from Italy, was tipped as Potemkin's successor at the War College. Grigory, however, had not yet recovered from a recent stroke of palsy, but was visited several times by Catherine. 'Two visits, which the Empress made to the prince during his illness,' writes Oakes, 'caused a very warm alterca-tion between her and the favorite, and though he seems at present to enjoy the plenitude of power, his fate is confi-dently foretold by many as an event at no great distance, but this, I presume, arises rather from its being universally wished than from any actual symptoms. A proof of the bad opinion that is entertained of his character, is the credit (however undeserving it may be) which the report of his having caused poison to be given to Prince Orlov, gains with numbers here. Indeed his jealousy of everyone who meets with any kind of distinction from the Empress, is excessive and seems to be expressed in a manner and upon occasions which cannot render it flattering to his mistress but, on the contrary, is likely to disgust her.'

A diversion was provided by the arrival in St. Petersburg of Prince Henry of Prussia, Frederick the Great's brother. The object of this visit was to endeavor to lure Russia back to Prussia's side. Although Frederick had behaved very badly to Catherine and had repeatedly betrayed her implicit trust, finally incurring her justified description of him as a 'disloyal scoundrel' through his anti-Russian machinations in Turkey, he was always hoping by mendacious flattery to re-establish himself in the good graces of the Russian Empress. Had he not helped to place her—as yet only one of his poor relations— on the throne of Russia? But that was long ago, and now she was a proud and powerful woman with a strong will of her own. Prince Henry was to see what could be done about it, and was to show special deference to Potemkin, since he was known throughout Europe still to have the strongest possible influence over the Empress.

The letters and messages written by Catherine to Potemkin before and during this visit show how completely all the outside observers were misjudging the nature of their relations, and how fundamentally unchanged these were. 'My darling, my dear husband,' she writes, 'I attribute your spleen solely to the fact of your taking cold baths. I have told you that they affect me the same way. I have just received news from Riga saying that Prince Henry must arrive here on March 21, that was last Monday. I think he will be here at the begin-

Prince Grigory Alexandrovitch Potemkin
(From an engraving by Charitonov)

The Empress Catherine II
(*From a painting by Levitsky*)

ning of Holy Week. My pigeon, my friend, be happy and get
rid of your spleen.' From the next *billet* it is obvious that,
despite everything, Catherine and Potemkin were still spending at least an occasional night together and that she was still
calling him by her special, tender, diminutive names: 'Grishi-
fishetchka, you are lying. I remember . . . for you were asleep
and I was not! Here is the letter from Prince Henry: he is not
coming.' The Prince finally arrived on April 2, 1776, and almost the first thing he did was to invest Potemkin with the
insignia of the Black Eagle previously conferred upon him
by Frederick the Great. They had a long talk even before
the Empress received her distinguished German relation, and
here again a *billet* from Catherine to Potemkin is significant.
'When the prince speaks to you please listen carefully to him
and tell me afterwards all he said, so that I could form a
proper judgment.' She attached particular importance to the
friendly relations that had existed between Potemkin and
Prince Henry ever since the prince's preceding visit to Russia,
and as will be remembered had even personally drafted the
letter by which Potemkin informed the prince that he had
been made a Knight of the St. Andrew Order. A week after
Prince Henry's arrival Potemkin gave a magnificent reception
for him, with a concert at which the famous French violinist
Joly played, the Empress and all the leading courtiers and
diplomats being present. Catherine had sent her husband a
little note saying: 'Your protectress and friend advises you to
wear the Prussian Order and this will be a courtesy and attention.' But according to Nolcken, Potemkin looked so gloomy
at his own party that when he approached the Empress she
glanced at him and the black ribbon he was wearing and then
said: 'My God, this color goes well with your expression.'

  Were they playing a comedy? It might almost appear they ·
were. For in public they seemed more and more estranged
from each other, while their private relations, judging from
Catherine's habitual messages, were the same as ever. Indeed, ·

they were conspicuous for their tenderness at the very time of this alleged rift. How little the outside world knew what was really going on can be judged from the following dispatch by Oakes. He describes Potemkin as a partisan of Prince Henry who, he thinks, 'contributed much towards retarding the removal of Prince Potemkin whom the ribbon has bound to his interests. It is possible, however, that in a few days an end will be put to those appearances of favor which are still preserved towards him.'

Meanwhile general interest had been focused on something else. The Tsarevitch's wife, the Grand Duchess Natalie, was just on the point of becoming a mother, and finally on April 15, died in childbirth. Catherine, who liked neither her son nor her daughter-in-law, felt bound to be present throughout this painful and tragic confinement, and kept sending messages with all the details to Potemkin who spent the whole of that night playing cards. She seemed deeply moved. Yet, no sooner was the young grand duchess dead, than Catherine decided to find the widowed Tsarevitch a new wife and availed herself of the presence of Prince Henry to take the necessary preliminary steps and discuss all the possible candidates. That these were to come from Germany, the acknowledged purveyor of consorts both male and female to all the thrones of Europe, was of course understood.

The court moved to Tsarskoe Selo, and Prince Henry was spending most of his time either in consultation with the Empress or the Tsarevitch, who seemed much overcome with grief.

But Frederick's envoy did not neglect Potemkin, and even presented him with a valuable ring as a token of his personal admiration and in memory of their interesting conversations. The court, however, interpreted this gift as a small farewell *douceur* before the imminent dismissal by Catherine of her no longer wanted lover. An unexpected move on the part of the Empress herself only confirmed that impression; she suddenly presented Potemkin with a large house or private palace in the Nevsky Prospect, St. Petersburg's main thoroughfare. It was he who had asked for a town residence of his own and they had been discussing the idea for some time. Finally, she had sent him a note: 'Will you, please, yourself say or write to Elaghin that he should find and buy you a house in accordance with your desires. And I will also confirm it to him, while in the meantime I gladly believe what you say, for your thoughts are kind and proper.' Before long Potemkin reported to her that he had his eye on the Anitchkov Palace, formerly the property of Bibikov and later of Rasoumovsky. Since Catherine was in no hurry to reply, he sent her a note: 'Ma'am, I have been waiting for four days that you should say something about our plans concerning the Bibikov house.' This is followed by a line written in the lovers' special code, and the meaning of these signs can only be guessed to have been something pleasant. For Catherine's answer was: 'If you are anxious for a little comedy I will tell Your Excellency that seeing your ill-temper I could not find an opportunity of speaking to you about the Bibikov house, whereas now, touched by your *billet-doux*, I have the honor to tell Your Excellency that . . .' and here too there follows a line written in code. He was growing impatient, and the following note from Catherine did not satisfy him: 'My sweetest soul, we shall talk of the Bibikov house later.' So he sent her a long letter which must have been full of reproaches. Her reply, written from beginning to end in French was: 'Listen to me, my friend, your letter would require some long discussions if I wanted to answer it in detail; I select the two main points from it. The first, Anitchkov's house. [This palace was continually referred to under the different names of its three previous owners.] In Moscow they wanted four hundred thousand rubles for it; this is an enormous sum and I would not know where to take it, but Elaghin need only inquire for the price; perhaps it has become cheaper; it is a house that is uninhabitable and is

threatened by ruin; on one side the whole wall is cracked; the
upkeep and repairs would, I think, amount to something considerable. The second point is friendship; I venture to affirm
that there is no friend more faithful than I am, but what is
necessary to be a friend? I always thought it was mutual confidence, and on my side it has been complete. I told you what I
think about that a very long time ago. It remains to find out
what weighted heavier in the scales; confidence or considerations, etc. . . . . but let there be no more discussions. I do not
wish either to argue or to annoy; I know how to respect and I
realize the price of things.'

Potemkin managed to get his way, and on June 22, 1776,
the Empress addressed the following official document to him:
'Prince Grigory Alexandrovitch, we are pleased to present to
you for eternal and hereditary ownership the Anitchkov house
purchased by us from Count Rasoumovsky; kindly take possession of it from Elaghin, who has been instructed to repair
and fit it up in accordance with your tastes, spending for this
purpose up to one hundred thousand rubles.' At the same time
Catherine who was not normally in the habit of haggling about
money, paid, not without complaints about his extravagance,
Potemkin's huge debts, which he kept on incurring despite the
large income he derived from his estates and the salary he was
drawing or the imposing monetary presents he was receiving
regularly in addition to his revenues. According to Baron Nolcken, Potemkin's debts at that period were estimated at something like 400,000 rubles; but these figures, based on gossip and
guesswork, are not very reliable. And whatever he did owe,
it greatly pleased Catherine that at the very time she was
settling his debts he presented her with a large spray of the
rarest emeralds.

Nobody could make out what their relations really were,
but the general assumption was that Potemkin's 'credit' as the
current phrase was, had fallen to its lowest point, and, now

that a town residence had been purchased for him, he was expected to be dismissed from the palace at any moment. 'Why does he not draw the conclusions?' the courtiers said. 'Surely the poor fellow ought to realize his position and leave for some trip or other.' And all his enemies—even the Orlovs and Panin, who had always loathed each other, now joined forces—were going out of their way to precipitate his fall. Alexis Orlov, availing himself of an old prerogative of speaking to the Empress frankly and bluntly, went to see her, and, in strong language, represented to her the general unpopularity of Potemkin. He emphasized the fact that Potemkin's haughtiness, when he was at work, made all co-operation with him impossible, while his apathy and neglect when he was passing through one of his depression periods, had a paralyzing effect on the normal transaction of state business. She should realize the damage her favorite was causing her, Alexis Orlov suggested, and dismiss him without further delay. At the same time he opened up a new vista to her; no one wished to deny the beloved Monarch a *liaison de cœur*, he said. But the happy man in possession of the almighty Empress's heart should be contented with that and not crave for supreme power over the people and the state at the same time. Any interference from that quarter could only exercise a most destructive influence on the peace and prosperity of the empire, creating discontent among Her Majesty's most humble subjects—that is the nobility, of course, for the rest did not count. As on previous occasions, Catherine listened to all this and said nothing that would commit her in any way. She also had something else on her mind, for in consultation with Potemkin she and Prince Henry, who was just about to leave for Berlin, were making the final arrangements for the Tsarevitch's proposed trip to Germany. The prospects of going abroad pleased Catherine's son so much that he almost forgot his recent bereavement and was running about the palace in Prus-

sian cavalry uniform, his headgear—according to Baron Nolcken—transcending in size and shape anything to be found in
Prussia itself.

When finally the grand duke, accompanied by Field Marshal
Roumiantsev and a large retinue of courtiers and soldiers,
started on his trip and a few days later Prince Henry also took
his leave—without even bothering to call on Count Panin,
who was, after all, still in charge of the Russian Foreign Office—Potemkin applied to the Empress for permission to go on
an inspection tour of some of the districts of which he was
titular governor, and the Empress authorized him to do so. It
was, of course, a little unusual that a fallen favorite should
leave at his own request and not be ordered to travel, but
nevertheless the various court cliques and the foreign diplomats interpreted Potemkin's departure from St. Petersburg
to the adjoining province of Novgorod as the final severance of
his romance with Catherine. Before long, however, it became
patent that Potemkin's 'disgrace' was not as complete as had
been anticipated. 'Notwithstanding the high degree of favor
in which the Orlovs at present stand with the Sovereign,'
writes Oakes to William Eden, 'and the resentment which
Count Orlov is supposed to entertain against Prince Potemkin, appearances are still preserved towards the latter which
are looked upon as extraordinary. In his trip to Novgorod he is
served in every article from court, and it is affected to be said
that he will return hither in a few weeks; but I cannot help
believing his favor to be absolutely at an end, and am assured
that he has already removed some furniture, belonging to him,
from the apartments which he occupied in the Winter Palace.
The haughtiness of his conduct while in power has created him
so many enemies that he may reasonably expect to be retaliated
upon in his disgrace, and it would not be surprising nor altogether unexpected to see him finish his career in a monastery,
a way of life for which he has always shown a strong predilection and which perhaps may be the best refuge from the despair

of an impotent ambition. His debts are said to amount to upwards of two hundred thousand rubles.' The British diplomat's
Swedish colleague seemed to be better informed or to have
more intuition, for in his reports he talks of Potemkin's
'feigned or real disgrace'; on the other hand Baron Nolcken's
estimate of Potemkin's debts was twice that reported by
Richard Oakes, and in all probability the correct amount was
neither two nor four hundred thousand rubles. But where
Oakes and indeed most of the gossips in St. Petersburg made
their greatest mistake was in assuming that Potemkin had lost
all his influence and was about to vacate his quarters at the
Winter Palace. His furniture was not being moved. He and
Catherine had parted on very tender terms and she had made
him promise he would not stay away longer than three weeks.
Everywhere he went he was received, on her explicit order,
with royal honors. And when, after a month's absence, he returned to the capital, he went back—to everybody's consternation—to his old apartments, immediately below those of the
Empress. The new house, on which a fortune had just been
spent, remained empty as before.

People did not know what to think. For during the time
the 'fallen favorite' had been away the Empress had openly
taken a new lover. About a fortnight after Potemkin had gone,
Catherine's young and able secretary Zavadovsky had been put
through the customary examination by the faithful Countess
Bruce and having successfully passed this test as well as the
equally traditional medical inspection by Dr. John Rogerson,
the Empress's Scottish private physician (in the case of Potemkin both these formalities were dispensed with), he had
been duly appointed personal adjutant general of Her Imperial
Majesty. An installation present of 20,000 rubles and 1,000
serfs were also given to him on the same occasion, but to the
court's surprise he was not made a chamberlain. Panin and the
Orlovs were pleased: Potemkin seemed to be completely
ousted from his imperial mistress's good graces, and, what

augured particularly well for everybody, the successor appeared to be quite happy with a comparatively modest scale of favors. But at this crucial point in their relationship Catherine and Potemkin succeeded in bluffing their entourage, watchful though it was, just as much as in the opening stages of their romance.

There is no record of a conversation between Potemkin and the Empress prior to his leaving, but from the large number of notes she wrote to him at the time it can be inferred that they did have a long talk. Whether it was then that they decided to adjust their liaison and adopt the new peculiar basis on which they soon placed their relationship, which gave each party physical freedom but preserved for both mutual affection and the political collaboration; or whether this new form developed, as it were, quite automatically during Potemkin's absence, the fact remains that nothing was changed in their association except its purely sexual aspect. Catherine wrote to him in the same tender strain in which she usually addressed him and seemed to miss him a very great deal. He repeatedly sent her various presents from the way; on one occasion it was a melon of unusual size and in acknowledging it she said: 'Thank you, my master—this is the first point of my letter. And to think that I thought you were in Voksha when you are at Schlüsselburg. Secundo: as to the marshals, we will talk about that when you are back. Tertio: I am burning with impatience to see you again; it seems to me I have not seen you for a year. Goodby, and God bless you. I kiss you, my friend. Come back happy and in good health and we shall love each other.' He got a cold, a message about which reached her at the same time as two pictures he sent her. Her reply was particularly affectionate: 'I am living very quietly awaiting your return. I am so sorry you are ill. Many thanks for the Italian and Swiss landscapes. I beg of you to recover as soon as possible and to return to me. We shall then be able to spend ten days in town without parting from each other. Goodby, my dear friend. I kiss you and I so much wish to see you because I love you with all my heart.' She moved to Tsarskoe Selo before he returned from his tour and, ever solicitous and loving, she wrote to him: 'I hear, my friend, that you are living in camp. I am scared lest you might catch a chill. Come to join me. Here you will be all right. It seems to me that I have not seen you a whole year. Hullo, my falcon, you are staying away too long.'

She was not accustomed to his absence, for normally even if either he or she happened to be indisposed, or if he was busy, they still lived under the same roof and there was always the closest of contacts between them. Throughout 1774 and 1775 he had never been away for longer than a day, and the first trip he ever took since they had become lovers only lasted eleven days and was in the spring of 1776. Four weeks seemed like eternity to her; she suddenly felt she had nobody to talk to, she saw how true it was when in amorous ecstasy she used to tell him that without him she would feel as if she had lost the use of her hands or her brain. Her new lover's position was hardly an enviable one. For with every fiber of her being she was still attached to Potemkin. And in all the years that followed, despite the frequent changes of her alcove heroes, she remained tender, loving, and amazingly loyal to her extravagant consort.

He, too, continued to love her in his own way. While the passion for the woman Catherine had died, the adoration of the Empress Catherine remained the same or even grew, and he loved her glory more than anything in the world. It became a strange relationship, for Potemkin now assumed the unsavory functions of director or supervisor of what might be described as Catherine's shifting male harem. He it was who, for the next thirteen years, made and unmade the Empress's new favorites—fifteen in number—and she would never have dreamt of going against Potemkin's advice in this delicate matter. The first and only time since their own romance had

come to a close that she ventured to take a lover, not on Potemkin's recommendation but actually despite his violent opposition was in 1789 when, aged sixty, she fell completely under
the spell of young Plato Zoubov, the last of her favorites. But
until that moment she and Potemkin seemed intent on helping
each other in every way to indulge the lust with which they
were both so richly endowed, and they talked or corresponded
about these things quite freely. Time and again in her letters
to him, which had lost none of their tender and loving quality,
she made a point of informing him that the favorite—whoever
it happened to be at the moment—sends his love or best
respects and she frequently reproached Potemkin with neglecting his various new mistresses. She even made her lovers write
to him too, mostly subservient and mendacious declarations
of how much they admire or even worship him, how they miss
him, how concerned they are about his health, and similar
obviously insincere effusions. They quite often sent him
presents, hoping to win his good graces that way, for they fully
knew that in the long run he alone, and only he, counted and
that their own influence compared to his was nil. Thus Mamonov sent him a golden teapot on which he had engraved: 'Plus
unis par le cœur que par le sang.' But he, for his part, was
treating Catherine's lovers with supreme contempt and never
bothered to reciprocate their signs of attention.

Afraid lest by remaining too long in the Empress's good
graces any new favorite should acquire too great a degree
of power and thus interfere with his own work, Potemkin was
throwing ever fresh supplies of eligible young men into her
insatiable bed, while he himself—with Catherine's blessing—
was continually transferring his affections from one young
woman to another. His five nieces, the beautiful daughters of
his sister Maria Engelhardt, formed the first and fairly permanent nucleus of his own—otherwise kaleidoscopic and
ambulant—harem. Alexandra, Varvara, Ekaterina, Nadeshda,
Tatiana—he loved them all one after the other, or simul-

taneously, and his liaison with most of them continued even after their astonishingly brilliant marriages, which his influence and munificence did much to bring about.

It was Varvara (1757–1815) who inspired her uncle with the greatest passion. Moody, capricious, and jealous, she was not unlike him in character, and at the age of nineteen she knew exactly how to dominate the seemingly indomitable Potemkin, who was now forty. She was almost as difficult as he himself had been with the Empress, and he not only accepted that but went out of his way to please, spoil, and cajole her. He called her 'Oulibotchka' ('Little Smile') or by the tender diminutive of her name, 'Varinka,' and he wrote to her the most ardent letters and *billets-doux*. Here are just a few specimens: 'Varinka, I love you boundlessly, my spirit knows no other food than you . . . you have promised to love me eternally; I love you, my darling, as I have never loved anybody before. Goodby, my dearest Goddess, I kiss you all over'; 'I have not forgotten you Varinka, and never shall. I kiss you all over . . . Sick though I am, I shall come to you. You are my life, nothing is as dear to me as you are . . . I kiss you lovingly . . . my sweet, my precious friend. . . . Goodby, sweetness of my lips, come and have dinner with me'; 'You were sound asleep, silly, and do not remember anything. When I left you I tucked you in, kissed you, covered you with a dressing gown, and blessed you with the sign of the cross'; 'Tell me dearest, my beautiful, my Goddess, that you love me; that will immediately make me well, gay, happy and content. I am entirely full of you'; 'My soul, my tender sweetheart, your victory over me is both overwhelming and eternal . . . I shall come anon to start kissing you'; 'Varioushetchka, my sweetest, my little smile, you dare not get out of health, I shall spank you for that. My beloved, I saw you in my dream quite clearly. When I am dressed, I shall come to kiss you'; 'My little doll, I kiss you twenty-two million times'; 'My angel, my lovely pink cheeks, I kiss you, dearest, and cannot get you out of my mind'.

Poor Catherine would have given anything to receive a letter or a note that was half so tender; but young Varvara Engelhardt, though occasionally reciprocating with equally passionate effusions, had no compunction about venting her moods and sulks on her loving uncle. It appeared that old Daria Vassilievna, Potemkin's mother and the girl's grandmother had expressed her indignation at this liaison in no measured terms, and Varinka complained that she was 'furious about grandmother'.

When Potemkin left St. Petersburg for the Southern Provinces Varinka pretended to be very sad and lonely, so much so in fact that the Empress wrote to him: 'Listen, my dearest, Varinka is very sick; if it is your absence that is causing it, you are wrong. You will kill her, while I am getting more and more fond of her; they want to bleed her.' Actually it was merely a ruse on the girl's part. She was by now deeply in love with Prince Serge Galitsin, a young nobleman of striking good looks, and she wanted to prepare the way for getting Catherine's and Potemkin's consent to her marriage with him. This duly took place in 1779 and for the rest of her days she was a devoted wife and mother, keeping the affection and good will of Potemkin, who bestowed the most lavish presents on her and her husband.

Alexandra, her elder sister (1754–1838), came next, but here the liaison between Potemkin and his young niece was of a very different kind. It was less turbulent than that with Varvara, but more durable. They were devoted to each other, and even after he had married her off to an influential Polish nobleman Count Xavier Branitsky, Alexandra or 'Sashenka' remained in almost permanent attendance. She accompanied her uncle on many of his journeys across Russia, and when she was not with him she was with the Empress, having become one of her favorite and most confidential ladies in waiting. She was by no means just a docile slave as she has usually been represented, but a woman of character, who combined good

looks with a keen intellect and a strong practical sense. Moreover, she had an innate dignity that was truly regal and a smile
that could conquer any obstacle. Both Catherine and Potemkin repeatedly used her for political missions of different kinds,
and the influence of her husband in Polish affairs also proved
of great value. Count Branitsky was both a leading figure in
the public life of Poland and a Russian general in Catherine's
service.

He and the countess were on their way to Warsaw in the
autumn of 1791 when she heard of her uncle's sudden illness.
Leaving Count Branitsky, whom she was to have supported in
his political activities at the Diet, the faithful Sashenka
traveled as fast as her horses would carry her and reached Potemkin just before he died.

It is to her that he bequeathed by far the greater part of
his estates, and in her old age she once said she thought her
fortune amounted to twenty-eight million rubles. While
Catherine was alive, she had her quarters at the palace and
only after the Empress's death she retired to one of her country
seats. There she lived in a large but simple wooden house, full
of the rarest art treasures and other invaluable possessions
given or bequeathed to her by Potemkin, whose memory she
cherished till the end.

The dullest, but also the prettiest, of the five Engelhardt
sisters was Ekaterina (1761–1829), Potemkin's youngest niece.
He fell in love with her, as he had fallen in love with the others,
and the gentle, phlegmatic, almost nostalgic girl yielded to his
passion more out of pity than out of reciprocity. She did not
wish to cause him any pain by refusing to accept his ardent
love-making. Although this liaison was less stormy in character
than that with Varvara, and less affectionate than that with
Sashenka, it lasted much longer. The Empress, too, liked
Ekaterina and spent much time in her company, all the five
sisters being in frequent attendance as ladies in waiting. During a trip on which Ekaterina accompanied the Empress in

1780 she met Count Paul Skavronsky, the eccentric nobleman whose servants had to speak in recitative. He fell in love with her at first sight, and though he knew of her liaison with Potemkin he married her a few months later. But when in 1784 Skavronsky was appointed Russian minister in Naples his wife refused to follow him and remained in St. Petersburg, much to the joy of her uncle, who did not wish her to go. Potemkin thus kept this 'embodiment of an angel' at his side and even managed to get her special honors and distinctions from Catherine. Only after he left St. Petersburg to take command of the armies in the second Turkish War, did the young countess consent to join her sick husband in Naples. There she spent her time in complete indolence and seemed almost glad that the count's illness made all social life quite impossible. Her only amusements were cards and the bedtime stories that her maid had to tell her every night before she would fall asleep, the subject being of no importance. She did not care about anything. Vigée-Lebrun who painted her portrait at that time was most enthusiastic about her beauty, but said that 'the countess's greatest joy was to remain all day reclining on a sofa, with no corsets on, and just wrapped up in a huge black fur coat.' She hardly ever wore the diamonds Potemkin had given her and looking at the many trunks full of new expensive dresses from Paris she would say: 'What is the use of all this? Who wants it?' She never saw Potemkin again, for he died while she was still in Italy. Two years later, in 1793, Count Skavronsky also died. Everything seemed finished. But soon after the death of her husband, whom she had never loved, and after her return to Russia, she fell violently in love for the first time in her life. The loved one was an Italian count by the name of Litta. Ekaterina was thirty-seven years of age when she married him, and it proved a singularly happy union.

The two other Engelhardt sisters, Tatiana and Nadeshda, were also their uncle's mistresses, and both of them made a double experiment in matrimony before settling down for good. Tatiana first married her kinsman, General Michael Potemkin and later Prince Nicolas Youssoupov. Nadeshda's first husband was Colonel Ismailov and her second husband Senator Shepelov, an influential courtier. There is no doubt that it was Alexandra who meant most to Potemkin. Of all his mistresses, only she and the Empress can be said to have preserved his loyalty and his affection till the end of his days. His feelings for both of them were something infinitely deeper and nobler than passing sexual desire, to the satisfaction of which no one in those days seemed to attach much importance; he never stopped worshipping his Empress and adoring his tender Sashenka. And perhaps the strongest bond between these two women was that both of them continued to love this fascinating but insufferable man, even after the purely physical aspect of their relations with him had given place to platonic friendship.

10

THE BUILDER

TO BUILD is an act of faith. Potemkin was not only an enthusiastic builder literally speaking, but he was, in the widest sense of the word, an empire builder as well. At an early stage of his career he had taken part in the fight for Russia's territorial expansion. But he had grasped even then that conquering a territory was not enough and that there remained the far more vital question of consolidating and developing it. During the first two years of his association with Catherine he had already shown great interest in problems of this nature and had done excellent work as governor general of the Southern Provinces, or New Russia as they were symbolically called. Yet his efforts, successful though they had been, could so far only be considered as just the initial attempts of putting into practice the grandiose schemes he had so often discussed with the Empress. In their joint imagination—they seemed to exercise a most fructifying influence on each other—Potemkin and Catherine had always envisaged a huge program for making this New Russia really worthy of its ambitious name. The time had now arrived to begin the realization of the dreams he and the Empress continued to share, even if they did no longer continue to sleep together.

From the earliest moment that Catherine had placed her unreserved trust in, and had also given supreme executive power to, her difficult consort, he had revealed what he could do as an organizer, reformer, administrator, builder and diplomat. Now that the disturbing factor of his sexual relations with the Empress was removed, Potemkin found himself able to concentrate on national affairs with even greater zest than before. Nothing was changed in the established arrangement through which the control and direction of practically all the affairs of state were vested in him. He was, as ever, unable to bear the thought of Catherine taking any decision, whether important or trivial, without first consulting him, and she, for her part, was only too glad to go on sharing the vicissitudes of power and responsibility with a consort who had proved such an able adviser and collaborator. She was grateful to him for staying at her side and she had a guilty conscience because she imagined that their physical association had come to an end through her own infidelity. Since she was anxious to make it up to him in many different ways, and since, moreover, some of the great foreign honors and decorations she had solicited for him also happened to arrive precisely at that time, Potemkin's position as her leading statesman became even stronger than it had been before their love relations were thus adjusted.

A variety of documents reveals that in the second half of the year 1776, when he had just vacated her alcove, or as most contemporaries thought, had been dropped out of it, and fallen into disgrace, their working association was closer than ever. He it was who corrected and even partly rewrote a very important letter the Empress sent at the time to her son, the Tsarevitch, with regard to his future matrimonial arrangements. It was through Potemkin that she invariably issued both the personal and the official instructions to her courtiers, statesmen, generals and provincial governors or other civil servants. Whether it happened to be a question of state or family affairs, whether it was a matter concerning the new favorite of the moment, or his string of predecessors; whether it was the planning of a trip or an excursion, a concert, theatrical performance, or other entertainment, it was always Potemkin who had to deal with these things and at the same time continue not only to advise on and carry out her decisions, but also draft documents, correct the Empress' style and spelling, and generally see to the proper functioning of the state machine.

His main work, however, now lay in a very different sphere; consolidating and expanding Russia's new dominions in the south was one of the vital problems to which he devoted himself. Making the empire strong on land and on sea, was another. Developing its economic and cultural life by creating new industries and centers of trade, learning, and local administration was yet one more urgent task. Finally, there was the question of Russia's place in the world, and, ever proud of and anxious for Catherine's glory—a thing he valued above everything else —he felt constrained to see to it that the empire's foreign policy should be conducted on lines in accordance with this fundamental consideration.

Each of these issues really demanded a man's full time and effort. But Potemkin saw in them merely the different aspects of one and the same problem: the future of the Russian Empire; and in dealing with them he displayed courage, vision, and an astonishing capacity for work. It is true that this was occasionally interrupted by his periodic fits of nostalgia and apathy, when he did nothing at all, but at the same time the accusation of indolence so often leveled against him by his enemies or foreign critics is wholly without foundation. Not only have some of the results of his great constructive efforts survived to the present day, but Catherine's state and private correspondence with him, as well as the unusually large volume of Potemkin's papers in the Russian state archives present so overwhelming a body of evidence that no further argument is possible. Indeed, his achievement during the thirteen years that separate the second from the first Turkish War must be acknowledged as truly stupendous.

Fortifying and developing the Southern Provinces was one

of the earliest tasks to which he turned. With regard to colonization, he was particularly anxious to utilize the various alien races inhabiting Russia, or indeed, to attract foreign colonists from abroad. In 1776 he was busy arranging for the settlement of Albanians in the Crimea, and in the Azov district. In the following year he encouraged certain Caucasian tribes to move there and was also anxious for the return of the so-called 'Nevkrassovtsi', or Russians of Cossack origin, who had emigrated to Turkey and had been utilized by the Turkish government in Asia and also on the Danube as light cavalry. In May 1777, he was instructing one of his generals to form a Serbian regiment, and said: 'Please recruit the new regiment entirely among the Serbians, and for that purpose you can take men of that nationality, from any other regiments where there happen to be any. I desire that other regiments should also be composed in accordance with the men's nationality, which should not be difficult with the Moldavians, Wallachians and Bulgarians.'

The most astonishing effort in that direction, however, was the creation first of a Jewish battalion and later of a whole regiment. Potemkin conceived the idea that some day, when in accordance with his most ardent desire, the Ottoman Empire would at last be destroyed and the Turks expelled from Europe, with Constantinople and the Straits firmly in Russia's possession, Jerusalem should not be allowed to remain in the hands of the infidels. Opportunely, then, he could remove all the Jews, whom he thought to be in many ways a source of trouble and nuisance, back to the Holy Land, to which, in his opinion, they were fully entitled. He had no doubt that back in their own country they would become completely regenerated, but he also thought that they would have to do a great deal of fighting against the infidels before they could firmly establish themselves and prosper. He therefore decided to begin their military training at once, and as a nucleus of this future Jewish army he formed an initial squadron which was placed

under the honorary colonelcy of Duke Ferdinand of Brunswick and called 'Isrælovsky', a name closely resembling in
sound that of the famous 'Ismailovsky' Horse Guards.

Armed with huge lances of the Cossack type, but still wearing their own traditional costume, with their long beards and
ringlets of hair moving in the wind, these Hebrews offered an
unbelievable sight, especially when ordered to charge an
imaginary enemy at breath-taking speed. But little by little
Potemkin's drill sergeants managed to shape this picturesque
and comic army unit into something more presentable and to
infuse much courage and enthusiasm into the bewildered sons
of Israel, who had at first shown nothing but apprehension
and obvious fear of the horses on which they were seated. It is
a fact that in 1794 the Jews in Poland themselves applied for
permission to form a cavalry regiment, and that its extremely
active commander, the Jewish Colonel Berkovitz, covered himself with glory, even getting the Legion of Honor for his bravery
when in later years he joined Napoleon's army; he lost his life
·in fighting the Austrians in 1809. But the original idea of
starting Jewish military service formations belongs to Potemkin, and in his arguments in favor of such an unprecedented
action, he can be said to have been the precursor both of the
·Zionist movement and of Lord Balfour.

Among the papers preserved in Potemkin's archives a
very large proportion belongs to letters, requests, and a
variety of other documents written in practically all the different languages of the multitude of alien, and especially
Asiatic, races inhabiting the Russian Empire. Tartars, Kal-
mucks, Georgians, Turks, Moldavians, Jews, and innumerable
others, knowing his predilection for their exotic looks and
qualities, continually approached him in connection with one
thing or another and usually wrote in their own vernacular;
their efforts were seldom vain. But while sponsoring their mi-
gration and helping them as colonists in the New Russia,
Potemkin was not ignoring the need of getting also purely

Russian settlers whose importance he fully realized. Thus he took the unusual step of prohibiting the extradition of escaped peasant serfs who had found their way to the Southern Provinces, and this measure was so contrary to the established practices and general spirit of the times, that it shows both courage and vision. His orders in that respect were precise: the local authorities should absolutely refuse to hand back to the noble landowners any former peasants of theirs whom they might be claiming, and it is hardly surprising that this resulted in a considerable influx of enterprising, daring fellows who took the risk of running away from their masters and settled down to be excellent colonizers.

In 1783 Potemkin formed a regular army of the various new settlers in the South, and before long his jurisdiction was extended to a number of further provinces. He was now governor general and viceroy of four of Russia's largest districts, and a very active one at that; despite the great accumulation of different duties he was not the type of man to be just a titular holder of a post and leave the work to others. He kept in close touch with his provinces and paid frequent visits to them, covering thousands of miles at great speed and with no apparent fatigue.

Meanwhile, in February 1784, he had been promoted to the presidency of the College of War and to the rank of field marshal and Chief of the Horse Guards. A year later the new special staff of the Black Sea Fleet and Admiralty was created and placed under Potemkin's direct orders. This meant the complete concentration in his hands of everything pertaining to Russia's relations with Turkey, for two years before that the Empress had ordered her ambassador to take instructions from Potemkin.

His diplomatic activities in those days were, as will be seen, of the utmost importance. But perhaps the greatest task he performed at the time was the introduction of far-reaching army reforms, which were expounded in his report of April 4,

1783—a famous date in Russian military history. Potemkin
completely changed the uniforms and footgear of the soldiers,
which hitherto had been a torture to them. He gave them comfortable tunics, wide breeches, lower boots and easy fitting
helmets. Further, he ordered them to cut off their tresses and to
stop powdering their hair. 'To put the hair into curls, to powder
it, to plait it—is that a soldier's business?' he wrote. 'They have
no personal valets. What is their need of curls? Everybody
must agree that it is much healthier to wash their hair and
comb it, than to make it heavy with powder, tallow, flour, pins,
and plaits. The soldier's dressing must be such that no sooner
is he up than he is ready.' These new regulations, which met
with the men's enthusiasm, soon became celebrated in a special
soldiers' song, and were also much to the taste of Catherine,
who issued a long manifesto of favorable comment. But it is
not without humor that while Potemkin was so anxious for the
men's hygiene, he himself—whenever he got a fit of apathy
and melancholia—neither washed nor combed his hair, but
scratched it mercilessly with his five fingers, which were invariably bitten to the quick, and was wont to appear in public
looking disheveled and dissipated without wig or powder.

His reform of the soldiers' dress was much ahead of the
times. Yet even more progressive were his instructions for
the actual treatment of men by their officers. He reduced the
various established punishments and was strongly against the
thrashing of recruits. Repeatedly he told the officers to be more
human. 'Tell Messieurs les Officiers,' he wrote to some of the
local chiefs, 'that they should be as moderate as possible with
their men, that they should endeavor to look after them, and
in punishments should not transgress the regulations; that
they should behave to them as I do, for I love them as children.' Potemkin absolutely prohibited the officers to use soldiers for their private needs under the threat of severe penal-
ties. He firmly believed in the old maxim that there are no bad
Russian soldiers, but only bad officers.

In 1786 he issued a statute in which the expenses of each

regiment were carefully laid down. He took a most active personal interest in the soldiers' food and equipment and in the strict application of the code of sanitary measures which he introduced in 1788. Potemkin was the second military chief in Russia after Peter the Great to introduce army inspectors.

Among the fighting units he first of all thoroughly overhauled the cavalry, increasing it by about one-fifth of its size and creating new regiments. Then he turned his attention to the infantry, which was also expanded and modernized.

In April 1786, on Potemkin's suggestion, special Caucasian and Siberian armies were created, their organization and direction also being entrusted to him.

Yet another great task he performed in these years was the annexation of the Crimea. He had had his eye on the Tauric peninsula for some considerable time and had already done a great deal towards colonizing it with elements favorable to Russia. But it remained as yet a Turkish vassal state, despite the Treaty of Kuchuk-Kainardje (1774), by which the independence of its ruler or Khan had been officially established. During the unrest that began under Khan Shaghin-Ghirey, an opportunity seemed to present itself to Potemkin to settle the Crimean question once and for all. He drew up a long memorandum for Catherine, which shows how strongly he felt about Russia's southern borders. He said: 'The Crimea, on account of its position, splits our frontiers. Whether we have to mind the Turks on the river Bug or on the Kuban side—in all cases there is always the Crimea. That explains why they do not like the present Khan; because they know that he will not allow them to pass through the Crimea and threaten, so to speak, our heart. Now imagine that the Crimea is yours and that this wart on the nose has been removed—then the position of the frontiers at once becomes admirable.' After explaining to Catherine the strategic position and the difficulty of effectively protecting Russia's southern frontiers while the Crimea remained outside the Russian Empire, he went on thus:

'Almighty Empress! My excessive devotion to you com-

pels me to say: Treat with contempt that envy of others which
cannot put obstacles in your way. It is your duty to raise Russia's glory still higher. Just look, whether those who have taken
possession of anything have had it disputed: France has taken
Corsica, the Cæsarians [Austrians] without a war have taken
more from the Turks in Moldavia than ourselves. There are no
powers in Europe that have not divided among themselves,
Asia, Africa, America. The acquisition of the Crimea can
neither make us stronger nor richer, but it will ensure our
peace.'

The suggestion of course fired Catherine's imagination, and
after several long discussions with him she signed in December
1782, a 'most secret' instruction calling on Potemkin to annex
the Crimea at the first suitable opportunity. In the following
spring he traveled down south to take command of the army
in case a war were to break out. Stopping on his way at the
estate of Count Branitsky, where he enjoyed the company of
his faithful Sashenka, and talked about Polish affairs with her
husband, he reached Kherson—his newly built city on the border—in June, and settled down there. The Crimea was being
affected by an epidemic of plague, and he anticipated that
delegates would probably be sent to him at Kherson offering
the peninsula's surrender without a fight. But while he was
still waiting, Catherine was growing desperate with anxiety
and was bombarding him with requests for news, which he
mostly ignored.

On July 15, 1783, for instance, she wrote to him in the
following strain: 'You cannot imagine how worried I must
be not having received a single line from you for over five
weeks. Besides, there were false rumors here and I have nothing with which to deny them. I was expecting the occupation
of the Crimea at the latest in mid-May, and now it is already
mid-July while I know no more about it than the Pope. This
inevitably leads to all kinds of stories which are by no means
pleasant to me. I beg of you in every way to keep me informed

as often as possible so that I could follow the thread of things. The natural activity of my mind and of my head forges a thousand ideas which often torment me. Various fables about the past have also reached us: you will give me back my peace of mind by frequent information: I have nothing else to write. Neither I nor anybody else know where you are; at a guess I send this to Kherson. Field Marshal Roumiantsev, as ever, is full of complaints about you. Goodby, my friend, keep well. When is this Crimea business of yours going to be finished?'

She for her part kept him regularly informed of everything that was going on in St. Petersburg, and solicited advice and guidance on innumerable questions of varying importance. He did not care. His mind at the moment was fully occupied with the immediate problem of how to get the Crimea with the minimum of loss and sacrifice. One day the information reached him that a Caucasian Khan with 6,000 Circassians had just crossed the Crimean border. The same night Potemkin also moved his troops into the Crimea and within no time had this chieftain captured, while the local population and the 6,000 Circassians were made to swear an oath of allegiance to the Empress Catherine. But during his short sojourn in the Crimea Potemkin got very bad malaria, moreover the plague was still raging in the peninsula, so that he was compelled to leave, entrusting the completion of the conquest and the command over his men to General Igelström.

The last resistance of the various Crimean tribes was soon broken down, and on July 21, 1783, upon hearing that all of them had now acknowledged her as Empress, Catherine announced the official incorporation of the Tauric peninsula in the Russian Empire. Two days later in a special document she expressed her thanks to Potemkin as the chief hero of this successful exploit and bestowed generous favors and decorations on his principal assistants. He remained in the South, and despite his acute ill-health, which was worrying Catherine a great deal, he threw himself with renewed energy into his

colonization and fortification schemes. It is then that he conceived the idea of settling English convicts in the Crimea; for
some reason he felt sure that they would be just the kind of
colonists required. But the Russian ambassador in London,
Count Simon Vorontsov, was horrified at the very suggestion
of such a possibility and did all he could to thwart this project.
Unable to dissuade Potemkin, Vorontsov wrote to the Empress
direct and also exchanged many letters on the subject with
Catherine's secretary, Bezborodko—whose influence, especially in foreign affairs, was rapidly rising—and it was with the
greatest of difficulty that they made Potemkin abandon his
plan.

Yet in the light of Australia's and Siberia's experience this
idea of colonizing a new continent with convicts does not
appear as senseless as Vorontsov thought it then. Under the
circumstances, Potemkin decided to redouble his efforts in attracting Russian and alien settlers of all kinds, and achieved
much in that direction. But he did not entirely abandon the
idea that the English might be useful, and having failed to obtain his convicts he managed at least to get a farming specialist
sent over by Vorontsov to teach the new colony the best
methods of agriculture. At the same time it is noteworthy that
within less than a month of the Crimea having become part of
the Russian Empire and of his more special dominion, he had
submitted to Catherine a scheme and received her approval
· for the industrialization of the new province. A textile factory
and other trades were to be established there forthwith, and to
Potemkin belongs the credit of having created a number of
· important industries not only in the South but all over Russia.

He also held strong views on the necessity of providing the
Southern Provinces, of which he was now supreme master,
with towns, and claimed that military preparations alone were
not enough to develop and consolidate these vital border-
lands. Kherson had been his first effort in that direction, and
within four years of the foundation of that important city the

following picture of it was given in a letter by Cyril Rasoumovsky who happened to visit it: 'As far as Kherson is concerned, apart from the famous lovely Dniepr, the northern shore of which is rapidly becoming populated, imagine a multitude of stone buildings that increases hourly, a fortress wall that encircles the citadel and the best edifices; an Admiralty with ships already completed or in the course of construction, a large suburb inhabited by merchants and commoners of different races on the one side and with barracks housing 10,000 military men on the other. Add to it almost adjoining this suburb a pleasant island, with the quarantine buildings, with Greek merchant ships and with canals that are being made for their convenience. Imagine all this and then you will not be surprised when I tell you that even now I have not yet recovered from my surprise about the rapid development of a place where only quite recently there was merely a winter hut.' Other travelers were equally impressed.

But Potemkin soon realized that now that the Crimea was Russian there was no longer any point in using Kherson as a naval base and that this could be moved to a more convenient spot. In 1784 he built Sebastopol, which remains to the present day one of the greatest military harbors in the world. Its foundation was epoch-making in the history of the Russian Navy. Potemkin corresponded a great deal on this subject with the Empress, and in one of his letters in which he asked her to send him men and officers, he emphasized the necessity of careful selection. 'You must order good ones to be sent, since what is the advantage of despatching a lot of scum to a new place? I must beg of you, Madam, to look upon this place as one where your glory is *original* and where you do not share it with your predecessors; here you are not following in the footsteps of another.' This is a remarkable reference to Catherine's fondness for proclaiming herself the continuer of Peter the Great's pioneering work. When Potemkin launched his first ship he informed Catherine that he was going to christen it

The Glory of Catherine, and added: 'This name, I am prepared to justify if it comes to a test.' But Catherine was a little
worried, and begged of him in her reply not to be too ambitious, and not to give his ships names that were too great,
since these might prove a handicap rather than an asset; 'It is
better to be, than to seem and not to be,' she concluded her
letter, which, however, left the naming of the boats to him.

In his shipbuilding activities Potemkin was now assisted
by Sir Samuel Bentham, the English naval architect and engineer, who had traveled in Russia and Siberia in 1780–82,
'studying methods of working metals.' Potemkin made him a
lieutenant colonel in the Russian Army and superintendent
of one of his main shipbuilding yards. Sir Samuel's more
famous brother, the great Jeremy Bentham, visited him there,
and it was in Russia that this economist, philosopher, and
sociologist wrote his *Defence of Usury* and *Panopticon.* Potemkin naturally seized the opportunity of meeting so distinguished a foreign scholar, and their ensuing discussions
gave him great pleasure.

Bentham was not the only British naval expert who put
his services at Catherine's disposal. Sir Samuel Greig, John
Elphinston, and the picturesque adventurer Paul Jones, a Scot
by birth and one of America's most famous naval heroes were
among her leading admirals, and all of them worked in close
collaboration with Potemkin. Jones, however, ended by quarreling with Potemkin, who turned him out. Another distinguished visitor from England was John Howard, the philan-
thropist and prison reformer. He first came to Russia in 1781,
but returned in 1789 and after a stay in St. Petersburg and
Moscow he came down to Kherson where at Potemkin's invitation he inspected the hospitals.

Two years after the foundation of Sebastopol, in 1786, the
construction of another important city was started by Potemkin. He gave it the proud name of 'Ekaterinoslav', or 'Cather-

ine's Glory' and he incurred much ridicule when it was found that only part of his fantastically ambitious scheme could be immediately realized. The site chosen for Ekaterinoslav, on the right bank of the Dniepr, and some 600 miles west of Moscow, was magnificent. It was the very heart of a region unusually fertile and beautiful, which was later destined to become one of Russia's most prosperous industrial centers. Potemkin wanted the new city to be something unique, fully justifying its name of 'Catherine's Glory'. So from the very start he included in the plans he submitted to the Empress the following items: a university whose purpose would be to attract Russian and foreign youth from adjoining countries, such as Poland, Greece, and Moldavia; a conservatoire and an academy of music; law courts in the shape of an ancient basilica; a row of shops 'built in semicircle like the Propylæan Athenian entrance', with an exchange and a theater in the center; further, twelve factories for making cloth, silk, wool, and other articles; and finally, chief of all, a cathedral 'to resemble the temple of St. Peter in Rome, as a sign that this region, thanks to Your Majesty, has been turned from a sterile desert into a fertile orchard and dwelling place for animals as well as a pleasant haven for people who come from all countries.'

In his opinion, enough building material was already in stock. The first steps he took were with regard to the university, and a number of professors were at once engaged, drawing regular salaries in anticipation of the building being erected and of the students arriving as foreshadowed by Potemkin, while the only erected part of the university was its chancellery and the professors' dwellings. At the same time, the famous Italian composer Sarti was invited to become director of the future musical academy, also drawing a salary, and ordered to do other artistic work until such time as the conservatoire was ready. Potemkin's arrangements in fact were not unlike those of the present-day film industry, which secures the services of innumerable people and pays huge salaries before it is ready to employ the celebrities and others who have been engaged at such unproductive cost.

But building work in Ekaterinoslav was progressing even though the more ambitious schemes of its founder were as yet far from realization, and before long his own magnificent palace, with two splendid hothouses containing the rarest plants, was ready. So too was a stocking factory, built at a cost of 340,000 rubles, of which no less than 240,000 were spent on erecting 200 houses for the workers and foremen. The silk stockings turned out by this factory were so thin that they could be placed in the shell of a nut, and in that strange vessel a pair was sent to Catherine. Before long a regular silk industry was also established under Potemkin's supervision and he was so pleased with the results that, in sending to the Empress a variety of silk articles, he could write: 'You have ordered the worms to work for humans. From the fruit of your endeavors you now get enough for a dress. If any prayers are heard, God will grant you a long life, so that when, my Merciful Mother, you visit the dominions over which I preside, you will see your path covered with silk.'

But many of Potemkin's Ekaterinoslav projects could never be carried out in accordance with his original plans: and this element of the impracticable largely contributed to the scepticism with which his other work was regarded. There is no doubt that the war which was soon to break out also did much to delay the realization of his projects, which the nineteenth and early twentieth centuries proved to be considerably less fantastic than had appeared in his own times.

It was actually during the second Turkish War that Potemkin founded his last important city, Nicolaev, a seaport in a particularly advantageous strategic position, about twenty miles northwest of Kherson. He immediately saw that Nicolaev offered better possibilities than Kherson or even Sebastopol, and decided to make it the chief naval station of

Russia on the Black Sea. This it has remained to the present day. Potemkin's original schemes for Nicolaev were as ambitious as those for Ekaterinoslav, and included a large public garden, factories, mills, model farms and even a monastery; but he started with the more essential buildings first, and within a year of its foundation, the first frigate was launched from the Nicolaev shipyards. By that time the foundations of a new Admiralty and a large church were also ready, but Potemkin died before these were completed.

During his lifetime and also in the memoirs of many of his contemporaries Potemkin has been frequently accused of having 'wasted large sums of money without any purpose' in developing southern Russia. Figures have since become available that show the utter falsehood of this accusation. By no means all the moneys granted for his work were actually paid out to him. Thus in 1787 the sum of 2,718,245 rubles was granted for building and developing purposes of the Ekaterinoslav and Tauric districts, but nothing as yet was paid out before the second Turkish War began; and with the beginning of hostilities the Council—always glad to find an opportunity of putting spokes in Potemkin's wheels—advised the Empress to delay the payment till a more opportune moment. Again, according to the instructions issued on September 1, 1785, to the Assignation Bank, this institution was to remit to Potemkin the sum of 3,000,000 rubles on account of development work in the Southern Provinces. The money, however, was not paid out as it should have been, but at the rate of 1,000,000 rubles a year and the third million, that should have been forthcoming, in 1787, was never paid at all. Further, there is a letter from Catherine thanking Potemkin for bargaining with the building contractors, and when it is realized that only nine years separate the foundation of his first city, Kherson, from the outbreak of the war, his efforts as a builder deserve the greatest admiration.

It is worth mentioning that on the eve of the Bolshevik ·

revolution, in 1917, Kherson had a population of over 100,000, Sebastopol about 75,000, Ekaterinoslav 300,000, and Nicolaev 200,000. Moreover, all these cities, which still preserved some of the original buildings put up by Potemkin, were rapidly growing and had more than justified both their strategic and their economic and cultural purpose. But even during Potemkin's lifetime or in the years immediately following his death, these cities, or indeed the whole of the Southern Provinces, had achieved a degree of development that was in itself a monument to his vision and his creative genius. An unexpected testimonial to that aspect of his work will be found in a delightful book, written by Mrs. Maria Guthrie, a contemporary and an obviously unbiased English lady who happened to visit southern Russia at the close of the century. This Mrs. Guthrie traveled in the very region that owed everything to Potemkin, and she saw with her open eyes the great constructive achievement he had accomplished in a remarkably short time and against tremendous odds. Thus, writing from the city of Nicolaev which she saw within barely five years of its foundation, she says: 'The streets are remarkably long, broad, and straight; eight of them intersect one another, at right angles, and may contain about 600 houses; besides 200 cottages and semblankies (habitations underground) in the suburbs, inhabited by sailors, soldiers, etc. There are likewise some handsome public buildings, such as the Admiralty, with a long line of magazines, workshops, etc., belonging to it, placed all along the bank of the Ingul, with the wet and dry docks; in short, every necessary department for the building, rigging, and victualing of ships of war, from a first-rate down to a sloop: a proof of which is, that a vessel of ninety guns was launched here last year . . . The public buildings before mentioned, with a pretty church, and even a number of private houses, are constructed of a fine white calcareous stone full of shells, which is soft when first cut out of the quarry, though it afterwards hardens in the air, like one that we have in Petersburg from the

Prince Grigory Grigorievitch Orlov
(*From a painting by de Bellay*)

Catherine II in 1789
(*From a painting by Schebanoff*)

James Harris, Earl of
Malmesbury, K.B.
(*From a painting by Sir Joshua Reynolds*)

Count von Panin
(*From a painting by Roslin*)

"Sashenka," Countess Alexandra Vassilievna Branitsky, *née* Engelhardt

"Varinka," Princess Varvara Vassilievna Galitsin, *née* Engelhardt

neighborhood of the palace of Gatchina. The rest of the houses are of wood, brought, as said before, all the way from White Russia down the Dniepr . . . I passed a winter in one of those mansions of recent construction, without either feeling or perceiving the effects of humidity, although my delicate frame is become of late a sort of animal hygrometer. . . . The number of inhabitants, sailors and soldiers included, may amount to about 10,000.'

In his desire to turn the Southern Provinces into a flourishing continent with gardens, orchards, and parks, cathedrals, schools, and universities; with imposing great cities and modern industrial centers, beautiful villages, and picturesque farms—densely populated, yet with plenty of room for everybody—Potemkin may have lacked a sense of proportion. He may also have revealed a degree of ambition that was not warranted by the practical possibilities with which he must have been familiar at the time. Yet the achievement, even allowing for mistakes and miscalculations, partly due to the general tendency towards extravagance so prevalent in those days, remains stupendous and shows that in time the most unreal dreams can come true.

11

DIPLOMACY

P OTEMKIN'S great effort in the Southern Provinces appears all the more remarkable when it is realized that it was only a part time occupation and that simultaneously with it he had to attend to a number of equally important problems elsewhere. In addition to the army reforms there were other vital changes in various departments, to the preparation and carrying out of which he had to devote much energy. Moreover, despite the fact that the rapidly aging Count Panin was still nominally in charge of foreign relations, the actual direction of affairs had passed very largely into Potemkin's hands. And of course there was the court, with its incessant intrigues; there were his various and somewhat complicated amours, by now no longer limited to the five beautiful nieces; finally, there was the infinitely complex and difficult question of his personal relations with the Empress.

With all this on hand Potemkin must have been one of the most hard-working men not only in Russia, but, indeed, in the whole of Europe, and it is hard to find any justification for the claim of his critics and detractors that he was slothful and negligent. His position at court and his multifarious activities in those years are particularly well recorded by two very shrewd observers. From 1775–1780 the Chevalier de Corberon was French chargé d'affaires in St. Petersburg and kept a diary—written in the form of letters to a number of fictitious addresses—in which he gives a most interesting picture of life in Russia, which he began by hating and, like so many foreign residents, ended by loving better even than his own country. This able and energetic French diplomat naturally had many dealings with Potemkin, who looms very largely in his diary. But even greater prominence is enjoyed by Potemkin in the letters and dispatches of Corberon's brilliant rival, James Harris—later first Earl of Malmesbury—who was British ambassador at the court of St. Petersburg from 1778–1783. Harris's dealings with Potemkin constitute one of the most interesting chapters in Anglo-Russian relations and were fraught with possibilities that might have changed the whole course of modern history, had the efforts of this great British diplomat met with the success he and his government so anxiously desired.

It must be borne in mind that Russia's international position, despite her many wars and internal difficulties, had been growing in strength almost without interruption from the beginning of the century, and now under Catherine it was so high that even that most sceptical and cynical of foreign monarchs, Frederick the Great, could not fail to be impressed. For a long time he had exercised a very strong influence on Russian affairs; and, to maintain it, had stooped to unprecedented excesses of servile flattery; but his double-dealing during the first twelve years of Catherine's reign, and especially during the Turkish War, had cured her of her morbid interest in this treacherous German ally, whom he now hated and despised. Her sympathies were now definitely gravitating from the Prussian to the Austrian court, and it was a matter of great annoyance to her that in 1777 she was forced by circumstances not only to renew her alliance with the hated 'Fredericus', but actually had to throw in the whole weight of her diplomacy on his side in Prussia's conflict with Austria over the Bavarian succession. Thanks to her mediation, this quarrel was ultimately settled in 1779 at the peace congress of Teschen, and that was the last service she rendered the Prussians. After that she went entirely over to the 'Cæsarean' or Austrian side, developing a great personal liking for the Emperor Joseph II, which resulted in the closest of co-operation and finally in an alliance. But meanwhile, France (whose alluring fashions and culture had given her a truly privileged position in Russia), Great Britain, Sweden, and other powers, were all fighting for the Empress's good graces, and most of the foreign diplomats in St. Petersburg were in a state of open or secret war with each other. In their struggle for Russia's sympathy and support no method appeared too reprehensible, and bluff, blackmail, corruption, and espionage were customary weapons. They also turned from one court clique to another, trying to use the influence of the Orlovs, Tchernishevs, and various others to sponsor their respective interests and, as has been seen, it was from that angle that they viewed the changes in Catherine's alcove. But the two most important men from these diplomats' point of view were without doubt Panin and Potemkin, while in later years Bezborodko—working in conjunction with Potemkin—became the principal instrument of Catherine's foreign policy, though less in an advisory than in an executive capacity.

The request made by England through Sir Robert Gunning for Russia's intervention against 'His Majesty's misguided subjects in America' in itself opens up an intriguing vista of what might have happened if Catherine had agreed to it. But the developments that followed this remarkable diplomatic interlude were even more astonishing, both in their character and in their far-reaching consequences. For the price England was prepared to pay for Catherine's support included, among other things, the cession of important British territory, and indeed it seems that in the fierce international struggle for Russia's friendship that was going on at the time England was determined to outbid the other powers, no matter what sacrifice this might involve.

With the appointment of James Harris, young in years but rich in experience, England hoped that her various previous efforts would at last be brought to fruition. No sooner had he reached the Russian capital than he received a long message from Lord Suffolk, in which the Foreign Secretary reviewed the whole international situation, especially with regard to Great Britain and Russia, and suggested that the time had now arrived 'for reverting to the idea of an alliance with each other'. In concluding his dispatch, Lord Suffolk wrote: 'From all these considerations thus detailed to you, I am by His Majesty's command to instruct you to take such methods as your experience in business, guided by the reception given to you at the Court of St. Petersburg, may induce you to prefer, to learn the sentiment of that court on the present situation of Europe, and to discover how far there is any practicable disposition in the Empress of Russia and her ministers, towards forming an *offensive and defensive alliance* with Great Britain. If Russia turns a deaf ear to the consideration of an alliance now in the disposition of this country and the particular situation of both, I own I don't foresee the conjuncture when an alliance can be formed between us.'

Harris set to work at once and not unnaturally directed his first efforts towards securing Panin's co-operation. The old Russian diplomat was friendly but evasive. Before long, Harris was presented to the Empress, who seemed to go out of her way to distinguish him personally and emphasize on every possible occasion her friendly feelings towards England, while at the same time remaining completely noncommittal.

So far, Harris had only met Potemkin casually and Potemkin's attitude was as yet rather negative. Harris thought that Potemkin and the then favorite (Korsakov) were 'creating eternal plagues' at the court. Potemkin's part in the making and unmaking of new favorites, his alleged difficulties with Catherine and invariably 'the return of Prince Potemkin into favor', were topics with which Harris dealt very fully in his early reports. He was paying a great deal of attention to gossip and to the unending stream of rumors current at the court and in diplomatic quarters, so that his information was not always reliable. Harris must sometimes have been aware of that, for in a long dispatch in which he describes what was obviously only one of the innumerable attempts by the Orlovs and others to dislodge Potemkin, he finds it necessary to state: 'The following conversation I can vouch to be authentic.' Then he goes on: 'Soon after Alexis Orlov's arrival, the Empress sent for him, and after the highest encomiums on his character and the strongest expressions of gratitude for past services, she told him she had now one to require of him, of more importance to her repose than any she had yet asked him. "Be friends," said she, "with Potemkin; prevail upon that extraordinary man to be more circumspect in his conduct, more attentive to the duties of the great offices he fills; to endeavor to conciliate to himself friends, and not, in return for the regard and friendship I have for him, to make my life a continued scene of misery. For God's sake," added she, "seek his acquaintance, increase my obligations to you, by contributing to my private happiness, as much as you have done to the luster and glory of my reign." If such a language from a sovereign to a subject was uncommon, the answer was equally so. "You know, Madam," said the Count, "I am your slave; my life is at your service; if Potemkin disturbs your peace of mind, give me your orders, he shall disappear immediately; you shall hear no more of him; but, Madam," added he, "with my character and reputation to engage in a court intrigue, to seek the good will of a person I must despise as a man, and regard as the greatest enemy of the state; your Majesty must pardon me if I decline the task." The Empress here burst into tears; Orlov withdrew, but returned in a few minutes, and went on by saying: "I know, Madam, beyond a doubt, that Potemkin has no real attachment for Your Majesty; that he consults in everything his own interest alone; that his only superior talent is

cunning; that he is gradually endeavoring to divert Your
Majesty from business, and lull you into a state of voluptuous
security, in order to invest himself with the sovereign power.
He has essentially hurt your Navy, he has ruined your Army,
and what is worse, he has sunk your reputation in the eyes of
the world, and alienated from you the affection of your faithful subjects. If you choose to get rid of so dangerous a man, my
life is at your devotion; but if you mean to temporize with him,
I can be of no use to you in the execution of measures where
flattery, dissimulation, and duplicity are the most necessary
qualifications." The Empress was much affected at this extraordinary speech; confessed her belief of all he said of Potemkin; thanked the count in the strongest manner for his zealous
offers, but said she could not bear the thoughts of such harsh
proceedings; acknowledged an alteration in her own character,
and complained of her health being essentially affected. She
desired the count not to think of leaving Petersburg, as she
certainly should now want both his advice and his assistance.'

But a fortnight later, on December 31, 1778, according to
Harris the situation looked very different. This is how he reported it to Lord Suffolk:

'My Lord, since the singular conversation I communicated
to Your Lordship October 5 and 16, 1778, the Empress has
gradually withdrawn her confidence and good will from Count
Alexis Orlov; she has refused him some trifling favors he asked
for his natural son; and, finally, has forced him by her behavior
to have recourse to the method commonly used by Russians
when they are not well at court, that of staying at home, under
pretence of illness. This must be accounted for, by her having
been weak enough to have repeated to Prince Potemkin, what
had passed between them, and to his having been artful enough
to have made it appear to her, as proceeding solely from personal ill will and jealousy. Prince Orlov has not appeared at
court for these three months, and the language of both
brothers, (and they speak their minds very freely) is that of

men disappointed, angry, and who foresee no hopes of reassuming their former stations.'

There follow some comments on a possible new favorite and on the then occupant of that position about whom Harris remarks: 'He is very good-natured, but silly to a degree, and entirely subservient to the orders of Prince Potemkin, and the Countess Bruce. These two seem now in quiet possession of the direction of the Empress' mind. He is supreme in regard to everything that regards either her serious or pleasurable pursuits; the other interferes only in the latter.'

Though Potemkin's power and influence were now quite clear to Harris, he continued his endeavors to win Panin's support, and every time the shrewd but dilatory and pro-Prussian old statesman chose to be pleasant to him, a note of optimism appeared in the British ambassador's masterly dispatches. Not until August 1779, or practically eighteen months after his arrival in Russia, did Sir James Harris, as he now was, come to the irrevocable conclusion that there was nothing to hope for from these quarters, and he even maliciously accused Panin of being bribed by the Prussians —a stupid and undignified statement, which was quite untrue. From that moment onwards Harris concentrated all his efforts on establishing himself in Potemkin's good graces and of winning both his personal and his political friendship.

This proved less difficult than he had anticipated. Not only did they share a number of dislikes, but in their more positive aspirations Potemkin and Harris, up to a certain point, saw eye to eye. Both of them were anxious to secure the dismissal of Panin—Harris because he saw an obstacle in him, Potemkin because he could not bear the old man's influence in foreign and other affairs. Moreover, both Harris and Potemkin were united in their hatred of France. It is true that individual Frenchmen had always appealed to Potemkin a very great deal, and in addition to those he had on his own staff he also employed or collaborated with a number of French people. He certainly liked the Chevalier de Corberon and not only often had him to dinner alone, but showed various signs of attention and friendship to the young French diplomat. He had even used his best endeavors to obtain Corberon's appointment as ambassador to the Court of St. Petersburg—an attempt which, to their mutual regret and annoyance, was thwarted by Panin. Yet apart from these personal exceptions Potemkin had little · use for France, and on the other hand was genuinely anxious for a close co-operation between Russia and England. In a · letter written to Bezborodko from the South a few years later, on July 30, 1783, he stated his views on the subject very clearly: 'My ideas with regard to counterbalancing the influence of the Bourbon courts: an alliance with England, which, the closer it is, the more beneficial it will be, since France has shown her good nature and her desire to see the Russian state reduced to inaction. Imagine what laws she would lay down if she became stronger; we need a maritime power which in its turn has realized its need of an alliance with us. There is nothing to be said against this truism, and if the Empress deigns to make up her mind you will see all that we can do. Therefore please let me know what the position of foreign affairs is. We must first build a fleet and then God will help us.' Thus Harris was quite justified when, from the very start of his new friendship with Potemkin, he reported that he found in him: 'a very acute understanding' and obvious sincerity.

In an almost interminable message to Lord Weymouth, who had become Secretary of State for Foreign Affairs after Lord Suffolk's death. Harris describes one of his earliest and most promising moves. It is so well written, that despite its length it deserves to be quoted in detail; moreover it throws some interesting light on that phase of Anglo-Russian relations. After some preliminaries, Harris begins by explaining to his chief how he was 'resolved to apply to Prince Potemkin, as the only person who could from his weight give activity' to Catherine's favorable feelings towards England, if these were not merely lip service. Then he continues: 'Some time passed, however, before it was in my power to address myself to him unaffectedly. On June 28 an opportunity offered itself in the Empress' antechamber, when I told him that the moment was now come when Russia might act the greatest part in Europe. . . . He told me there needed no eloquence or deep logic to persuade him of the truth of what I said; that neither Her Imperial Majesty nor himself were deficient in their good will, but that the event was too recent for the Empress to have thought it over maturely; and that, if I would have a little patience, he would soon speak to me more fully. . . . He then was pleased to pay me a most flattering personal compliment, by saying the Empress had the greatest confidence in me, and that she would listen to what I said as readily as if it came from one of her own ministers. This emboldened me to ask a very uncommon, and, till now, ungranted favor, namely, *that of being allowed to converse with Her Imperial Majesty myself on business.* He told me he would endeavor, however unusual and novel such a step would be, to procure me this satisfaction, but promised the necessity of its being a profound secret. . . .

'On the following Friday he appointed me to dinner at a country house of his nephew, where no one was present but part of his own family and dependants; and there, my lord, we discoursed very amply, as well on the critical position in which England stood, as on the influence the consequences of the present war necessarily must have on the balance of power, and of the means the most efficacious to be used to prevent a general disorder taking place, or at least to counteract the operations of the force of the House of Bourbon united against England alone.

' . . . I take upon me very little merit in bringing him over to my opinion. He was so well-informed, and thought so judiciously, that there remained very little for me to convince him of. . . .'

Harris explains how he evolved a complicated plan, the initial stage of which should be that Catherine should make a strong declaration against the Courts of Versailles and Madrid, and then continues:

'The Prince seemed struck with this idea; he admitted the propriety of it, and did not doubt its efficacy; but said—and here, my lord, I come to a very confidential and singular part of his conversation: "Whom shall we trust to draw up this declaration, or whom for preparing the armament? Count Panin has neither the will nor the capacity to serve you; he is *Prussian*, and nothing else. Count Tchernishev (at the head of the Admiralty) is a villain, and would betray any orders given him; nothing can be done with either of these, yet they preside at the head of the departments through which the whole must pass."

'I proposed, in answer, that as I wished the transaction to be his alone, and that he should share the honor of it with nobody, the declaration might be drawn up under his eye; that he might carry it when done, himself, to Count Panin, as from the Empress, whose orders he very well knew how to enforce. That as for the equipment of the ships, I understood, in the last war, Her Imperial Majesty always settled this with the admiral who was to command them; that the same measure might be observed now, which would not only prevent any tricks being played by the person he mentioned, but also avoid giving any umbrage to the grand duke, who possibly, as high admiral, might be offended if not consulted on this occasion. He replied: "You seem to have made good use of your time in this country, and to understand it perfectly well."

'There now remained for me to ask him whether I should ever be admitted to converse with Her Imperial Majesty; he said, "undoubtedly; that she was not only willing, but desirous to hear me, particularly if I would not approach her with the mask and cunning of a foreign minister, but with the sincerity and frankness of a good and honest Englishman.

I assured him I never wore the mask he spoke of but when I
had to do with artful and insidious people; that before Her
Imperial Majesty I was ready to open my whole heart, convinced that I could not do my country a more essential service
than by letting her see in me a sentiment which prevailed
throughout the whole nation; that I was very impatient for
this honor. I hoped Her Imperial Majesty would fix an early
day. He assured me she would.'

There follows a detailed description of the British Ambassador's conversation with Catherine a fortnight later. His
eloquent plea seemed to impress her. 'The Empress,' writes
Harris, 'who had heard me with great attention, replied that
she admitted everything I said relative to the situation of
Europe; that she saw the critical position in which we stood,
and felt, both from political motives and from her own particular sentiments, the strongest desire of serving us; that she
had withheld from it merely from the reluctance she had of
plunging her empire into fresh troubles, and probably either
ending her reign in a state of war, or else of committing herself
to all Europe; that she had the highest opinion of our national
strength and spirit; and did not doubt that we should still over-
match the French and Spaniards. Her Imperial Majesty then
discoursed on the American war, lamented at our not having
been able to stop it in the beginning, and hinted at the possibility of restoring peace by renouncing our struggle with our
colonies. I asked her, if they belonged to her, and a foreign
power was to propose peace on such terms, whether she would
accept it? She replied, with great vehemence "J'aimerais mieux
perdre ma tête." "Admitting what you say," replied she, "what
right have I, after all, to interfere in a quarrel foreign to my
own concerns, on a subject I am not supposed to understand,
and with courts at such a distance from me?" I answered Her
Imperial Majesty by saying that if, in the last century, a
sovereign of Russia had held this language to me, I should
have been puzzled for a reply; but since Russia was becoming

a leading power in Europe, the answer was obvious; she was too great to see any great events with indifference.

After another conversation with the Empress, Harris again approached Potemkin.

'. . . Prince Potemkin, who, contrary to his usual custom, had heard me without interruption, told me, when I had finished speaking, that he had been so little conversant in foreign affairs that a great deal of what I said was entirely new to him; that he should make use of it in discoursing with the Empress, whose thoughts were constantly occupied with our concerns, and who certainly would already have subscribed to what I proposed, if persons ill-disposed towards us, and high in office, were not perpetually raising doubts in her mind, and representing to her that interference would be highly prejudicial to her own empire, and not even operate those salutary effects towards us I attributed to it . . . He strongly advised us, in any future plans we might propose, for connecting the two courts, to be particularly attentive to the personal character of the Empress, and not leave any room for our ill-wishers to say, we treated her with inattention, *fierté*, or *froideur*—accusations they were continually laying to our charge, and which the Empress was sometimes inclined to give credit to. He added, that as she was as yet come to no resolution, I must wait with patience, and although he was sorry to see the season advancing so fast without anything being determined on, yet it was not in his power to forward the decision. Her Imperial Majesty intended to hear the sentiments of her Council of State, and till then would certainly not be influenced in her opinion by the advice of anybody.'

There followed a long interval, when for a number of reasons it was impossible for Harris to see either Catherine or Potemkin. The truth of the matter was that Catherine, as Harris soon began to realize, was shifty in her foreign policy. She was certainly partial to Great Britain, yet at the same time she was by no means sorry to see the English engaged in a war against the

French, the Spaniards, and others while Russia was recovering from the exhausting efforts of the first Turkish War and gathering strength for the second one. There were moments when the idea of England being crushed genuinely alarmed her, and on such occasions she was almost ready to offer the desired assistance. But whenever the British position improved, her sympathies with, and anxieties for, England receded into the background. She did not wish to risk an adventure; she did not altogether trust England's promises; and subconsciously she felt the exact counterpart of what Disraeli openly expressed one hundred years later, namely that an England that was too strong was not in the interests of the Russian Empire.

At the close of the nineteenth century Disraeli feared lest a strong Russia might prejudice Britain's position in India; at the close of the eighteenth century Catherine was afraid, and not without reason, that the British would interfere with Russia's continued expansion along the shores of the Black Sea. The annexation of the Crimea had by no means satisfied her romantic imagination. She was still yearning for the realization of the daring plans she and Potemkin had so often discussed in the early days of their romance. These dreams included the conquest of Constantinople and the final ejection of the Turks from Europe. Strategically and economically this would have given Russia the much-needed free access to the Mediterranean; politically it would have enhanced her empire's own prestige beyond measure, and morally it would have given her, and especially Potemkin, the satisfaction of witnessing the triumph of Christianity over the infidels. Though absorbed by other and more immediate issues, the Empress and Potemkin had never forgotten or given up this ideal.

But in the meantime, another monarch, though for entirely different reasons, had also conceived a most ardent desire to accomplish the destruction of the Turkish Empire. For years the Austrian chancellor, Kaunitz, had been preaching to his Emperor, Joseph II, the desirability of dismembering Turkey.

The Emperor, anxious to avenge the humiliation inflicted on Austria by Frederick the Great, and longing to eclipse the hated Prussian king's fame and glory, was now willing to accept the scheme carefully prepared by Kaunitz. According to this project, the desired object was to be achieved through a joint effort of Austria and Russia. It was not without a struggle that the scheme was made palatable to the Empress Maria Theresa, Joseph's mother and coregent, who was profoundly antagonistic to Catherine on personal and moral grounds. It was finally decided that the Emperor should pay a personal visit to Russia, and Catherine was informed that he would like to make her acquaintance. She replied that she would be delighted. As she was about to take a trip to western Russia, it was agreed that she and Joseph should meet in Moghilev, a city not very far from the Austrian border, on June 7, 1780. Catherine sent Potemkin to make all the necessary preparations. He was also to hand the Austrian Emperor, who was expected to arrive first and who was traveling incognito under the title of Count Falkenstein, a very warm letter of welcome.

With pomp and splendor Catherine entered Moghilev, which Joseph, for his part, thought 'a vile city, built of wood, and the streets full of mud'. In a large wooden palace, Potemkin presented the Emperor of Austria to the Empress of all the Russias. The two monarchs liked each other almost at sight, discovering from the very start a community of ideas and interests. Joseph was not a Viennese cavalier for nothing. Both he and Catherine knew how to fascinate and to bewitch, and both made full use of their art of coquetry. No doubt, Catherine was also impressed by the fact that the head of the ancient and powerful House of Hapsburg, the Holy Roman Emperor in person, had taken the trouble of journeying all this way to Russia for the sake of making her personal acquaintance—hers, who started life as a poor little provincial German princess. She was intent on showing him how greatly she appreciated the compliment.

That, in itself, annoyed Potemkin, for he considered his
Empress as superior, or at any rate equal, to any other ruler
in the world, and he did not in the least care whether the
House of Hapsburg was more important than that of Zerbst
to which Catherine belonged, or whether 'Count Falkenstein'
had any other claims to Catherine's special consideration.
Moreover, the two men had taken an instantaneous strong
dislike to each other, which they hardly took the trouble to
conceal, even though both deemed it wise to preserve the outward forms of courtesy and etiquette. It is significant that in
this case Potemkin was no exception, for the Emperor 'went
down' very badly with all the Russians. He openly showed his
contempt for them, treated them like a lot of barbarians, and
was altogether so tactless that even Catherine could not help
being irritated. Joseph was not in the least interested in the
opera and military parades Potemkin had improvised for him
in Moghilev, and he only wanted to talk politics. Potemkin,
on the other hand, seemed determined to avoid political discussions, and invariably changed the subject whenever Joseph
made any attempts to draw him into serious conversation. In
the case of the Empress, however, it was quite different. At
Catherine's request, Joseph came with her to St. Petersburg,
and on the way they discussed their anti-Turkish plans very
freely. In the capital, where he stayed three weeks, he also succeeded in having important conferences with Potemkin.
Despite their mutual dislike, they even exchanged presents
and promises in a solemn manner, but Joseph's private opinion
was that Potemkin 'is a very indolent person, extremely cool
. . . and *insouciant*'.

Potemkin, for his part, resented the Emperor's reserve, aloof-
ness, and arrogance; nevertheless, following Catherine's instructions, he stage-managed Joseph's five-day visit to Tsarskoe
Selo in a way that was intended to please this distinguished
guest. 'Count Falkenstein,' who traveled without the usual
retinue of courtiers, flunkys, and attendants of all kinds, was

wont to sleep only at ordinary inns, and had refused the hospitality of Catherine's royal apartments. At Tsarskoe Selo, therefore, the 'upper bathhouse' or 'soaping room' in an annex of the palace, was transformed for him into an inn. The servants were put into fancy dress suitable to the occasion. Busch, Catherine's German gardener, was given the role of innkeeper, and a sign was even placed outside, describing these apartments as an inn or roadhouse.

By the time Joseph left, the foundations of a future alliance were established, and a regular correspondence now began between him and Catherine, which culminated in 1782 in a formal understanding for the partition of Turkey. The appetite of both sovereigns for new territory, as revealed by their correspondence, was insatiable. Catherine saw visions of the restoration of the Greek Empire under her grandson Constantine, with Constantinople as its capital, while Joseph coveted most of the Balkans and all the insular and continental possessions of Venice. But while the authorship of this grandiose 'Greek project' was generally attributed to Potemkin, the publication of Russian state papers shows that he took comparatively little interest in it, spending most of the year 1782 in the South, and that it was Bezborodko who drafted most of the documents relating to the 'Greek project' and stimulated as much as he could Catherine's ambitions in that direction. These, for a time, even included the creation of a 'buffer' kingdom of Dakia between the Russian and the future Greek Empire, and foreign observers freely forecast that the object pursued by her was to provide Potemkin with a suitable crown.

She certainly corresponded with him about her plans, sought his advice, and kept him informed of the smallest details of her every diplomatic move. Yet, either on account of his dislike of Joseph II, who was to take such a leading part in the realization of all these projects, or for some other reason, Potemkin was rather lukewarm about the whole thing. At any rate, Har-

ris was quite wrong in assuming that all Potemkin's interest
and energy were monopolized by the 'Greek project' and that
Western politics did not appeal to him in the same measure.
At that juncture of Russia's foreign relations, almost exactly
the opposite was the case. Potemkin believed in the desirability
of an English alliance and was anxious to secure it. In addition
to that, he was moved by his antagonism towards Panin and
towards the various other court cliques, most of whom were
pro-French. His knowledge of European affairs, as Harris soon
discovered, was far greater than could be anticipated. He also
gave Harris ample proof that he was not only partial to Great
Britain, but to her ambassador personally as well. Although
he could see through Harris, whom he once described as 'per-
fidious, a liar, and of very unsavory parts', Potemkin admired
him for his brain, energy, and endless resource; he actually
quite liked Harris, and in that respect his attitude was somewhat similar to Corberon's, who had written about his British
rival as follows: 'Harris is a large political fish that feeds on
shoals of small ones and then vomits them back again. I am
quite convinced that he despises the scum he sometimes uses
and whom he manipulates as he pleases. Despite the practices
in which he indulges, I like this man, for he has got character.'

But Corberon's feelings were scarcely reciprocated, as is
shown in the following typical outburst in a long dispatch
by Harris, giving a most vivid, if entirely negative description
of the *corps diplomatique* in St. Petersburg: 'The present
chargé d'affaires, le Chevalier Corberon, who, though he has a
very moderate capacity, has, by being used to the country,
got access to all the *valets de chambre* and inferior agents in
the Russian houses who, being chiefly French, and having,
some of them, great weight with their masters, very often con-
jured up evil spirits where I least of all expected them.' Harris
and Corberon were always spying on each other, intriguing
against each other, and accusing one another of the most
improper practices. One day Harris indignantly reported that

Corberon 'has been indiscreet enough to boast of having where-
withal to buy Prince Potemkin and, with the arrogance inseparable from his nation, talks of nothing less than uniting
this court to France. Every day produces fresh difficulties and
new enemies; as long, however, as I hold my ground at court
I trust their attempts will prove ineffectual'.

   With his zeal undamped by the absence of any tangible ·
results, Harris was now using all his powers of persuasion
on the British as well as on the Russian side to bring about
the desired understanding. He was pressing his government ·
to make some spontaneous friendly gesture towards Russia.
At his suggestion King George III wrote a very warm personal
letter to Catherine, and, as another sop to her, England's right
to search Russian ships was unconditionally suspended. At the
same time Harris was doing his utmost to work up Potemkin,
whom he now always described in his dispatches as 'my friend'.
Though occasionally overcome with doubt whether his 'friend'
was really as helpful and as sympathetic as he seemed to be,
Harris invariably came back to the conclusion that his sus-
picions were unjustified, and that he could rely not only on
Potemkin's support but actually on much confidence and consideration not shown to many other persons. Potemkin was
frequently informing him of various things that had no direct
bearing on their immediate interests, but which he thought
might be—and often were—of great use to the British ambassador. No wonder Harris was 'very assiduous in keeping up' his
intimacy with Potemkin, and they were now seeing each other
practically every day. He was continually trying to induce Potemkin to use his influence with the Empress to force matters
to a head. In a dispatch to Lord Stormont, who was now his
immediate chief, Harris described with an almost incredible
wealth of detail one of these regular attempts. He found Potemkin as friendly and eager as ever: 'I must do him justice to
say,' he continues, 'that on opening myself to him, which I endeavored to do with an appearance of the most unreserved con-

fidence, he gave the strongest marks of satisfaction. He made me repeat to him my propositions, and, as in this first conversation I confined them *solely to those of an alliance, and request of immediate assistance*, he said, though he approved entirely the measure himself, yet he feared it would not readily gain admittance with the Empress, as the dread she was under of embarking in a fresh war was stronger even than her thirst for glory; and although her predilection for us was perfectly sincere, yet Count Panin and other emissaries, of less weight in themselves, though equally capable of doing mischief, would take care to keep that under, by malevolent misrepresentations and falsehood, particularly calculated to pique her; and, added he, so susceptible is she of these impressions, that it requires the most dexterous management to efface them.'

Potemkin also told Harris to keep in touch with Panin so as to avoid giving the old count the impression that something was being done behind his back. Much though he disliked him, he had no wish to antagonize him unnecessarily.

Harris did as he was told, but soon found that Panin, despite his usual outward friendliness, was doing all he could to thwart the projected Russo-British alliance. 'I did not lose a moment', continues Harris, 'in returning to Prince Potemkin, to whom, as he always receives me without ceremony, I found easy admittance. He anticipated the motive of my visit, by saying, he had seen the strange proof, as he termed it, of Mons. de Panin's political creed, and weakness of mind; and that though he himself most thoroughly condemned it, yet that it still lay on the Empress's table and he was doubtful whether she at length would not be induced to acknowledge these sentiments for her own. I asked him with great eagerness, and no small anxiety, what could have operated so singular a revolution; he replied, "You have chosen an unlucky moment. The new favorite lies dangerously ill; the cause of his illness and uncertainty of his recovery have so entirely unhinged the Empress, that she is incapable of employing her thoughts on any subject, and all

ideas of ambition, of glory, of dignity, are absorbed in this one
passion. Enervated to a degree, she repugns everything which
bears the features of activity or exertion. Your antagonists well
know how to make use of this opportunity, and Count Panin,
who has numberless emissaries at court, times his counsels with
more address than falls to his share in other concerns. "My influence," added he, "is suspended, particularly as I have taken
on me to advise her to get rid of a favorite who, if he dies in
her palace, would do her reputation an essential injury." '

As usual, Harris tried to play on Potemkin's ambition to be
the only man capable of influencing the Empress and as usual
he promised to do his best. But the atmosphere was not
propitious: young Lanskoy was worse, Panin was also ill and
finally Harris himself developed the first symptoms of jaundice.
When after a considerable interval, Harris once again tried to
work up Potemkin he found his 'friend' rather impatient.

'Prince Potemkin had more than once attempted to interrupt me, when I begged leave to be heard out, and when I
had ended, he said: "You should say this to Count Panin, not
to me; you speak exactly my sentiments, and although I had
them not so ready in my mind as you, yet I have made use of
most of them to the Empress. She has ordered me to tell you to
give in a paper expressive of your notions and instructions, and
I trust we shall, at least, mollify the answer which has been
prepared for her." I gave him in, the next day, the paper marked
B, and myself fell so ill the following one so as to be obliged to
keep my house for three weeks. Nothing, however was lost, as,
had I been in perfect health, I could not have advanced a single
step. Your Lordship is not unacquainted with the reasons; and
I had no other way of filling up this space usefully, than by
keeping Prince Potemkin regularly informed of all news I received from England, which I did at the Empress's request, and
by writing him short notes to keep up his good disposition,
which I all along have believed, and still do believe, to be
perfectly sincere.'

Having recovered, Harris immediately called on Panin, who was as yet confined to bed and whose health seemed to be greatly impaired. This time the old diplomat refrained from any lip service to Great Britain but simply proceeded to read out to Harris what he claimed to be Catherine's own words. The British ambassador wrote it all down very carefully, but felt alarmed and disappointed and once again he rushed to Potemkin for help and advice. It must have been a very bad winter, for not only had Harris himself barely recovered from influenza and been constrained to visit Panin in his sick-room, but Potemkin too was so ill that the interview had to be postponed for several days. He then received Harris in bed, and, having read several times the paper dictated by Panin, said, while handing it back: 'Such will ever be the language of this indolent and torpid minister; cold professions of friend-ship; false logic and narrow views. I can assure you, the Em-press' feelings are very ill expressed and I recognize in this abstract nothing which she would own but the last paragraph. It is true, from a timidity contrary to her general character, and arising from the impulse of the day, she refuses your pro-posals; but she never meant to do it in a cold and reserved style.' With all his eloquence Harris pleaded that Potemkin and the Empress should override whatever opposition there was to the proposed English alliance, and pointed out that perhaps a day would come when the position would be re-versed and Russia would be soliciting the friendship and good offices of England as urgently as England did at the moment those of Russia. Potemkin saw all that and tried to explain to his friend the nature of Catherine's difficulties: 'You must have patience,' he said, 'depend on it, the chapter of accidents will serve you better than all your rhetoric. Improve events as they arise, and be fully convinced that if you ever can furnish her with a specious and plausible pretext, Her Imperial Majesty will embrace your cause with the greatest eagerness.'

But the British ambassador was not a man to be satisfied

with such friendly advice, much though he appreciated it. Once he had started his attack nothing could force him to abandon the effort, and stubbornly he renewed his plea. What added weight to his argument was that during the very time of these negotiations he received information that an order had been issued by the Court of Madrid to bring all neutral ships destined for the Mediterranean to Cadiz, and to sell their lading to the highest bidder without even bothering to obtain the consent of the proprietors or the respective foreign consuls. Harris writes: 'As, fortunately, the singular conduct of His Catholic Majesty came at this moment to my knowledge, I inserted it [in a memorandum he was drawing up for Catherine at Potemkin's suggestion] as a proof of what was to be expected from the House of Bourbon if they acquired that maritime superiority they were contending for. On reading this paragraph, Prince Potemkin said, "Par Dieu, vous la tenez, The Empress abhors the inquisition, and never will suffer its precepts to be exercised on the seas. If what you advance is confirmed by our letters from Spain, you may depend on it we shall be no longer inactive." ' Upon hearing that the Spaniards really were seizing neutral, i.e. also Russian ships, the Empress sent a very strong note to Madrid and also handed one to the Spanish chargé d'affaires in St. Petersburg. Further developments seemed to bring Harris and Potemkin nearer to the realization of their desire: this time Catherine really did show the intention to act.

'By the post of February 6,' writes Harris, 'there arrived letters from the Russian consul at Cadiz, that a Russian vessel, with a Russian flag, bound with corn to Malaga, had been brought in, confiscated, the cargo disposed of to the best bidder, and the crew very inhumanly treated. It was no unfortunate circumstance for me to learn that this same ship had been visited by our cruisers, but treated in the most civil manner, and dismissed, as having an innocent cargo. I was going to expatiate on this to Prince Potemkin when he sent for me

(Tuesday last, February 11), and with an impetuous joy, analogous to his character, he said, "I heartily congratulate you; orders will be given to arm instantly fifteen ships of the line, and five frigates; they are to put to sea early in the spring, and though they will be supposed to protect the Russian trade, *envers et contre tous*, they are meant to chastise the Spaniards, whose insolence and arbitrary conduct the Empress cannot put up with." '

Harris was somewhat sceptical as to the benefits to be derived from this step by Britain, but Potemkin assured him that it was worth a great deal more than even the strongest declaration. The ambassador retorted that it was really no more than the three northern courts just protecting their trade. His report continues: 'Prince Potemkin, almost out of humor with my objections, and with my backwardness to admit the great advantage we should derive from this step, said, "I am just come from the Empress: it is by her particular orders I tell it to you; she commanded me to lose no time in finding you out; she said she knew it would give you pleasure, and, besides myself, you are at this moment the only person acquainted with her design." He ended by desiring me to dispatch my messenger immediately, expressing his impatience for this event being known in London. I begged him to assure Her Imperial Majesty how grateful I was for this additional mark of her goodness; that I would repeat it exactly in his own words, and would convey, as accurately as lay in the power of my pen, the satisfaction he expressed on the occasion; that I was still free to confess to him, that this circumstance gave me more pleasure than the armament itself, since there could be no doubt, that while we had so powerful and able a friend near the Empress' person, we might hope for everything.'

12

ENGLAND'S OFFER

BOTH Catherine and Potemkin were behaving in such a manner that Harris was once again full of hope, and thought he was on the eve of achieving final success. Potemkin informed him that the Empress was disgusted with Panin, and that the English were the only nation towards whom she was partial. 'I am so convinced of this,' he added, 'that if it was not my own opinion, it would be my interest to support you, as a contrary conduct would deprive me of the Empress' favor.' Catherine, for her part, made a point of telling him that if Rodney were to defeat the Spanish fleet, she would celebrate the occasion by distributing money to the poor. She not only kept her word, but when news of the British naval victory off Cape St. Vincent reached St. Petersburg she gave a 'ball and entertainment on account of Rodney's successes'. At the same time, however, she said to Harris: 'You have given me insomnia; the several papers you have given in to Prince Potemkin, joined to the interest I take in everything that concerns your country, have made me resolve in my mind every kind of means by which I could assist you. I would do everything to serve you, *except involving myself in a war*; I should be answerable to my subjects, my successor, and perhaps to all Europe, for the consequences of such a conduct.' She also added that perhaps if she were younger she would not be so wise. Thus despite all the personal compliments and distinctions enjoyed by Harris, both in his private and in his official capacity, the position was fundamentally unchanged.

He ascribed Catherine's reluctance to take England's side, and assume great military and political risks, to the intrigues of his enemies and to insufficient zeal on Potemkin's part. Strangely enough, it did not occur to Harris, or else he was unwilling to admit it, that Russian and British interests were by no means identical, and that if the positions were reversed England most certainly would not have moved a little finger to help Russia under such precarious circumstances. The proclamation of the 'armed neutrality' contributed to convincing him that Catherine and Potemkin were bluffing, and in his blind rage Harris conceived the grotesque plan of bribing Potemkin.

'My Lord,' he wrote to Lord Stormont, 'If, on further inquiry, I should find, as I almost suspect, that my friend's fidelity has been shaken, or his political faith corrupted, in the late conferences by any direct offers or indirect promises of reward, I shall think myself, in such a case, not only authorized but obliged to lure him with a similar bait, since, if it ever should come from that quarter, every hope of success here will be cut off, and the tide will turn powerfully against us. I shall, however, take care to use only general terms, and by creating expectations, keep up the good will till I hear from Your Lordship. You will be pleased to recollect that I have to do with a person immensely rich, who well knows the importance of what is asked, and whose avidity, not necessity, is to be paid. He will require, perhaps, as much as Torsy proposed, but without success, to Marlborough.'

This is a reference to the offer of 2,000,000 francs that Louis XIV's minister, Torsy, had made in May 1709, at the Hague to the Duke of Marlborough, to bring him over to the French side. Needless to say, Harris was equally unsuccessful; but having failed to bribe Potemkin, he managed to purchase the services of one of his menials, whose name, however, he does not give. He bombarded this man with questions, and in reporting the results of his interview to Lord Stormont, he wrote:

'Prince Potemkin is sincere in what he does and says; he dislikes the French, is piqued against the King of Prussia, and has turned a deaf ear to some very advantageous proposals that monarch lately made him. He, however, is not sufficiently zealous in the cause of England, to depart from his habits of indolence and ease; and unless he is roused to activity, by the opposition of Count Panin, he will not use his whole influence in our behalf . . . I asked what he meant by the advantageous proposals made by the King of Prussia to Prince Potemkin? He said, a promise of assistance to obtain the Duchy of Courland, and, if he chose it, to find him a wife among some of the German princesses, none of whom, however, were named. I inquired how the prince came to reject so flattering an offer. He replied, because he did not believe it sincere, but calculated solely to gain his good will during the interview at Moghilev. I asked him what Prince Potemkin thought of this interview, and how he was disposed towards the Court of Vienna. He answered that the prince had no regular system of politics; that he was led by impulse of the moment, and he had seen him almost adopt the political principles of every country . . . He concluded by saying, that if she [the Empress] was fairly embarked she would never retract, and that if we could contrive once to make her declare herself avowedly our friend, we might be assured of being assisted, if necessary, with the whole force of her empire.'

Writing to his father a few days later, Harris attributed the blame for his lack of success to the fluctuations of the Russian court and the inattention of the British Government. But despite the unsatisfactory nature of their joint diplomatic endeavors, the personal relations between Potemkin and Harris were as close as ever. Knowing that Harris's father was an enthusiastic Greek scholar, Potemkin gave the ambassador a number of valuable Greek books, the music of a Greek hymn, five pounds of coffee just arrived from Constantinople, and other valuable presents for transmission to Mr. Harris, senior. Harris even felt constrained to report to Lord Stormont that the doubts he had had of Potemkin's fidelity being shaken had proved groundless, and that he had wrongfully accused his 'friend' of duplicity. He complained, however, of Potemkin's moodiness, which made it impossible even to guess what particular person or cause he would be championing at any given moment. At the same time, Panin's inveterate anti-English and pro-Prussian sympathies were causing Harris great anxiety. 'With such a friend and such an enemy, I have much to fear and little to hope,' he wrote, and suggested that his recall, and the appointment of some other British representative, might perhaps facilitate the desired end, 'which it was my greatest and sole ambition to effect, but to which my abilities and zeal have been found inadequate.' But Lord Stormont refused to recall him, and asked him to persevere still further in his endeavors. England's need of Russia was too great to drop the project on which so much time and effort had been spent, and it was premature to give up hope that Catherine's favor would find no other expression than mere words. Once again Harris concentrated all his forensic abilities and all his diplomatic skill in a fresh attempt to get some action out of Potemkin. Finding Potemkin alone and for once at leisure, Harris immediately got down to business. They had a long talk, when the British ambassador restated the position very fully and made a most eloquent plea for his 'friend's' help. He found Potemkin as ever eager and understanding, full of 'uncommon attention' to every word he said, but, as on so many previous occasions, Potemkin could only counsel patience and perseverance. A few days later, in a private letter to his friend and colleague Joseph York, at the Hague, Harris thus summed up the situation:

'I, however, stand better than ever at court, and enjoy Prince Potemkin's entire confidence and support; and, could I cure him of the most unaccountable carelessness and inattention, we should soon triumph. These vices hurt him as much as me; and if he does not bestir himself we shall fall together, though with this difference, that his fall will be somewhat more severe than mine.'

But Potemkin's fall was by no means imminent, and he did not seem to fear in the least the adverse criticism and intrigues his intimate association with the British ambassador was provoking among both his Russian and foreign enemies. When Corberon and the Spanish envoy one day called on him and jointly complained of his obvious predilection for Harris, the French chargé d'affaires even producing a list out of his pocket on which all Potemkin's meetings with the British ambassador were carefully enumerated, Potemkin was furious, and abruptly broke off the conversation by declaring to the two 'Bourbon' diplomats that he was busy. In open defiance of the anti-British cliques at the court and of Harris's rivals among the other foreign diplomats, Potemkin even invited Harris to spend a long week end at his country house. The dispatch describing this visit gives so admirable a picture of 'Serenissimus' that it deserves to be quoted in full.

'I spent part of last week,' writes Harris, 'at a country house of Prince Potemkin's in Finland. Nobody was with us but a select part of his family, and I had him, when not employed with them, in a manner entirely to myself . . . I had an opportunity of investigating his character to the bottom, and that I really believe he spoke freer and more openly with me than he would have ventured to have done with any person in the empire. He certainly is strongly disposed to be our friend, and has never deceived me. He recapitulated with an incredible accuracy, everything which had passed between us, and pointed out from conference to conference all he had said to the Empress, and attempted to do, in our behalf. He told me, that at certain moments she seemed determined to join us; but that the idea of bringing on herself the sarcasms of the King of Prussia and of France, and, above all, the dread of losing the reputation she enjoyed by ill success, restrained her, and that under these impressions the enervating language of Count Panin was better listened to than anything which fell from him. That, however, in the present instance, she began to feel she had been influenced by her minister too far, and though she was too proud to recant yet he was persuaded she repented of having embarked so far and so inconsiderately in this neutral league. He called it "the child of faction and folly", and that if left to itself it could not last.

'He added, that she began also to be tired of the favorite, and that his fall was not very distant. "When things go on smoothly," continued the Prince, "my influence is small; but when she meets with rubs she always wants me, and then my influence becomes as great as ever." This will soon be the case, and I shall certainly take advantage of it in some shape or other. He ridiculed the Danish and Swedish fleets, particularly the latter, which, he said, was so rotten that a royal salute would shake it to pieces. He seemed piqued with the King of Prussia, and to have a natural aversion for the French and Spaniards. It would be endless if I was to write all he said. He was in perfect good humor, the whole time, and discovered a mixture of wit, levity, learning, and humor, I never met in the same man. His way of life is as singular as his character; his hours for eating and sleeping are uncertain, and we were frequently airing in the rain in an open carriage at midnight.

'This visit of mine will give the greatest uneasiness to the Prussians and French, particularly as not only no strangers, but even no Russian but his nearest relations, were ever admitted to be of this annual party. Indeed, it is my intimacy with him that gives me importance, and induces them to attack me with such inveteracy.'

The struggle between Harris and Potemkin on the one side

and practically the whole of the diplomatic corps and all the court cliques on the other side was approaching its final stages. Harris found out through his spies that Count Goertz, the Prussian envoy, had instructions from Frederick the Great to obtain the British ambassador's removal at any price. The 'Bourbon' ministers and the Dutch representative were using all their influence in the same direction, and Panin was helping them as much as he could. This struggle had resulted in frightening all Harris's colleagues from his house, but when he complained to Potemkin the reply he got was: 'Have patience, conceal your uneasiness, they have overshot the mark, and if you let them alone, they will destroy themselves.' That was the principle on which Potemkin had often acted towards his own enemies, and it had usually proved successful. But Harris was too impatient, and the pressure exercised on him from London obviously too great, to abide by such dilatory tactics. He would not admit that Potemkin had other and more urgent things to do, that his manifold activities absorbed much of his time and energy, and because his 'friend' would not devote himself entirely to the promotion of British interests or the counteracting of those of England's enemies, Harris was accusing him of indolence.

It is at this juncture that in her desire to secure the Russian alliance, England made her most astonishing move. In a dispatch dated October 28, 1780, Lord Stormont directed Harris to find out whether the British Government could hold out to Catherine 'some object worthy of her ambition, some cession of a nature to increase her commerce and naval strength and that would engage the Empress to conclude with His Majesty an alliance, making the present war, the *casus fœderis* and assisting us *totis viribus* against France and Spain, and our revolted colonies.' But Harris had already anticipated his chief's wishes and had on his own initiative broached the subject to Potemkin; his dispatch—marked "Most secret" in cipher—crossed with that of Lord Stormont and said: 'Prince Potemkin, though he did not directly say so, yet clearly gave me to understand that *the only cession*, which would induce the Empress to become our ally, was that of Minorca.'

The Balearic Islands had in the previous centuries seen many battles and had changed hands several times; from 1708–1756 and again since 1763 Minorca with its fine harbor Port Mahon was a most treasured British possession. Yet, in the course of the negotiations that followed, England was prepared to part with it to Russia, no price being too heavy to obtain Catherine's much coveted support. The negotiations that proceeded on the subject, first between Harris and Potemkin, then between the British ambassador and Catherine direct and finally again between the two 'friends' are very fully recorded by Harris in his dispatches. In his regular daily conferences with Potemkin Harris had carefully prepared the ground and through him he was seeking to be received at a private audience by the Empress. On Harris's own admission, Potemkin did everything in his power to persuade her to see the British ambassador in private, but for a long time his efforts met with unprecedented and unaccountable resistance on her part, 'He imputed it,' reports Harris, 'in part to the idea his enemies had fixed in her mind, that he was aspiring at unlimited power; to the imbecility of the favorite, who was an idle tale-bearer, and particularly to the adroit flattery of Count Falkenstein, who, though certainly he meant him no harm, had essentially hurt him by teaching her to believe that she was the greatest princess in Europe, and that she wanted neither ministers nor favorite to direct her councils; he added, that this language would at any time have turned her head, but that she was within these two years so greatly sunk, her intellects so weakened, and her passions so increased, that it now operated with redoubled force. "Sometimes," said he, "when I speak on foreign affairs, she lets me remain without any answer at all, and at others replies to me with warmth and displeasure." '

One morning, however, Potemkin sent for Harris and showed an exchange of communications that had just taken place between himself and the Empress. The British ambassador reports on this important interview as follows: 'His note was short. It set forth his zeal for her service, his concern for the situation in which persons less zealous than himself for her glory had placed her, and requested if she had doubts of what he said, that she would be pleased to perform the promise she had so long ago given him, of seeing me in private. Her answer was equally short; she consented to see me, but first desired to see him. He accordingly went down to her, and remained upwards of two hours alone with her. I had with impatience waited his return and was happy to see him come in with a countenance full of satisfaction and joy. He began by telling me, Her Imperial Majesty would see me at ten the next morning; that she heard him with particular attention and pleasure, and that he evidently saw she was coming round.

'He told me to be unreserved, open and candid: "for," said he, "she has excessive penetration, and if she perceives any inconsistency or prevarication she will suspect your sincerity: let her feel that you use no other weapons than those of truth and justice, and that you argue from these principles, and from love of your country. Flatter as much as you can; *you cannot use too much unction*; but flatter her for what she *ought to be*, not for *what she is*. Do not expect that you can break off the Dutch negotiation, or that it is in the power of any person living to prevent her from concluding her favorite plan of armed neutrality. Content yourself with destroying its effects; the resolution itself is immovable. As it was conceived by mistake, perfected by vanity, it is maintained by pride and obstinacy; you well know the hold of these passions *on a female mind*, and if you attempt to slacken you will only tighten the knot. Let me repeat to you," said he, "Be open and unreserved; make her feel you have full confidence in her; it is because she supposes your nation has not this confidence, that she is displeased." '

Armed with this advice, Harris had his interview with the Empress, which he reported verbatim and in dialogue form, the conversation naturally being in French. Out of this interminable discussion, in the course of which both the Empress and the ambassador seemed to be finding unlimited new arguments in support of their respective points of view, the following statement made by Harris deserves to be extracted: 'You can demand from us whatever you like; we could not refuse anything to Your Imperial Majesty, if we only knew what could please you.' But Catherine was as stubborn as before in her determination not to become involved in England's domestic and international difficulties at any price, and much though she sympathized with the British she had several reasons to complain of their attitude towards her and her people. Harris was shrewd enough to understand this, and commenting on his interview with the Empress he made the following recommendations to his chief:

'On this point we must humor her. Our arguments, though the best human reason ever used, will avail nothing; we must condescend to flatter her, to grant a free passage to her ships, to make an exception in her favor. She then immediately, and before any advantage will arise to her trade from this act of complaisance, will become our warm and zealous friend; and if the conditions on which the last Peace of Paris in 1762 was made, are such as may suit Her Majesty's approbation, I am positive will support us in insisting on them and become, in spite of these terms a willing mediator. If what I was writing was my own opinion solely, and if it arose from no other circumstance but from the conversation I have just related (however explicit this may have been) I should not dare to assert thus positively, what I say; but I am confirmed in it by Prince Potemkin, who knows too well Her Imperial Majesty to be mistaken in her character.

' "Let them reflect on the *character* and *sex* of the person to whom they are speaking; let them consider that there is no

disgrace to indulge a weakness, from which they may draw
the greatest advantages; let them imitate what first the King
of Prussia has done, and since the Emperor; let them talk to
her *passions*, to her *feelings*; she from that moment becomes
your lasting and most active friend. But supposing," said he,
"even this should not be so, where is the evil of speaking out?
Your secret will not be betrayed, and the terms you propose
will be such as will do you honor in Europe. For God's sake
do not be ashamed to flatter her; it is the only road to her
good-will, and she has so high an opinion of your nation, that
a pleasant word from you will go further than a studied phrase
from any other people. She asks for nothing but praise and
compliment; give her that, and she in return will give you the
whole force of her empire." These, my lord, are the prince's
own words, and they contain the *whole* secret of this court.'

Meanwhile, in pursuance of Lord Stormont's message, instructing him to raise the question of a possible territorial
cession by Great Britain to Russia as a possible inducement,
Harris once again approached Potemkin on this delicate matter. But although Harris used a great deal of circumlocution,
Potemkin came straight to the point:

'Prince Potemkin caught with eagerness at the idea,' writes
Harris. "What can you cede to us?" said he. I told him we had
extensive possessions in America, in the East Indies, on the
Sugar Islands; perhaps some of these might please the Empress; and though I had not the smallest right to dispose of
them, or even a shadow of authority for what I was saying, yet,
in my own private opinion, we ought to gratify her with such
part of them as she chose, if by it we could obtain a lasting
peace. I said such as she chose, because I was sure she would
be moderate, and because in my own mind, such a cession
would only be an exchange of masters, and that the utility and
advantages of the possessions would, when it was in the hands
of the Empress, still remain to the English.

'He shook his head at all this. "You would ruin us if you

gave us distant colonies; you see our ships can scarce get out of the Baltic, how would you have them cross the Atlantic? If you give us anything, give us something *nearer home*."

'I told him we could not dismember our own island, and that we set an immense value on our Mediterranean possessions.

' "I am sorry for it," added he; "for, if you would cede *Minorca*, I promise you, *I believe I could lead the Empress any lengths*."

'I told him I had no authority to say we would cede anything, but that I believed the cession he required, impossible.

' "So much the worse," replied the prince; "it would insure us to you for ever."

'The next day, and several days after, he always got on this subject, and I found it had made a very strong impression on his mind. I, however, affected not to encourage him to talk on it, and generally turned the conversation on other subjects. About a fortnight ago, we were sitting alone together very late in the evening, when he broke out all of a sudden, into all the advantages that would arise to Russia from a possession in the Mediterranean; that we ought to wish it, because it would be a perpetual source of enmity with France, and that we should never suffer by it, since, for every possible political use, it would be as much ours as theirs. He then, with the liveliness of his imagination, ran on the idea of a Russian fleet stationed at Mahon, of its peopling the island with Greeks; that such an acquisition would be a column of the Empress's glory erected in the middle of the sea, and that he would be responsible he could lead her to any lengths under the promise of such a cession.

'I told him what I had said before, that the idea of any cession at all was purely my own; that I was happy it had given him some pleasing reflections, but that these were but reveries, since I was perfectly ignorant of the sentiments of my court on this subject.

'"Find them out," added he with eagerness, "as soon as · you can; persuade your ministers to give it to us, and we will give you peace, and then unite ourselves to you by the firmest and most lasting alliance."

The negotiations that followed revealed both Harris and Potemkin at their best. So eager was the British ambassador to achieve at long last the desired object, on which he had spent so much energy, time, and money—on several occasions he had felt compelled to ask for fresh funds to combat the alleged corruption practiced by his enemies—that he was using all his influence with his own government to make the cession of Minorca palatable to them. Finally, he got a message from Lord Stormont expressing England's willingness in principle, and the conditions on which this unprecedented step could be taken. Lord Stormont's letter to Sir James Harris is dated January 20, 1781, and reads as follows:—

'My Lord, Prince Potemkin has pointed the views of his Sovereign to a very great object indeed, to a most valuable possession which this country was eager to acquire, and has been ever anxious to maintain. Minorca, besides its many real advantages, stands very high in the esteem of the nation at large, a circumstance that must be attended to in a constitution like ours; if ever a minister in this country parts with such a possession, it must be upon grounds that will fully warrant the propriety in the public opinion.

'It is true, that there is a most material difference between ceding a valuable possession to an enemy, and yielding it to a neutral friend and ally, as a return for great and essential proofs of friendship, and as a bond of perpetual union; the sacrifice would certainly be a great one, even in that view, but every sacrifice consistent with honor and dignity may have its price. Prince Potemkin saw at once the many advantages that would accrue to Russia from such an acquisition, but he spoke in very loose and general terms of the service the Empress would engage to render this country, yet, it is very clear, such a sacrifice cannot possibly be made but for great and essential service actually performed. However unusual it may be to go deep into a negotiation of so delicate a nature upon the first general opening, yet every consideration of that sort gives way to the desire of treating with that unreserved confidence which the Empress so much recommends, and which we are persuaded she will ever return.

'Upon this principle it is, that the King goes at once to the root of this business, and His Majesty, after taking the opinion of his confidential servants, has empowered me to authorize you to mention the conditions upon which alone so great and important a cession can be made. (You will decipher with the utmost attention what follows.) The Empress of Russia shall effectuate the restoration of peace between Great Britain, France, and Spain, upon the following terms, viz., The Treaty of Paris in 1762 shall be the basis of the treaty to be made; it shall be renewed with such alterations only, respecting the possessions of the contracting parties, as the events of the war have made; with regard to all which, the present *uti possidetis* shall be the rule, unless where the parties shall choose to vary it for mutual convenience.

'It shall be an express condition, that the French immediately evacuate Rhode Island, and every other part of His Majesty's colonies in North America. No stipulation or agreement whatever shall be made with respect to His Majesty's rebellious subjects, who can *never be suffered to treat* through the medium of a *foreign power*.

'If the Empress of Russia will effectuate such a peace as is here described, the King will, in that case, cede to Her Imperial Majesty and to the Imperial Crown of Russia, the Island of Minorca, this cession to take place as soon as possible after the preliminaries of the above-described peace are signed. A treaty of perpetual defensive alliance between Great Britain and Russia, of which treaty the cession and guarantee of Minorca shall make a part, and shall be signed on the same day as the above-mentioned preliminaries; though the cession must be conditional, and cannot be made till after the service performed, yet the effectual engagement may be entered into immediately, but must, for many reasons, be kept absolutely secret for the present. When the Empress of Russia takes possession of Minorca, she shall purchase all the artillery, military stores, etc., that shall be found there; she shall also expressly engage that the port and harbors of Minorca, shall, at all times, be open to His Majesty's ships of war, as also to all privateers; and all ships belonging to His Majesty's trading subjects shall have free entry there, and pay no other duties than common port duties paid at present.

'To prevent the danger of a sudden attack upon Minorca during the present war, the Russian fleet in the Mediterranean shall receive orders to be attentive to its protection.

'You see with what frankness we have gone at once is as far as it is possible to go; a little time will now show whether Prince Potemkin is, or is not, mistaken in the opinion he entertains of Her Imperial Majesty's intentions. A great field is open to her, worthy of her talents, and a rich harvest of real glory must attend her in the completion of such a plan. You will take care to let it be fully understood, that no other court has the least knowledge of this business, and we expect that the whole should at present be an inviolable secret, trusted only to the Empress, Prince Potemkin, and yourself.'

In the promotion of this scheme, Harris was now indefatigable. Since Potemkin was ill and, though he received him in bed on several occasions, could not himself convey all the necessary messages to Catherine, Harris also applied to Bezborodko and even to Alexis Orlov, both of whom did what they could for him.

Catherine was eager, yet adamant. The refrain of all her arguments was 'I will not be led into temptation'. Finally she drafted in her own hand a declaration which Potemkin was to read to Harris. It was written in Russian and had been corrected many times. She expressed her gratitude for England's offer, as usual emphasized her friendly feelings and her desire to be helpful, but flatly turned down the whole proposition.

'My friend's commentary on this text amounted to this: that she has a longing desire to have Minorca, but that she has not courage to subscribe to the means by which alone it can be got.'

Thus ended one of the most picturesque episodes in Anglo-Russian relations. If the cession of Minorca had taken place, there is no end to the strategic and political developments that might have followed.

It is interesting that much later, in a long letter to his old friend Lord Grantham, Harris attributed a large part of the blame for the failure to secure an alliance with Catherine to the ambiguous and insincere policy of the British Government. He not only pays a very warm tribute to Potemkin for his genuine and enthusiastic support of the scheme but also expresses his belief that Catherine was on the point of accepting the offer of Minorca. On the other hand England was 'equally afraid to accept or dismiss' Russia's position, and he was instructed 'secretly to oppose, but avowedly to acquiesce' in Catherine's notions. An indiscretion in London had revealed to the Empress the true nature of the British offer.

But there were other reasons as well. Catherine's mind at the time was absorbed by a number of issues that appeared to her even more important than Minorca. Her *rapprochement* with Austria, which had been progressing during the last two years, had taken such shape that the conclusion of a formal alliance now became possible. Moreover, her alcove affairs were passing through a crisis, and this was having the most peculiar effects on her. 'The Empress,' reported Harris, 'grows every day more suspicious and hasty; tenacious to a degree of her own power, and obstinately attached to her own opinion, she is jealous or displeased with almost every one that approaches her. From being the most easy and pleasing mistress to serve,

she is become the most difficult, and her domestics, as well as
her ministers and favorites, feel this singular change in her disposition. It makes itself so sensibly felt, that several of the
leading people of state have asked, or mean to ask, their dis-
mission from their offices. . . . My friend, too, who is more
exposed to the effects of this revolution in her temper than
anyone, has, I have good reason to believe, expressed to her
his earnest desire of throwing up his many employments, and
it was not till he received the flattest refusal, that he desisted
from his solicitations. I am, however, very far from believing
that he was earnest in forming this request, and that, knowing
the impossibility of the Empress's doing without him, he
made it with a view, if possible, of recovering his influence over
her which, for some time past, has to me visibly diminished,
and in which, if he has failed (for I think it still in a state of
decline) he has completely succeeded in another point (not
less interesting to him), by having induced her to purchase of
him for Lanskoy (who seems to be now reinstated in favor) a
considerable estate, for a sum not less than 500,000 rubles; and
indeed, if anything could make me suppose he had it in con-
templation to leave the court, it is the loads of ready money
he is heaping up, by selling his estates, horses, and jewels, and
which looks as if he either wished, or was apprehensive he
should be forced, to retire, and that it was wise to place in time
a large capital in some foreign funds.

'He is to me most perfectly friendly and cordial, and assures
me that whenever he can, he will serve me, and that, in the
meanwhile, he is free to confess that it is not in his power,
either to direct his sovereign's conduct, or to prevent her from
being imposed on by false representations. I should not do
him justice if I was not to say that I believe him perfectly sincere, and that he has never deceived me, or withheld from me
any secrets he was not enjoined by the Empress to keep. I in
some measure partake of his fate, and, for some time past, I
have remarked a very material change in the Empress's behavior

towards me, particularly since my conference with her in November, when I have reason to believe, she was displeased with the freedom I made use of.'

She was also annoyed that her offer of mediation between England and Holland had been turned down by the British Government, and both Potemkin and Bezborodko told Harris that at the moment she was determined to conduct her own foreign relations, without anybody's help or advice. Potemkin, according to Harris, 'sees in as strong lights as Your Lordship or any of His Majesty's ministers the many inconveniences attending her ideas but was unable to suggest a remedy'. He was very frank and candid in explaining to Harris the cause of all these changes in the Empress, and gave him some sound advice how to behave in the future.

'My Lord,' wrote Harris, 'Prince Potemkin, in some of the late conversations I have had with him, spoke of the Empress in freer terms than he ever used before. He had often accused her of levity, of perpetually altering her opinion, and never acting up to a system; and indeed, so many proofs of this appear in the course of my correspondence, that his authority was not necessary to constitute the veracity of the fact. He now, however, made no scruple of saying that increase of years by degrees destroyed all her great qualities; that she has become suspicious, timid, and narrow-minded; that in all great objects which were held out to her, she suspected some deep selfish design in him who proposed them; or if she supposed him sincere, she saw only the peril, not the glory attending the attempt; that her ambition disappeared before the most remote probability of risk; and that she was sensible of nothing but the flattery of the hour, because it was obtained without danger. "It was for this reason," said he, "that she declined the very advantageous offer you made her last February, of a cession of the Isle of Minorca, a possession," added the Prince, "she would have purchased a few years ago by lending you the whole force of her empire, if you had required it; and," added he, emphati-

cally, "what have you to fear from her, even suppose she meant
you ill? when now she has not spirit enough to accept it, when it
was given her for nothing, and when, instead of acknowledging the generosity of the offer, she thought it was a snare to
draw her into the war? Be sure," continued he, "that nothing
will induce her to be your avowed enemy, or your avowed
friend. He that knows best how to please her will have the appearance of her friendship; and in this," he said, "though, from
her predilection for your nation, you have an easier game to play
than your enemies, yet they are more adroit than you are." '

Summing up Russia's international position and pointing out
the great influence Joseph II was now exercising over Catherine,
Potemkin suggested that Harris might try that channel. According to the British ambassador's dispatch he said: ' "Cultivate, therefore, on one side the good will of the Emperor; it
is through him alone you can get at the Empress; on the other,
do everything you possibly can to please her. Never contradict
her, in the first instance; affect to accept her offers, to follow
her councils; and if her offers and councils are incompatible
with your interests, or contrary to your opinions, wait an opportunity in the course of business, of imperceptibly deviating
from them. I am reduced," ended he, "to give you advice, for
I cannot give you assistance; and recommend to your Ministry
to follow it, and I am sure they will find their account in it."
Such was the very confidential and, I may say, extraordinary
language of my friend; and what he says is so strongly confirmed
by everything I have related that I am satisfied that on the
whole he speaks truth.'

Despite Potemkin's advice, Harris, more tenacious than
ever, continued to make every endeavor to obtain what he had
set out to achieve. He was using all his arts of bluff and persuasion on both the Russian and the British side, making
further eloquent appeals to Lord Stormont for new concessions
'to the dangerous whims of this singular court,' and still clinging to Potemkin as the principal channel of British influence.

Finally, the British Government consented to accept Catherine's offer of separate mediation between England and the Netherlands. 'The turn of your dispatches, backed by the weight of Prince Potemkin's opinion, greatly influenced the decision upon this difficult point,' wrote Lord Stormont to Harris; and a little further, in the same dispatch: 'Prince Potemkin's advice is followed in communicating to the Empress our ultimatum.' Thus, despite Potemkin's declaration to the effect that his influence was no longer of any avail, both the British ambassador and the British Government were still attaching the greatest importance to his opinions, and were obviously relying on his assistance. But although this, and repeated further attempts to come to some definite understanding with Catherine, at times appeared to be on the verge of success, nothing definite was ever achieved, and this state of affairs was obviously irritating both Harris and Potemkin. They were still very friendly and still kept in close contact with each other, but their joint 'post-mortems' on what might have been—not unnaturally followed by a certain amount of recrimination—could scarcely improve matters or add new zest to their endeavors. Moreover, Potemkin was becoming increasingly absorbed by a new outbreak of court and alcove intrigues, which demanded his undivided attention, and at the moment appeared to him far more vital than even the most important issues of foreign policy. Battle royal was raging around the proposed trip of the Grand Duke Paul and his grand duchess abroad, and one of the most astonishing moves in this welter of plots and counterplots was Potemkin's sudden intervention on behalf of his oldest and most hated rival, Count Panin. To everybody's amazement it was Potemkin who prevented Catherine from dismissing Panin—whose close friendship with, and influence over, the Tsarevitch Paul she always dreaded—and ordering him to leave St. Petersburg. In fact the two men, who had striven to jockey each other out of office for years, suddenly came together again. But a few weeks later, after the grand duke and duchess had gone, Catherine all of a sudden instructed Panin to deliver his papers and to consider himself henceforward only titular and no longer an active member of her Council. Even Potemkin's position was uncertain: 'It is my duty to inform Your Lordship,' Harris reported to Lord Stormont at the close of 1781, 'that I receive no longer the smallest assistance from Prince Potemkin. He repeats nothing I say to him to the Empress; never conveys to me her sentiments; gives me no information; nor can I prevail on him to prevent the most egregious misrepresentations getting to Her Imperial Majesty's ears, and gaining a degree of credit with her. Whenever I talk to him on business he grows inattentive and impatient; and instead, as formerly, of entering with great cordiality into everything I said relative to our concerns, it should appear as if they had become perfectly indifferent to him.

'This change in his conduct does not, I believe, arise from a variation of his political principles; and I am persuaded he is not converted by the French or Prussian party; for, had this been the case, I must have discovered some trace of it in my researches, which have been particularly directed to this object. It arises from a very material change in his own situation, which makes it necessary for him to abandon every other consideration but the support of his own influence. This has lessened since the beginning of the year; and as he imputes it, though, I believe, wrongfully, in some measure to his having taken too great a share in foreign concerns, he is determined no longer to interfere in anything relative to them.'

No crisis at the palace, however, could last eternally, and a few weeks later Harris was reporting that 'Potemkin has lost neither his favor nor his power, but I do not like the manner in which he employs it so well as I did formerly.'

Once again a change in Catherine's alcove had been carried out with consummate adroitness by Potemkin who—despite their occasional 'rubs' as he himself put it—was still the only person to whom the Empress would listen. And Charles James

Fox, who had just become Foreign Secretary upon Lord Rock-
ingham's forming a new British Government, hastened to write
to his old friend Harris a letter in which he bluntly inquired
'whether there are any hopes from your friend, or if there are
none?' He also wished to know whether any other channels
could be tried.

The immediate answer to that letter is of no great interest,
even though it does stress the renewed influence of Potemkin.
But scarcely a month later Harris reported to Fox an unexpected, and yet typical episode, in the checkered history of his
relations with Potemkin. There were various urgent issues the
British ambassador was anxious to discuss with his 'friend',
whose return from the Southern Provinces was expected at any
moment. Harris had heard that the Empress had issued important secret instructions to her fleet; moreover, news of
Rodney's great victory over the French off Dominica in the
West Indies had only recently reached St. Petersburg, and it
was hoped that it could be turned to profitable use in the further
negotiations with Catherine. Here is an extract from Harris's
long dispatch which—like so many others—gives a most striking pen picture of Potemkin:—

'I passed the greatest part of that night and yesterday in his
company, during which time he frequently went up to the
Empress, and ever returned in the highest spirits; he constantly
made me fresh reports of her regard for England, of her esteem
and approbation of its ministers, and though our conversation
naturally wandered, in so many hours, from one subject to another, yet he ever brought it back to our successes, on which he
spoke with an enthusiastic satisfaction that, till now, I thought
none but an Englishman could feel. Various collateral circumstances leave me no doubt of his sincerity. If you ask me, why
this sudden change? I shall be at a loss for a reply. It is certainly
not attributable to any efforts of mine, neither is it to be de-
duced from any system he wishes to pursue. It must be sought
for in the character of this very extraordinary man, who, every

day, affords me new matter of amazement and surprise. Our conversation took place immediately on his coming off a journey of three thousand versts, which he had performed in sixteen days, during which period he slept only three times; and besides visiting several estates, and every church he came near, he had been exposed to all the delays and tedious ceremonies of the military and civil honors, which the Empress had ordered should be bestowed on him wherever he passed, yet he did not bear the smallest appearance of fatigue, either in body or mind, and on our separating I was certainly the more exhausted of the two.'

The end of Harris's momentous, if not altogether successful Russian embassy, was, however, approaching, and the British ambassador directed his observations to other subjects, contriving to find a deep political reason even for the change in feminine fashions at St. Petersburg:—

'The dress of the ladies has lately undergone a severe reform,' he reported to the Foreign Office. 'All trimmings, flounces, blondes, etc. are to be laid aside. The hair is not to exceed the height of two inches and a half, and the whole of the regulation (wise and judicious for more than one reason) tends to reduce the ornaments of the female person to a natural and decent standard.

'The immense increase of the importation of French modes, millineries, and other similar productions, which, without exaggeration, run away with the whole benefit of the trade of Russia, was the first and serious reason for the reform I mentioned in my other despatch, as ordered to take place in the dress of the Russian ladies. Its being published at this particular moment, which, from the navigation being at an end, seems an improper one, was aimed at the grand duchess, who returns passionately fond of the French nation, their dress and manners, and who, besides having settled a correspondence to be carried on in her hand with Mlle. Bertin, and other French agents of a like cast, has no less than 200 boxes arrived or arriving here, filled with gauzes, pompons, and other trash, from Paris, together with new *valets de chambre*, and various designs for preposterous new headdresses. It is impossible the Empress could have wounded Her Imperial Highness in a more sensible part. I am certain when the news of it reaches her, which it will at Riga, that it will hurt her more feelingly than any event which might have affected the glory and welfare of the empire.'

Harris was now urging his chiefs to recall him, since on the one hand the state of his health, and on the other the change in Russia's international position, had robbed him of his last hopes of success. Despite their renewed friendship, Harris felt that Potemkin was so much absorbed by his manifold duties, that diplomacy was outweighed by his activities as a builder, administrator, and supreme defence chief. 'The character and conduct of Prince Potemkin,' he wrote, 'are so materially changed within these six months, that it is very worthy of re-mark. He rises early, attends to business, is become not only visible but affable to everybody, and, what is still more extraor-dinary, he is now endeavoring to reconcile himself with his most implacable enemies. Bezborodko (in this case Harris appears to be wrong: Potemkin was never Bezborodko's enemy), and the Vorontsovs, whom he has been uniformly attempting for these last three years to overset and disgrace. His temporary connection with Count Panin did not last long; he soon per-ceived the insincerity of this artful and unforgiving minister, and that if he raised him too high, he would immediately em-ploy his influence in a way directly contrary to his views. He therefore has abandoned Count Panin to his fate.

'Thus, my lord, we are threatened with a turbulent winter on all sides, and I trust, before the storm begins, that I shall be well enough to be a spectator of what passes, and to report it faithfully to Your Lordship.'

What was actually going on was that Potemkin and Cath-erine were making hasty preparations for the annexation of the Crimea (described in an earlier chapter of this book), and this was absorbing their attention to such an extent that England's peace negotiations with America, France, and Spain attracted singularly little attention. Harris succeeded, however, in persuading the Empress to refuse to receive Mr. Dana, America's unofficial envoy, until England's treaty with America was ratified. It is astonishing with what perseverance even then, with his departure from Russia so imminent, Harris was still cultivating Potemkin and still trying to induce him to act as a sponsor of British interests. One day he reproached him with having treated England's representations with levity and never having stated them properly to Catherine. 'Prince Potemkin's reply was remarkable,' he writes. ' "I did state them, upon my honor," said he, "in as strong a manner to her as you had stated them to me, but here we never look forward nor backward, and are governed solely by the impulse of the hour. A good and faithful subject never can tell how to regulate his conduct. If I was sure of being applauded when I did good, or blamed when I did wrong, I should know on what I was to depend; but these discerning faculties are wanting, and if the passions are flattered, the judgment is never consulted." I said I was sorry to see him in this temper, since I was afraid something unpleasant had happened. "Nothing more," replied he, "than what I am every day used to. But," subjoined he, with an oath, "I shall soon be seen in another light, and then, if my conduct is not approved, I will retire into the country, and never again appear at court." '

Before long Potemkin left for the Crimea, and when he returned—a conquering hero—his friend Harris was gone.

Potemkin's diplomatic activities had, of course, never been limited to his dealings with the British ambassador and the sponsoring of an English alliance, even though he took the matter very much to heart and devoted an astonishing amount of time and energy to it. Relations between Russia and Poland were a subject of special interest to him, and through the husband of his niece Alexandra, the Polish aristocrat Branitsky, he had a unique possibility of exercising his influence and of obtaining information.

It is untrue, however, that he was responsible for the partition of Poland. At the time of the first partition in 1772 he was not as yet in power, but was at the front during the first Turkish War; the second partition of Poland took place after his death. He also kept a watchful eye on Sweden, which he knew since his visit there at the time of Catherine's accession, and in 1784 he drafted a long report on measures to be taken in case of a Russo-Swedish war. Two years later he negotiated Russia's trade agreement with France. Though he never liked that country, he was full of admiration for individual Frenchmen, and was in regular contact with Mirabeau. He called him 'Mirabobotchka' ('Mirabobbie') and must have found him profoundly congenial, since both these great statesmen shared brilliant intellectual powers with a complete laxity of morals. It is a pity they never met; such a meeting would certainly have been full of intriguing possibilities.

Having a strong instinctive aversion to the Prussians, despite the high honor Frederick had conferred upon him, Potemkin deliberately snubbed the various Prussian princes who visited Catherine in quest of an alliance, and on the occasion of Prince Frederick William's sojourn he even demonstratively left St. Petersburg—ostensibly to entertain a hunting party at one of his country seats.

At one time he contemplated visiting Italy and the Archipelago, and on another he seriously intended to go to Constantinople. Boulgakov, the Russian ambassador there, who had been for years under Potemkin's direct orders, and with whom Potemkin conducted a regular and voluminous correspondence, had the greatest difficulty in persuading him to abandon the project. He wrote to 'Serenissimus' that his arrival would create a state of turmoil and upset in Turkey, where people regarded him as a kind of grand vizir. Potemkin's knowledge not only of everything going on in Turkey, but in

Persia, the Caucasus and the Danubian countries as well—
he maintained an army of private agents in all of them—was
quite remarkable. He found time to discuss by word or correspondence with statesmen, scholars, and even the Grand Duke
Paul, whom he loathed and despised, the affairs of all these
southern and oriental regions, drafting plans for a colony here,
a trade agreement there, a military alliance or plain conquest
somewhere else. Together with Greig he prepared a memorandum on seizing the Dardanelles, and in many letters addressed
to Bezborodko, Roumiantsev, and chief of all to Catherine
herself, he expressed his views on Russia's foreign relations,
which were so strongly intertwined with military and economic problems. Though the Empress had by now become 'her
own foreign minister', the diplomatic activities of Potemkin
remained for a long time a factor of the utmost international
importance.

13

SERENISSIMUS

WHEN the physical association between Catherine and Potemkin came to an end, one of the principal causes of their frequent quarrels vanished with it. Yet, remaining as they did, not only the most intimate of friends, but also the closest of collaborators, they found plenty of other things to quarrel about. With two such temperamental people this was hardly surprising. Moreover, as Catherine had herself admitted, it was not love but the question of power that had so often stood between them, and in that respect nothing had changed since Potemkin's withdrawal from the imperial alcove.

Their conflicts were still as violent, and Potemkin was as ever reluctant to take the first step towards reconciliation: he just sulked in the accustomed manner and left it to Catherine to make things up again. Not even the passing of years had taught the court or the diplomats the simple lesson that these estrangements could only be temporary and always ended in Potemkin's 'return to power', as they pleased to call it, although actually he had never lost any of it. But the courtiers never missed the chance of prejudicing Catherine against her consort and principal statesman, hoping against hope that their intrigues might one day achieve Potemkin's dismissal.

In the memoirs of his kinsman Engelhardt is related the following episode which took place in 1783: 'For a number of reasons the Empress showed him [Potemkin] her disfavor, and he was actually about to travel in foreign lands; the coaches were already being prepared. The prince stopped visiting the Empress and did not appear at the palace, and on account of this nobody either at court or among the other noblemen called on him, and following them everybody else also left him; near his house not one carriage was to be seen, yet before that the whole Millyonnaya used to be blocked with carriages, so much so that it was difficult to pass. Princess Dashkov, through her son, who was a colonel A.D.C. to the prince, informed the Empress of different delinquencies in the Army; that owing to his weak administration the plague had developed in the Kherson province, that the Italians and other foreigners settled there on sterile lands practically all died because no houses or anything else essential had been prepared for them, that the distribution of lands had been made without any order and with much abuse by his entourage, etc., etc.; Princess Dashkov was supported by A. D. Lanskoy [the favorite]. The Empress did not entirely believe these denunciations of His Serene Highness, and, through special, confidential men, secretly found out that his enemies had wrongly maligned Serenissimus whom she respected as a man who helped her to govern the state; she deprived Princess Dashkov of her favor and returned her confidence to the prince.' Engelhardt then relates how Potemkin was made president of the War College and field marshal, and continues: 'Even two hours had not yet elapsed before all the · rooms of the prince were filled with people and the Millyonnaya Street was blocked again with carriages; the very people who had snubbed him most were now crawling at his feet.'

This reference to his house in the Millyonnaya requires a little elucidation. Although the Empress had presented Potemkin with the Anitchkov Palace in June 1776, and on several occasions spent considerable sums of money in decorating it for him, Potemkin continued to live with her at the Winter

Palace. For a long time after he had ceased to be her lover he still occupied the so-called 'favorite's quarters'. Then in 1777, he moved into a house adjoining the palace and connected with it by a special gallery; it was really a part of the Hermitage museum and like the Winter Palace and the Hermitage it faced both the Neva and the Millyonnaya Street.

Although he continued to use the whole palace as his headquarters, that is where he actually lived when he was in St. Petersburg—until nearly ten years later the Empress built him the most magnificent palace of Taurida, on a huge site facing the river and not very far from her own residence. He also had his rooms in the various other imperial palaces, at Tsarskoe Selo, Peterhof, Moscow, and many others. In the course of a quarrel he must have reproached her with trying to drive him out of the house in the Millyonnaya and—it sounds quite incredible in view of her breath-taking munificence to him—with never having provided a residence for him or given him anything. Catherine's reply to that fantastic and most unfair of accusations was as humble and as loving as ever. She wrote: 'My darling, God is a witness I have no intention of driving you out of the palace. Please live in it and be content; that is the reason why I have not given you so much as a brass farthing. If, for your diversion, you find it useful to visit at the appropriate time your various provinces, I have no objection. But on your return, please take up your usual quarters in the palaces as before. And I appeal to God as a witness, that my attachment to you is solid and knows no limits, and that I am not angry; but please do me a favor: *ménagez mes nerfs*.'

This little note does not differ very much either in contents or in style from the daily or even hourly messages she used to send him at the time when their romance was at its height—especially the pathetic appeal at the end, to spare her nerves. Yet whenever he happened to be away Catherine felt lonely and miserable, bombarded him with letters, and seemed to miss him terribly.

He was constantly on the move, an indefatigable traveler, finding time not only for visiting his own numerous estates scattered all over Russia, but also the various huge dominions of which he was viceroy and governor general. To speed up work, much of which he did while traveling, he had a portable printing shop added to his already voluminous baggage. He took a childish delight in it. The years 1782–83 he spent principally in the South, and got so ill there that he very nearly died. A priest was constantly in attendance, and even gave him the last sacraments, while a special courier was dispatched from St. Petersburg in order to seal up all Potemkin's papers and bring them to the Empress in case he died. But much to the annoyance of his enemies who would not even grant him the right to be sick ('Moins moribond que fou' reported a foreign diplomat), Potemkin recovered, and at the close of 1783 was back in St. Petersburg. In March 1784, he was again on his way to the Southern Provinces while in July he was once more in the capital.

In the autumn of 1783, he visited the Caucasus, and the following year, after some months in St. Petersburg, left for the South—traveling via Riga, where great celebrations were organized in his honor. How little these exertions affected his iron constitution or his agile brain was recorded with surprise by Harris in a dispatch already quoted.

When in St. Petersburg, he invariably became the center of everything. Not only life at court, but the very atmosphere of the capital seemed to change in his presence. This is how an observant contemporary describes it: 'When absent, he alone was the subject of conversation; when present he engaged every eye. The nobles, who detested him, and who made some figure when he was with the Army, seemed at his sight to sink into nothingness, and to be annihilated by him.' He gave the most lavish of parties. Harris mentions an entertainment staged by Potemkin which cost him 50,000 rubles. His French rival, Corberon, describes a fancy-dress ball, 'superb to watch,' at which

Catherine and Potemkin participated in a Turkish quadrille, he looking 'mellow and voluptuous'.

The same diplomat gives a very full account of another party at the Anitchkov Palace, which Potemkin sometimes used for entertaining his friends. The large conservatory was turned into a garden 'in a pleasant fashion. In front, or facing the entrance door, there was a little Temple of Friendship, with the statue of a goddess holding a bust of the Empress. The small private rooms are charming; one of them is entirely decorated in the finest Japanese lacquer and in Chinese style. Another cabinet, where the Empress took supper, was furnished in the loveliest painted Chinese taffeta and arranged in such a way as to resemble a tent. Around the walls of the cabinet, which can hold at the most five or six persons, was a little sofa. I noticed a particularly beautiful crystal chandelier manufactured by Potemkin's own glass factory. Another small cabinet is furnished with a sofa for two persons, with a rich cloth embroidered by the Empress herself. This feast was as pretty as could be . . .'

He would think nothing of dispatching Baur or some other member of his staff to Astrakhan to fetch some fresh caviar, or some fruit from the Crimea or a special fish from the Volga, or some foreign delicacy from France with which to regale his guests. Himself an omnivorous eater, he could enjoy the simplest kind of Russian peasant food as much as the most refined of meals. But at his great receptions he always had quite astonishing fare, both from the point of view of quantity and quality. The whole of St. Petersburg talked about a certain sterlet soup which was supposed to have cost three thousand rubles and was served in a bath tub of massive silver.

In the summer of 1779, Potemkin gave a fancy-dress ball in Catherine's honor at Ozerki, one of his several villas near St. Petersburg—the powerful stream of the Neva forming a particularly picturesque background to the illuminations and fireworks. A floating cathedral bore the names of the various members of the imperial family in fiery signs. On a small island in the middle of the stream were some magnificently illuminated buildings. Supper was served in a 'Caucasian cavern' which was decorated with myrtles and laurels intertwined with the most gorgeous of roses. A hidden orchestra played soft music, and a choir sang Greek songs in honor of the Empress.

Even Potemkin's enemies were impressed, and had to admit that the exquisite taste of Serenissimus was unrivaled, and that his genius for showmanship was unsurpassed. How much Catherine herself valued it, can be judged from the fact that not only were all her own court entertainments in Potemkin's hands, but whenever any foreign visitor of distinction whom she wanted to impress was expected in St. Petersburg, it was invariably left to Potemkin to make the necessary arrangements. When in 1777, her cousin, King Gustavus III of Sweden, who was himself a connoisseur of art and theatricals, was about to arrive in Russia, she enjoined Potemkin to make a very special effort, and he did not fail her. Gustavus, unlike the Austrian Emperor, 'went down' extremely well with the Russians. He, too, traveled incognito, as the 'Count of Gothland'; but the pleasant disposition and charming manners of this gifted and picturesque sovereign immediately won him universal sympathies. Baron Nolcken, his minister at Catherine's court, was hard of hearing; when at a reception, in the King's presence, he asked for some question to be repeated twice and in a louder voice, Gustavus remarked: 'Madam, the King of Sweden has sent you a minister who seems to me to be both deaf and blind!' Catherine and Potemkin were delighted with their witty visitor, but this friendship did not prevent Gustavus from suddenly making war on Russia a few years later.

Meanwhile, however, there arrived in St. Petersburg another visitor, whose glamorous personality by far transcended even the most famous foreign guests—royal or otherwise—whom Catherine and Potemkin had ever had the privilege to entertain. Charles Joseph François Lamoral Alexis, Prince de Ligne, a Belgian by birth, a Frenchman by culture and education, a

Spanish grandee and a field marshal in the service of the Austrian Emperor, a true cosmopolitan, or 'a diplomatic jockey' as he once described himself, one of the greatest ambulant soldiers of the eighteenth century, who contrived to be present wherever an important battle was fought, came to Russia in August 1780, primarily to order some family affairs. His son Charles was about to marry a beautiful young Polish aristocrat whose dowry consisted chiefly of claims on the Russian Government, and the Prince de Ligne journeyed from Vienna via Prague, Dresden, Berlin, Warsaw, and Cracow to St. Petersburg, with a view to obtaining some ready cash in settlement. This is how he himself describes what followed: 'I arrived in Russia. The first thing I do there is to forget the object of my visit, because it seemed to me indelicate to take advantage of the infinite favors shown me every day to obtain some further ones!'

No sooner had they met him, than both Catherine and Potemkin were absolutely bewitched by this brilliant talker, glorious soldier, and diplomat, who knew everybody and everything, had been everywhere, and yet had a zest for life that made him anything but pretentious or *blasé*. Curiously enough, it was left to Potemkin, who had proclaimed himself 'his loyal friend for the rest of life', to write to Ligne: 'My dear Prince, do not forget the interests of Prince Charles!' Thus it is obvious that Ligne deliberately forgot the business that had originally brought him to St. Petersburg. From the very start he managed to establish the closest of relationships with the Empress and Potemkin, who discussed their own, Russia's, and Europe's affairs with him very freely, valued his advice, and went out of their way to honor and please him. Yet not everybody shared their enthusiasm about the urbane, cosmopolitan, omniscient, and ubiquitous prince, who entered into the diplomatic and other intrigues at St. Petersburg with the ardent zeal that characterized him in everything he did. Here is an amusing extract from Corberon's diaries: 'The Prince de Ligne did not end up

as well as he began. His waggish tone did not seem decent to
the Russians; Count Panin, always smiling and applauding,
shrugged his shoulders on several occasions in observing a great
nobleman, aged forty-five, a Knight of the Golden Fleece,
playing *broche-en-cul* and adorning his posterior with paper
spills.' Not only did Corberon, and according to him many
Russians, object to the frolicsome prince, but his son, the
younger Prince Charles, was judged even more severely. According to the French diplomat, the young man was 'stupid,
ill-mannered, a gambler, and with the bad tone of German
garrisons. You can judge him . . . by the swinish thing he did
at Count Panin's table. He wanted to prevent his father from
eating something he had on his plate, and being unable to take
it away from him, he proceeded to spit into his father's plate,
who thought the joke excellent'.

It would be hardly possible to invent such a story, and it
throws curious light on the manners of the day. The Princes de
Ligne, father and son, were representatives of all that was most
refined and cultured in eighteenth-century Europe, noblemen
of ancient lineage, and yet they behaved like a couple of barbarians. The eccentricities of some of their Russian contemporaries appear far less inexcusable in the light of this little
episode recorded by Corberon.

This French diplomat set down faithfully all he heard and
saw. He naturally followed the activities of his British rival,
Harris, with particular care, and notes with malicious pleasure
that a ball followed by a large supper given by England's ambassador was mediocre, and that Harris tried to borrow the
necessary plate from Potemkin. In the absence of Potemkin,
his servants refused, and Harris got what he wanted from the
French ambassador, who was not even informed—his servants
lent everything without bothering to ask their master.

Meanwhile, Potemkin's mother, Daria Vassilievna, died of ·
stones in the liver (1780), and although his relations with her
had been strained for many years, he was greatly affected by

· the shock. He happened to be staying at his villa in Ozerki, near St. Petersburg, and Catherine herself took the trouble to journey there from Tsarskoe Selo to inform him of his bereavement. The burial of the embalmed body of poor Daria Vassilievna was delayed for several weeks, because Potemkin could not pull himself together and give the necessary instructions.

The fact that she had so strongly disapproved of his way of living—especially his love affairs with the five nieces—had irritated him during her lifetime; now that she was dead, he seemed most upset by this thought. But it did not alter his accustomed mode of amorous promiscuity; he had always adored women and women simply raved about him.

Here are a few specimens of the love letters received by him. One lady wrote in French: 'How did you spend the night, my dear? I hope that for you it was more peaceful than for me; I could not close my eyes . . . the thought of you is the only thing that animates me. Goodby, my angel, I have no time to tell you more, goodby, I have to leave you—for my husband will be back at once.' In another letter from a lady: 'My sweet, how annoyed I am that I only saw you in the distance . . . tell me at least whether you love me. When shall I see you, my beloved? Please come to me. I would like to spend every minute with you; I would kiss you all the time and love you.' Yet another letter says: 'I love you to the point of madness; let me kiss you a million times before you start your trip . . . I kiss you thirty million times with tenderness that is growing every minute. In my thoughts I kiss your little fingers and white feet.'

Next to this passionate correspondence, however, there exists a most sober and friendly exchange of letters with various women—as, for instance, that with the Princess Dashkov, whose intellect Potemkin greatly admired. He revealed himself on more than one occasion a good friend to this somewhat over-ambitious lady—at one time his open enemy—and did much to bring about a reconciliation between her and the Empress.

It is an interesting fact that Potemkin was time and again

credited with all sorts of matrimonial intentions, which he never bothered to deny. Perhaps he and Catherine were quite pleased that people around them should be so ignorant of the secret bond of marriage existing between them as to take the rumors of Potemkin's impending betrothal seriously. But the fact that he remained 'single' as far as the outward world was concerned, and, despite his love for pomp and pageantry, denied himself the satisfaction of staging a spectacular wedding ceremony, is one more proof that he was not free, and that the secret ceremony at the St. Sampsonievsky Church did take place in 1774.

Catherine was as ever longing for his company, and when he was in St. Petersburg or one of her other residences, they used to spend practically every evening together, playing chess and discussing their usual range of topics, i.e. anything from international affairs to the next court entertainment.

Potemkin was now openly having a *liaison* with one of St. Petersburg's loveliest and admittedly most intelligent women, the fascinating Praskovia, who was the wife of his kinsman, and close collaborator, General Paul Potemkin. One day he received the following note from the Empress: 'Though you appreciate billets from me less than letters from your dear cousin, whom you consider so intelligent, I cannot refrain from writing to you . . . [there follows some of their accustomed¹ signs in code]; that is I love you excessively, and as a sign of my love I send you a present: your toothpick, which you forgot in my room. Goodby, my heart.' Both the tone and the contents of this note show that singularly little had changed since the now distant days when Catherine used to reproach her lover with throwing about and forgetting his handkerchiefs in her apartment.

Potemkin's own 'court' was now as great and as glamorous as that of any Eastern potentate. His antechamber was always crowded with people, among whom many had traveled from the most distant corners of Russia, and not infrequently from foreign lands, just to see him. Wherever he was, he held a regular levée, attended by all the local authorities, visibly bored with the whole procedure and yet submitting to it as the inevitable. But if a visitor—especially an ecclesiastic or a foreigner—happened to interest him, he immediately became animated and was prepared to interrupt even the most important work or dismiss a mistress just to have a good talk. 'Money is dust, people are everything,' he used to say, and he spent money on a scale as if it really were dust. On one or two occasions attempts had been made to question his right of drawing on the state funds, but when Catherine was asked by the officials she angrily replied that 'the prince's orders were as good as her own'.

To his family and friends he was the most munificent of donors. One day he presented Harris with a lovely large garden in St. Petersburg, specially arranged for the British ambassador's private use. To a neighbor in the country, who used to supply him with a particularly tasty brand of homemade mead, Potemkin gave an invaluable collection of Turkish arms. He spent a fortune on presents to Catherine. His generosity knew no bounds, but he liked to anticipate requests or desires, and invariably felt adamant if an attempt was made to persuade or force him to come to anybody's assistance or to gratify somebody's wish.

He was constantly besieged by people begging for favors or help, ranging from those suffering genuine hardship to seekers who just hoped to benefit by his influential support. To those who inspired him with confidence he was infinitely kind; if, on the other hand, he saw that he was being tricked, he was ruthless. One day, insisting that a certain government office should pay the legitimate claim of a poor merchant, he sent down the following lines in verse:—

> 'Pay Y. without further hitches,
> You . . . sons of bitches.'

The money was instantly paid. But when his old school friend, the self-seeking Von-Visin, remarked to him that there was no need for a man in his exalted position to receive common people, Potemkin instantly ordered that henceforward this very Von-Visin, and he alone, should no longer be admitted to his presence.

He could be vulgar and cynical beyond belief. One day he was passing through his dressing room with two important courtiers who stopped to admire his famous silver bath. 'If you can excrete enough to fill it,' said Potemkin to one of them, 'I will give it to you.' The courtier turned to his companion, who was notorious for his voracity, and said: 'How about attempting this business on a fifty-fifty basis?'

Yet coarseness was—like everything else—only a mood with Potemkin. An ardent patron of the arts, he was himself richly endowed with delicate artistic perceptions—as his musical programs or the general decorative arrangements at his own and Catherine's receptions, or again as his love and knowledge of poetry, frequently showed.

His eccentricities, however, were getting worse. People never quite knew what to expect from him next. During one of his innumerable trips to the South, when throughout the whole journey he was being celebrated in the now accustomed way with receptions, fireworks, and triumphal arches, he suddenly felt weary of the whole thing. His carriage was approaching the city of Moghilev—the scene of so many of his past glories—when it was met by a particularly noisy and disturbing outburst of salvos and glaring fireworks which so frightened the horses that they shied, and nearly upset the whole vehicle. Only the prompt intervention of Potemkin's three grooms, who always had to stand on the footboard behind the carriage with pistols and daggers drawn, saved the situation. They jumped off in time and, giants all of them, bodily propped up the heeling carriage.

The procession stopped dead. An invisible hand drew the curtain on the carriage's window, and a huge unkempt head appeared. With his one eye Serenissimus gave the assembled crowd a sinister look. 'Popov,' he yelled. The faithful factotum appeared within a fraction of a second. In a plaintive voice Potemkin continued: 'Are they all mad, Popov? What is the matter with them? They have scared the horses, they have nearly upset me together with the carriage, and now they just stand around gazing at me. What do they want? I have been sleepless for three nights, and the moment I doze off a little they make this infernal noise. Who is responsible?' Popov left his master's window and came back a few minutes later with the officer in charge. 'Who are you, sir?' snarled Potemkin. The man, more dead than alive, gave his name. 'Fool,' said Serenissimus, and then turning to Popov: 'Take this gentleman's name and rank and regiment. Also tell the coachmen to get going again.' He turned once more to the wretched officer: 'Can you tell me, my good sir, what induced you to stage all this rumpus in such a Godforsaken place?' 'My devotion to Your Serene Highness,' muttered the officer. 'Fool,' repeated Potemkin.

He closed the window, pulled the curtain, and the procession went on. But he was to have no peace. When he arrived in Moghilev he found that most elaborate arrangements had been made to welcome him.

Three miles outside the city a triumphal arch had been put up. On one side the road was lined by the troops in full uniform, with their flags and colors. On the other side were all the most notable citizens, and especially the members of the merchant guilds, with their picturesque signs and emblems. The military and municipal authorities and the governor were waiting on the steps of the cathedral, where Serenissimus was to call first, while the viceroy and his staff were expecting him at the palace. The Roman Catholic archbishop and his clergy had taken up a position in the old Franciscan chapel, just over the gate of Moghilev's ancient city walls, thus having an opportunity to welcome Potemkin before the Russian archbishop who was waiting at the cathedral.

In the city square the Jews had built a platform covered with green foliage and adorned with an enormous banner: 'Rejoice, oh Israel, as in the days of Solomon.' They had brought their flutes and cymbals and fiddles, and were making a most terrific noise, while some of them were even dancing to this bewildering accompaniment. Out of gratitude for his attention to their religious interests and invariably benevolent attitude to their various requests, they were preparing to present him with a pair of scales made of massive gold and mounted on a large diamond—the symbol of justice and right. But they were not without hope of securing some profitable business in connection with army supplies and the equipment of the new Southern Provinces with all the things required by the colonists. In anticipation of such transactions they had even 'raffled' not only Serenissimus but even Popov or various other people of his retinue, and they were proudly referring to him as 'Our Potemkin'.

When Potemkin's carriage reached the town, and on its way to the cathedral was pelted with flowers, while the crowds in the streets, the Catholic prelates in their niche, the Jews on the platform, and the Russians on their church steps were getting more and more excited, the curtained windows remained shut, and no one could even catch a glimpse of Serenissimus. But when finally the coachman pulled up at the cathedral and the salvos, the church bells, the music, and the shouting suddenly stopped dead, and Potemkin's grooms jumped off their footboard, opening the carriage door and lowering the folding steps with speed and dexterity, the crowd beheld a most strange spectacle.

An enormous shapeless body with a sinister looking one-eyed disheveled head emerged from the carriage, and for a moment it seemed as if this were some quaint biblical or mythological character come to life rather than the omnipotent Serenissimus, consort of Catherine the Great and almost her coregent.

His velvet jacket, trimmed with sables, was unbuttoned at the neck and so was his shirt, revealing a powerful hairy chest. Potemkin's clothes seemed tumbled and dusty; his face looked tired and unwashed. He seemed bored and quite unaware of the incredible impression made by his appearance.

Slowly he ascended the steps of the cathedral, threw a quick glance at the holy icons, made the sign of the cross, and then proceeded to take up a position not in the place of honor specially reserved for him and where he was asked to go by the governor, but in the very center of the nave.

The holy gates of the altar opened, the archbishop appeared and began an elaborate service. Potemkin was now deep in thought, while his one eye was fixed on the priest's face. From time to time he seemed to be chewing something. When the service was over he gave the cathedral another quick glance, and then, visibly relieved, proceeded to drive with the various local dignitaries to the viceroy's palace.

There followed interminable presentations, but throughout this tedious ceremony the expression on Potemkin's face remained distrait and glum. He appeared to listen with patience and even benevolence to the endless and exasperatingly obsequious speeches of welcome, occasionally uttering a few friendly words or just slightly bowing his head. But those who knew him well could see that something was upsetting him, and when suddenly he started biting his nails furiously or just tapped the table with his diamond-bedecked fingers his ill-temper became a certainty.

The municipal, military, and government officials were followed by various deputations, and finally by representatives of the academic world and even poets who delivered orations and recited specially written odes in honor of Serenissimus not only in Russian, but in Polish, German, Greek, and Latin.

When finally all this was over Potemkin got up and slowly walked through the crowd of visitors until he found a chair in the adjoining ballroom, where he wearily sat down again while all the others lined the walls and looked at him in breathless suspense. For a long while he was silent, and no one else dared to utter a word. His private valet arrived and with a deep bow handed Serenissimus a golden beaker of his favorite Russian cabbage soup. Potemkin, who in recent days had suddenly developed a special predilection for this beverage and had lived almost entirely on it, gulping down as much as fifteen large beakers a day, began to sip the cabbage soup without looking at anybody. When he finished it he put down the beaker and resting his chin on his fist remained silent and immobile for a quarter of an hour, when his valet brought him a fresh supply of cabbage soup. This time he gulped it down, and suddenly jumping to his feet he said in a sulky voice: 'I want some coffee.'

These were the first words he had spoken since his arrival. The viceroy beckoned to his liveried attendants, somebody among the guests also ran to the pantry to fetch Potemkin's coffee, while Serenissimus repeated impatiently: 'Coffee! I want some coffee.' This time they all ran to gratify his wish, while he was repeating like an obstinate child: 'Coffee! Where is that coffee? I want some coffee.' Finally they brought him what he wanted. He glanced at the coffee pot on a golden plate and said with a disappointed sigh: 'You can take it away. I only wanted to long for something and even here I have been done out of my pleasure.' Amidst general consternation he withdrew to the private apartments that had been reserved for him.

Meanwhile the three highest church dignitaries of the province arrived: the Russian archbishop, the Roman Catholic archbishop, and the Grand Rabbi. A few minutes later Serenissimus, still unkempt and unwashed, came out of his room, this time clad in the filthiest of old dressing gowns. Silently he beckoned to the priests and also to the representative of the dissidents' sect who was there, inviting all the four ecclesiastics with a gesture to follow him to his apartment. There, in a monotonous drone, he delivered to them a long oration on the futility of public life and informed them that his mind to withdraw to a monastery was made up. His only doubt, however, was that he could not grasp how God, who was one, could be worshipped in so many different ways through so many conflicting religions; could the prelates enlighten him on that point?

There began an animated theological discussion and Potemkin seemed to be enjoying the dialectical duel between the ministers of these four rival religions so much that he forgot entirely about the further ceremonies of the reception organized in his honor.

Finally the viceroy took it upon himself to interrupt the priests and invited Serenissimus to join the ladies. He was full of hope that owing to Potemkin's known susceptibility to feminine charms the reception might yet be made a success, and he had assembled all the loveliest ladies of the province to meet Serenissimus. With a sigh of regret Potemkin dismissed the priests, who had become quite excited during their discussions, and promised the viceroy to join the party in a few minutes.

The viceroy was certain that Serenissimus wanted to wash and to dress. This was particularly essential because he could not help having noticed that under his old dressing gown the disheveled Potemkin wore no pants. This habit of going about in the palace or even traveling with little or no underwear was by now a known thing. But still the viceroy felt sure that at a reception Serenissimus would appear in full dress.

To his horror he saw a few minutes later, when Serenissimus returned to the ballroom, that he was exactly in the same condition as he had been most of the day. He had done nothing to tidy up his appearance, nor had he added any garments to his unbelievable toilet. In this strange costume, with an open neck and no pants, Potemkin talked for a while to the guests, said a few charming compliments to the ladies and

finally sat down to supper next to a pretty young Polish girl
to whom he talked for the rest of the evening.

Next morning he appeared in a dazzling elegant uniform,
covered with jewels, orders, and decorations, beautifully
groomed and smelling of rare French perfume, a gay and enchanting man of the world. After attending to state business
and signing a lot of documents he left Moghilev a few hours
later.

Whether he was traveling or whether he was in St. Petersburg with the Empress, Potemkin was now supreme. He had
succeeded where Orlov and so many others had failed; Catherine was his wife. His power to sway her, within limits, of course,
was as great as ever, and in most things he could get his way.

Only quite recently he had had a new proof of this. After
the death of her lover, Lanskoy, he had installed a young
officer called Ermolov as her favorite. His choice had triumphed
against the rival candidates of the various other court cliques
who had many nominees of their own for this key position.
But no sooner was young Ermolov installed than he allowed
himself to engineer a filthy intrigue against his benefactor, trying to persuade the aging Catherine of Potemkin's financial
irregularities, malversations of state funds, and neglect of duty.
Potemkin did not even take up the challenge or attempt to
justify himself. He withdrew in proud silence. He was silent
for days on end. His cold and austere manner on those occasions made him particularly formidable and impressive. 'In-
accessible as the desert, cold as ice,' people said at court. But
when this had lasted longer than usual, no move coming from
Catherine's side either, the rumor spread that this time Potemkin had overstepped the mark, and had fallen from the Empress's favor for good. Once again all those who used to swarm
at his levées deserted him; no one bothered to call on him any
more; his antechamber stood empty. The only exception was
the new French envoy, the Comte de Ségur, who alone in St.
Petersburg continued to cultivate him; he was obviously the

shrewdest of diplomats. Ségur took the liberty of asking Potemkin, with whom he had soon become close and intimate, whether this contempt for his detractors was very wise, and whether it would not be better to break the silence and clear the matter up. 'What?' cried Potemkin. 'You too wish me to yield shamefully after so many services rendered, to the caprice of an offensive injustice? They say that I am working for my own destruction, I know it. But believe me, it will not be a *child* who will cause my overthrow, and I do not know who would *dare* to do it.'

This was in June 1786. Some weeks later, on the anniversary of Catherine's accession, during a celebration at the palace of Peterhof, Potemkin suddenly appeared in Catherine's anteroom. Resplendent in his gold-embroidered uniform, covered with invaluable jewels, and bedecked with decorations, his head higher than ever, a giant towering both physically and intellectually over the petty courtiers who stood petrified at this unexpected sight, Potemkin proudly passed through the apartment, when, at the other end, he ran into young Ermolov. There followed a quick but violent altercation. Then Potemkin, to everybody's consternation, left the favorite, and entered unannounced Catherine's private boudoir. 'He or I,' he roared at the Empress. 'If this young monkey, if this white nigger (Ermolov was fair, but had a rather flat nose and thick lips), if this nonentity of nonentities is allowed to remain favorite, I quit the state's service.' The man who had conquered the Crimea, reorganized the Army, who had built cities and created the Black Sea fleet; the man who for years had helped the Empress to rule her empire, who alone had enjoyed her supreme confidence, who, moreover, had not spared himself in her service, and had worked harder for her glory than anybody else, would not stand for any further humiliating insinuations or intrigues. If she could not see that justice was done to him, he would rather go. But what would Europe think of this scandalous ingratitude?

Catherine was petrified. It was years since she had seen Potemkin in such a state of excitement. She was speechless, and surrendered without even trying to protest. She agreed to everything. Ermolov was dismissed forthwith, and ordered abroad. Even a farewell audience was refused to the fallen favorite; he never saw the Empress again. Potemkin's triumph was complete, and before long he surprised Catherine with a new and more reliable bed companion, the intelligent but docile Mamonov, aged only twenty-six; Catherine was fifty-seven at the time.

It is typical of the man that he never availed himself of his power to persecute his enemies. He bore them no malice, and a lust for revenge was not in his character. When Radistchev published his famous *Journey from St. Petersburg to Moscow*, which in those days appeared as a daring revolutionary pamphlet, and publicly besmirched both Catherine and Potemkin, he not only did not demand a prosecution and banishment of the culprit, but appealed to the Empress for mercy. His own deeds, said Potemkin, and those of the Empress were by far the most eloquent reply to such detractors. On another occasion, when the retired hussar Basil Passetchnikov was similarly accused of having abused the Empress and Potemkin, and Catherine placed the final decision with regard to the punishment in his hands, he overruled the judges who had sentenced the man to death and decided to send him to a monastery.

He was straight, magnanimous and loyal beyond comparison, and Catherine knew how to appreciate these qualities.

Thus Potemkin remained the most powerful man in the Russian Empire and in many neighboring states as well. But his spleen, his passionate yearning for something he himself could not have possibly defined, pursued him and made him miserable. Satiated with success, he was bored with life— despite his apparent zest for it. One night, when his nephew Engelhardt happened to be dining with him, Potemkin seemed to be in a particularly good mood, cheerful, courteous, talkative, and gay. Suddenly, as if overcome by a grim thought, he turned somber and pensive; the conversation stopped abruptly. Then, breaking a long silence, he said: 'Can anybody be more happy than I am? Everything I have wished for, every whim of mine has been realized as if by some magic: I wanted high ranks—I have them; orders—I have them; I liked to gamble—and I did gamble away sums that are incalculable; I loved to give feasts—and have staged some magnificent ones; I loved to buy estates—I have them; I loved to build houses—I have built palaces; I loved jewels and precious things—I have so many of them that no private individual can boast as much or such rare ones; in a word, all my passions have been fully satisfied.' With these words he seized a precious porcelain plate and smashed it on the floor with vigor, after which he rose from the table and marched off to his bedroom, where he locked himself in for the rest of the evening.

Modern medical science would probably describe Potemkin, with his perplexing contradictions of character and alternating moods of exuberant activity and gloomy indolence, as a 'cyclothymic type'. But it seems impossible to reduce so complex a man, so rich a personality, to a simple medical formula. He was a diamond with so many facets that it was difficult to appreciate all of them simultaneously.

But Ségur, who saw a great deal of Potemkin in those years, and not only liked, but almost understood him, has given the following brilliant description of him:—

'In his person were combined the most opposite defects and accomplishments of every description. He was avaricious and ostentatious, despotic and popular, inflexible and beneficent, haughty and obliging, politic and confiding, licentious and superstitious, bold and timid, ambitious and indiscreet; lavish of his bounties to his relations, his mistresses, and his favorites; yet oftentimes obstinately refusing to pay either his household or his creditors; always attached to some female, and always unfaithful. Nothing could equal the vigor of his mind, or the indolence of his body. No dangers could appall his courage; no difficulties force him to abandon his projects; but the success of an enterprise never failed to disappoint him.

'He wearied the empire by the number of his dignities and the extent of his power. He was fatigued with the burden of his own existence, envious of everything that was not done by himself, and disgusted with all he did. To him rest was not grateful, nor occupation pleasing. Everything with him was desultory; business, pleasure, temper, carriage. In company, he looked embarrassed; his presence was a restraint wherever he went. He was morose to all that stood in awe of him, and affable to those who accosted him with familiarity.

'Ever lavish of promises, seldom performing them, and never forgetting what he had heard or seen. None had read less than he; few were better informed. He had conversed with eminent men in all professions, in every science, in every art. None knew better how to draw forth and to appropriate to himself the knowledge of others. In conversation, he astonished alike the scholar, the artist, the mechanic, and the divine. His information was not deep, but extensive. He never dived into any subject, but he spoke well on all.

'The inequality of his temper was productive of an indescribable singularity in his desires, in his conduct, and in his manner of life. At one time he formed the project of becoming Duke of Courland; at another, he thought of conferring on himself the Crown of Poland. He frequently gave intimations of an intention to make himself a bishop, or even a monk. He engaged in building a superb palace, and desired to sell it before it was finished. One day he would think of nothing but war; and only officers, Tartars, and Cossacks were admitted to his presence. The next day he was busily employed in politics; he would partition the Ottoman Empire, and set all the cabinets of Europe in motion. At other times he played the courtier; dressed in a magnificent suit, covered with ribbons, the gift of every potentate, displaying diamonds of extraordinary magnitude and brilliancy, he was giving splendid entertainments without any motive.

'For whole months together, neglecting alike business and decorum, he would openly pass his evenings in the apartments of a young female. Sometimes shut up in his room for successive weeks with his nieces and some intimate friends, he would lounge on a sofa without speaking; play at chess or at cards with his legs bare, and his shirt collar unbuttoned; wrapped up in a morning gown, knitting his eyebrows, and looking like an unpolished and squalid Cossack.

'These singularities, though they frequently put the Empress out of humor, rendered him yet more interesting to her. In his youth he had pleased her by the ardor of his passion, by his valor, and by his masculine beauty; at a more advanced period of life, he continued to charm her by flattering her pride, by calming her apprehensions, by confirming her power, by caressing her dreams of oriental empire, and by promising the expulsion of the barbarians, and the restoration of the Grecian republics.'

Such was Serenissimus.

14

SOUTHERN SPLENDOR

POTEMKIN'S career had reached a crucial point. The whole of his work for Catherine and the empire was soon to undergo two severe tests. But while the first of these—the journey of the Empress with a large retinue of Russians and foreigners to the Southern Provinces, was to be Potemkin's greatest triumph, the second—which soon followed, in the guise of a new and exhausting Russo-Turkish war—was a sore trial.

Responsibility for the whole of the Russian Empire rested on his powerful shoulders. Yet his detractors would not even grant him the successful building of a few cities in the South. All right, he said, he would show them. And, what was even more important, he would show Catherine and he would show the whole world his achievements accomplished for her glory. He would extend his arm to the beloved monarch and take her for a walk through the flourishing provinces of the South, the new cities and the miracles of the conquered Crimea. Europe should watch this picnic with breathless attention and at last understand that Russia was rich and powerful, capable of developing her own resources, that living under the rule of Mother Catherine—the 'Semiramis of the North', as Voltaire had called her—was a blessing for her newly acquired millions of faithful subjects. This picnic, moreover, would be fraught

with the greatest political, diplomatic, and even military consequences, and the proper staging of it would be no mean
achievement in itself. Stanislas Poniatowsky, the vassal King
of Poland, had better be produced somewhere *en route* to pay
his homage to the Empress by whose grace, as well as the grace
of God, he held his crown. That noble ally of Russia, His
Apostolic Majesty the Emperor Joseph, should also participate
in this expedition and the Prince de Ligne, too, as well as a host
of other foreign princes, diplomats, and state dignitaries. On
seeing all this, the 'sick man at the Bosphorus' [Turkey] can
jolly well make a note of the fact that he has a neighbor who is
to be taken seriously. What a spectacle for Europe! This piece
of international publicity is to cost 10,000,000 rubles? That is
not too heavy a price for a world pageant of Catherine's glory.

With these thoughts in mind, Potemkin had been preparing
the expedition to the South for some considerable time. Ever
since 1780 he had set his mind on it, and even then Catherine
had mentioned the possibility of such a trip to Joseph II. But
after the annexation of the Crimea in 1783 Potemkin became
determined to carry out this gigantic plan and personally
worked out all its minutest details. His talents for showmanship and organization revealed themselves at their best. During his various visits to the South in those years he had innumerable conferences with the local authorities, chose sites
for the various festivities, determined where his huge caravan
should stop for the night or change horses, what special palaces
should be built for the principal guests and simpler houses for
their retinue.

The new wharves on the Dniepr were busy building a whole
fleet of luxurious galleys to carry this distinguished company
part of the way. Potemkin's draft of all these preparations
was completed as early as the autumn 1784 and he had a special
guidebook or gazetteer printed for the Empress giving a detailed description of all the districts, towns, and even principal
villages she was to pass on her way. A complete itinerary, show-

ing the distances to be covered each day, a map and other useful information were contained in this handy volume, which appeared early in 1786. In August of the same year Catherine wrote to the Emperor Joseph informing him of her intention to visit the Southern Provinces and inviting him to join her on the way, in order that she might continue the trip in his company. But her invitation was so informal, being contained in a postscript to a letter dealing with other subjects, that Joseph was furious with the lack of deference shown by this 'Catherinized Princess of Anhalt-Zerbst' as he described his faithful ally. The advice of Chancellor Kaunitz prevailed, however, and once again Joseph accepted. So did all the other foreign guests. Potemkin's ambitious scheme was now nearing its realization.

He worked feverishly on it, finding time to attend to everything himself. The special ode composed for the occasion by the Italian musician Sarti was played to him before he accepted it; he wrote a personal letter to the Archbishop of Ekaterinoslav telling him exactly what he wished him to put into his address of welcome; there was not a Chinese lantern or a triumphal arch on the whole way of many thousands of miles he did not examine. Finally, he himself left for the South at the close of 1786 to supervise the last preparations on the spot.

Catherine was looking forward to this trip. She was as anxious as Potemkin to show both Russia and the world what he could do and how stupendous had been his achievements in a remarkably short time. On New Year's day, 1787, she received the congratulations of the Diplomatic Corps at the Winter Palace, appearing to be in a particularly good mood and then, accompanied by a thunder of farewell salvos, she drove off to Tsarskoe Selo whence on January 18 she started on her great expedition.

In brilliant sunshine, with icy cold weather, the caravan of sledges glided away on the crisp snow, which made traveling easy and pleasant. Fourteen great sledges had been prepared, with 124 smaller and forty in reserve. Five hundred and sixty splendid spare horses were waiting at each station, with an army of smiths, carpenters and others to attend to any possible repairs.

In the first sledge, drawn by thirty horses and the size of a house, was Catherine with her lady in waiting, Mademoiselle Protassov and Mamonov, the favorite. This sledge consisted of a drawing room, a study, a library and a bedroom—the forerunner of a modern saloon railway carriage. In the other sledges were all the principal courtiers and state dignitaries and—with special attention paid to them—the foreign diplomats:—the Comte de Ségur, a witty, urbane, accomplished Versailles courtier—young, keen, and happy, with the success recently achieved through the signature of a Russo-French trade agreement, a dazzling *raconteur* and impromptu poet; the new British envoy, Alleyne Fitz-Herbert (later Lord St. Helens), a highly cultured but somewhat melancholy and phlegmatic gentleman; Count Cobenzl, a typical Viennese nobleman, with a rare talent for entertaining his own and other people's guests —a most popular member of any society. 'Philosophers' all of them, which meant they had read Voltaire in the original; 'enlightened' and slightly sceptical gentlemen with a special aptitude for coining happy phrases, telling anecdotes, and composing light verses.

The part Catherine wanted them to play in connection with this trip was threefold: as representatives of their respective countries they were to carry on their diplomatic duties during the trip and inform their governments of what they had seen; as courtiers they were to contribute to her entertainment during so long and exhausting a journey, and finally, as prolific letter writers—like all the cultured people of the day—they were to spread the news of Russia's glory throughout the world. In that respect their rôle was that taken in the modern world by the special correspondents, and Catherine was her own—extremely active—press chief. She saw to it that these foreign diplomats got all the necessary information about the regions they were passing, or on what was awaiting them further ahead; talked to them, individually and collectively, throughout the journey about politics and other things; watched carefully their reports and letters, and denied strenuously any rumors or facts that appeared detrimental.

In this picturesque and imposing company, only the Tsarevitch Paul and his family were conspicuous by their absence. Catherine and Potemkin had simply left the powerless and naturally embittered grand duke with his wife and children in St. Petersburg, obviously not wishing him to see so important a part of his future empire, and not even bothering to conceal this open outrage by at least outwardly delegating to him some authority in the capital during his mother's long absence. But while her heir, whom she loathed, and her grandchildren whom she adored, were lingering in forced inactivity in St. Petersburg, Catherine and her caravan were covering over a hundred miles daily, gradually approaching the city of Kiev, where a halt for some considerable time was to be made before embarking on the Dniepr galleys.

The journey did not affect Catherine's habitual mode of living. She invariably rose at six, worked with her secretaries and ministers till breakfast time, after breakfast received the courtiers and diplomats, while at nine sharp the whole company re-entered the sledges and proceeded once again to glide through the Russian winter scenery at breath-taking speed. At two the cortège would stop for luncheon and then, after a few more hours of traveling, arrive at the appointed place for the night about seven o'clock. On the whole, it was possible to observe the timetable Potemkin had worked out with such astonishing accuracy; delays were only very occasional. In the late afternoon or early evening the darkness of the Russian winter was relieved by torches and bonfires lit at frequent intervals. The night was mostly spent in the palaces of local governor generals and in other public buildings; if there was no adequate accommodation, special luxurious mansions were built for housing this vast company. Potemkin had thought of everything, even laid down the exact quantity of material to be used in illuminating each palace at which Catherine stopped. They were to have 500 pots of tallow, ten lanterns, and two barrels of tar. At all the main stations, beginning with Smolensk, there were receptions and entertainments: the tour seemed to be an uninterrupted stream of festivities. But at the same time the Empress managed to get a great deal of solid hard work done. She endeavored to find out from the foreign diplomats, especially Ségur and Fitz-Herbert, how their countries would view a new conflict between Russia and Turkey, and conveyed to them her determination to act in this matter according to her own lights. She was also anxious to ventilate her literary tastes and philosophical views with so accomplished a retinue. But when Ségur, a rare lapse on the part of so polished a diplomat, tried to tell her a somewhat spicy story, Catherine was profoundly shocked and gave this impudent Frenchman promptly to understand that she was 'not amused'. She never liked dubious subjects of conversation, but in this case, in addition to a subconscious streak of prudishness, there was a strong determination not to allow people abroad—who were already sufficiently critical of her morals—to gain the impression that she was a libertine.

On February 9, 1787, the procession at last reached Kiev, 'the mother of Russian towns,' the most ancient capital of Holy Russia, an exceedingly picturesque city situated on the high banks of the Dniepr's powerful stream. Here the aspect of the journey changed completely. The Empress was received by Potemkin's two nieces, the Countesses Branitsky and Skavronsky, as well as a host of Polish noblemen, who joined the local aristocracy and the authorities in a tumultuous welcome.

Since several months would have to be spent in Kiev until the ice melted and the Dniepr became navigable, special care had been given by Potemkin to the question of accommodation and entertainment. Each one of the foreign guests was provided with a separate palace, with an army of servants and attendants, private coaches with horses and liveried grooms; in fact, they were treated with quite oriental splendor. Since the palace assigned to Count Cobenzl happened to be the largest of the lot, and since, moreover, the Austrian diplomat was endowed with such outstanding social qualities, his quarters soon became the central meeting place of all the foreign guests. It was promptly nicknamed 'Café de l'Europe', and there they took their meals, danced, gossiped, and talked business. Catherine herself occasionally honored this 'café' with her presence, and meanwhile the ranks of the foreigners had become reinforced by a large number of fresh arrivals. Among the celebrities who joined the party at Kiev were the Prince de Ligne and another glamorous international ambulant soldier, the Prince von Nassau-Siegen. Ligne and Ségur made friends at once, and were inseparable for the rest of the journey.

As to the Russians, there was hardly anybody of note in Catherine's vast empire who was not there. Two eccentric figures, Souvorov, frail, yet energetic, even then an almost legendary war hero, and General Kamensky, a notorious tyrant on his manifold estates, attracted special attention among a galaxy of state, church, and army dignitaries.

But where was Potemkin, who was responsible for all this splendor and who, according to plan, was also to meet the procession in Kiev? He had arrived there in time and had seen to all the final arrangements. But characteristically enough he, the viceroy of the Southern Provinces, the *deus ex machina* of the whole trip, and the impresario of this show of shows, had chosen as his headquarters in Kiev the ancient Petcherskaya Lavra, or monastery, situated on the outskirts of the actual city and consisting of a mass of churches, chapels, and cells, some of them plain caverns cut into the rock of this hilly region. While the two main poles of attraction were Catherine's palace and the group of palaces built for her guests, Potemkin, who should have been in the very center of things, was gratifying one of his eccentric moods by staying in the seclusion of a monastery and keeping as far away as he could from all the pomp he had created for the others. People who wanted to see him flocked to the monastery, but they achieved little or nothing.

Ségur gives the following picture of Potemkin in Kiev:—

'Either by reason of a natural indolence, or of an affected *hauteur* which he thought useful and politic, this powerful and capricious favorite of Catherine, after having made his appearance once or twice in the full uniform of a marshal, covered with decorations and diamonds, bedecked with lace and embroidery, curled and powdered like the oldest of our courtiers, was most usually dressed in a morning gown, open at the neck, his legs half-bare, his feet in wide slippers, hair flat and badly combed; he remained lounging on a wide divan, surrounded by a crowd of officers and of the greatest personages of the empire, scarcely ever inviting one of them to take a seat, and nearly always pretending to be too busy playing a game of chess to notice the Russians or the foreigners who were arriving in his salon.

'I was acquainted with all his peculiarities; but, as hardly anybody of those present knew the intimate familiarity which had grown up between this strange minister and myself, I must admit that my pride suffered to some extent, when I thought that so many foreigners would see the minister of the King of France being subjected, like any other man, to his *hauteur* and to his caprices.

'Therefore, so that there would be no mistake, this is the attitude that I took; when I had arrived at the monastery and had been announced, seeing that the prince took no notice, and never raised his eyes from his chessboard, I went straight up to him, took hold of his head between my hands, embraced him cordially, and sat down without further ado by his side on his divan. This familiarity astonished the onlookers a little; but, as it seemed natural to them, all was explained . . .

'The days when Prince Potemkin, in his monastery, did not grant public audiences, or, one might say, did not hold his Asiatic court, I saw him privately with more pleasure, surrounded as he was by his fair nieces and by a few friends. At that moment he was quite another man; always original, but witty, and capable of adding a piquant interest to all kinds of conversations, however varied.'

The occasions when he ventured into society, however, and displayed his gifts of a charming, brilliant conversationalist were comparatively rare. Nor did he spend all his time in playing chess or in religious meditation. Indeed, during those weeks of the Kiev stay he had to perform an almost superhuman effort in directing, completing, and supervising all the intricate arrangements for the further success of the trip. Officers, merchants, contractors, engineers, civil servants and clergymen, special couriers, and others were summoned to his quarters, provided with personal instructions by Serenissimus, praised or scolded, and then ordered to proceed to their particular jobs posthaste. There was still an enormous amount of work to accomplish before the procession could embark on its fleet of galleys and travel farther south. And meanwhile ever new and attractive entertainments had to be provided for all these people to pass away their time in Kiev. Some of them were only too anxious to find shortcomings in his organization or in the way he was managing their trip. However much he had endeavored to look ahead, he could not have foreseen everything, and it was only natural that unexpected difficulties should arise almost daily in connection with so vast an enterprise.

Through overwork and worry Potemkin was most of the time in a terrible temper. Those who could avoid him preferred not to come into contact with him. They were all scared of Serenissimus, and Catherine, who knew better than anybody else what he could be like when annoyed, remarked: 'The prince is slinking around looking like a wolf.' The Polish gentle-men seemed to irritate him at sight, and he covered them with invective whenever he happened to run into them. When his favorite niece Alexandra Branitsky, at some reception, showed insufficient deference to Count Stackelberg, the Russian envoy at Warsaw, Potemkin took her by the nose and proceeded to lead her up to Stackelberg in order that she should apologize for her apparent discourtesy.

The responsibilities and anxieties of the trip weighed heavily on him. But, in addition to that, he was greatly concerned by the question of how all this would affect Russo-Turkish rela-tions, and his correspondence with Boulgakov in Constanti-nople was at the moment more intensive than ever. He realized that war was unavoidable, and he was determined sooner or later to kick the Turks out of Europe; but the whole question was whether he would be able to do it in his own way and his own time or whether events would be forced on him before he was ready.

Meanwhile, on May 1, 1787, Catherine and her guests at last boarded the galleys and started on the second part of their great journey. Seven huge Roman galleys, painted red and gold, were heading the procession, followed by seventy-three others of different sizes; altogether eighty craft manned by 3,000 sailors in picturesque uniforms. These galleys were the last word in comfort and luxury, and each had its own orchestra that struck up a tune every time a guest came on board or went on land. The orchestra on Catherine's galley, called the 'Dniepr', was conducted by the *maestro* Sarti in person. Her traveling com-panions, as in the sledge, were Mademoiselle Protassov and young Mamonov, the favorite. The next galley was occupied by the English and Austrian envoys, the one after that by the Comte de Ségur and his now inseparable friend the Prince de Ligne. Behind them, on the galley called the 'Bug' came Potem-kin with his nieces; another galley, specially fitted out for large receptions, followed suit, and then came the rest of the flotilla.

Slowly this 'Cleopatra's fleet', as Ligne christened it, moved down the majestic stream of the Dniepr, whose shores were lined with multitudes of cheering people almost all the way. There is no evidence whatever to support the contention of Potemkin's enemies that these crowds were forced to be there; throngs have always collected to watch a royal procession, especially one so unique and picturesque. Indeed, there was nothing in the staging of the whole of this progress that was in any way different from the usual preparations made when a royal visit or some other impressive celebration is intended to be particularly picturesque and glamorous. Triumphal arches, floral and other decorations, illuminations and fireworks form an integral part of such festivities, which invariably not only attract local crowds but induce people to journey even long distances to catch a glimpse of it all. Nor is there anything unusual in the fact that existing buildings are given a fresh coat of paint, that towns and villages on the route of the procession are cleaned and tidied up, and that new special buildings— sometimes of a temporary character, like the coronation annex at Westminister Abbey—are erected to provide additional accommodation or serve some other definite purpose.

Potemkin's detractors have asserted that he built whole sham villages, with cardboard houses and paste palaces, or that he drove millions of unwilling slaves, dressed up as farmers, and their cattle to the various places passed by Catherine, in order to create a false picture of progress and prosperity, abandoning these wretched victims to starvation and even death when his pageant was over. The originator of these stories that found a willing echo in many circles hostile to Potemkin was the Saxon diplomat Helbig, and the legend of 'Potemkin villages' (*Potemkinsche Dörfer*—a stock phrase in colloquial German) as a synonym of sham owes its inception to him. Yet neither Helbig nor anybody else has produced so much as a vestige of evidence in support of these vile accusations.

There is, on the contrary, ample evidence that they are not

true. Ségur, an intelligent and sceptical observer, who had the courage of his opinions and did not hesitate to criticize Potemkin on various scores, was full of admiration for his achievements in the South. The Prince de Ligne, equally shrewd, on hearing of these insinuations, indignantly denied them. Contrary to the assertion made by some that Catherine was 'taken in by the prince's bluff', or by others that 'although she had seen everything, she had noticed nothing', the Empress was fully aware of the wanton calumnies, and being genuinely impressed by Potemkin's great work, was particularly angry. She resorted to her usual weapon, the pen, and herself wrote a parody of the slanders in circulation. Here it is: 'The cities of Moscow and Petersburg, and even more so the foreign newspapers have invented a great deal during our trip; now it is our turn: when one has come from afar, lying is easy. Here is a list of what I am going to tell people: I deem it necessary to inform of it those who traveled with me not only to get their approval but also in order to invite them to communicate their own ideas to me.

'First of all, I who am speaking to you, saw how the Tauric mountains walked in a heavy gait towards us and bowed to us with a languishing expression. Let those who do not believe it go and look at the new roads that have been built there: they will see that everywhere steep descents have been turned into comfortable slopes. In a story, however, the heavy gait and the bowing sound better.'

The legend of gigantic malversations—Helbig said that Potemkin had simply pocketed the 3,000,000 rubles paid to him to organize this trip—is equally devoid of foundation. Russian state papers reveal that although the decision to organize Catherine's visit to the South was taken in 1784, and the sum of 3,000,000 had been envisaged, by the time the Empress and her guests embarked on their journey in 1787, not even 1,000,000 rubles had been actually paid out to Potemkin. Indeed, it is more than probable that, in order to 'get a move on', he spent large sums of his own money. The state certainly did not suffer the losses alleged by his enemies.

The best test of his achievements, however, is the fact that not only the flotilla of galleys was built at the entirely new wharves created by him, and served their purpose without a single mishap, but within barely a few years Potemkin's shipping yards produced a navy that covered itself with glory in the second Turkish War. Not less remarkable is the fact that it was possible for Catherine and her guests to perambulate in the Southern Provinces, 'scattering rubles and epigrams in every direction,' with the utmost safety within less than four years since the wild tribesmen of the steppes and the Crimea had been conquered by Potemkin; that thanks to Potemkin's genius for organization the choicest food and the most luxurious of lodgings could be provided for months on end for this enormous gathering of spoiled and capricious people, and to their complete satisfaction. No one complained of discomfort or bad catering, yet everything had to be brought or newly installed within a very short time.

In the light of all this it is hard to conceive how anything more could have been achieved by Potemkin, especially having regard to the financial means and human material at his disposal. If he was really only a cynical trickster it is hardly possible that his outwardly imposing and internally hollow superstructure—so his critics said—could have survived till the end of the tour, or indeed parts of it to the present day.

There is too much documentary evidence that the achievements he showed the Empress and the other visitors were genuine, to make it necessary to argue the point any further. But there is no doubt that with his gift of showmanship, so often revealed before—in Moscow more than ten years earlier, or at Catherine's and his own parties—he managed to endow everything appertaining to this Crimean journey with special pomp and splendor.

Six days after leaving Kiev, 'Cleopatra's fleet' reached Kaniev, at which spot the Dniepr in those days formed the frontier between Russia and Poland. That is why it was chosen as the meeting place for Catherine and her ex-lover, King Stanislas Poniatowsky, who was precluded by the Polish constitution from leaving his own country's territory.

Potemkin had already seen him some weeks earlier, to discuss all the details of this momentous meeting. King Stanislas had made a most favorable impression on him, and he had promised to support him in his political negotiations with the Empress. Curiously enough, these preliminary negotiations between Stanislas and Potemkin had ended in a long discussion about the advisability of uniting the Churches of Russia and Rome—one of Potemkin's pet ideas. His interest in the Roman Church, and the protection he afforded its members in Russia even earned him a personal papal bull from Pius VI expressing the Vatican's thanks. Potemkin's knowledge of Catholic ecclesiastical history did not fail to commend itself to Poniatowsky, but the matter never went any further.

The meeting between Catherine and Stanislas was not devoid of dramatic tension. A special sloop was sent by the Empress to fetch her ex-lover. When the King—traveling incognito—stepped on board her galley and said, 'Gentlemen, the King of Poland has ordered me to commend to you Count Poniatowsky', feelings were running very high; but, since unfortunately he had been soaked *en route* by the pouring rain, some of the effect was lost.

After the formal greetings the two monarchs withdrew for half an hour's conference *en tête-à-tête*. When they came out, Catherine was aloof and monosyllabic and remained so throughout the gala lunch that followed, while Stanislas was visibly excited.

After lunch came a graceful little episode, quite in keeping with Poniatowsky's exquisite manner. He took from a page's hands Catherine's fan and gloves and offered them to the Empress; she for her part handed him his hat, whereupon

Stanislas with a deep bow said: 'Thank you, Madam, and also
for the still lovelier one you gave me on a previous occasion.'
This was an allusion to the Crown of Poland which he owed
her, and the whole of Europe soon heard of this witty political
epigram.

After dinner Poniatowsky visited Potemkin on his galley
and had a long political discussion with him, complaining
among other things about the behavior of Count Branitsky,
who was causing him so much trouble. Potemkin promised to
remonstrate with his niece's husband, and sending for Branitsky reprimanded him there and then. After that he and the
king visited together the various galleys of the foreign diplomats, where Stanislas deposited a card that read 'Le Comte de
Poniatowsky'. Later in the evening Catherine held a reception
and finally in dismissing her guests said a few empty and cold
words of courtesy to the man who had once been her dreamy
lover. There followed a ball on shore at Poniatowsky's palace
which she did not visit, preferring to watch the fireworks from
her galley. Next morning, on her express instructions, the
flotilla lifted its anchors and resumed the stately procession
down the Dniepr, much to Poniatowsky's humiliation and
Potemkin's annoyance. When he tried to remonstrate with the
Empress, and, having failed, sent her a few strongly worded
billets from his galley ('You are compromising me before the
King and the whole of Poland' one note said), Catherine remained adamant, and coldly told Potemkin that the King of
Poland bored her. An unconvincing excuse, to the effect that
she was suffering so much from the heat that she could not
possibly dress in the robes of state, was sent to the bitterly
disappointed ex-lover. Meanwhile, to vent his rage on somebody, Potemkin hit Branitsky with his fist and covered him
with invective in the presence of various courtiers who
thoroughly enjoyed this ugly scene.

Town after town, village after village, welcomed them, each
with some new surprise carefully thought out by Potemkin. In

the intervals, to pass the time away, the Russians and the foreigners visited each other on their respective galleys, talked business and gossip, played cards or other parlor games and generally seemed to enjoy a most excellent holiday. This life on board the galleys is beautifully described by Ségur, and Ligne, too, has given a fascinating account of the trip in his letters.

The witty cosmopolitan prince was thoroughly enjoying himself. He relates, among other things, how the Empress in her desire to create as informal and convivial an atmosphere as possible, invited her guests one day to drop the more official 'Vous' and to address her as 'Tu'; arguing that even God is addressed as 'Thou' in prayers. It was left to Ligne to find the correct formula when to her joy and many people's dismay he called Catherine 'Ta Majesté'.

When the fleet neared Kaidak, a courier arrived bringing news that the Emperor Joseph II, traveling once more as 'Count Falkenstein', was not far away. Hastily Catherine left her boat and drove to meet her friend and ally, thus completely upsetting the program for this particular occasion that had been prepared by Potemkin. The two monarchs met in a simple cossack's hut and then went to Kaidak together. The next day with great pomp they inaugurated at Ekaterinoslav the building of a cathedral modeled by Potemkin on St. Peter's in Rome, only a few feet longer. It is about this ceremony that Joseph sceptically remarked that Catherine had laid the first and he the last stone of a cathedral, and Ségur, too, gloomily prophesied that nothing would ever come of Potemkin's ambitious schemes in that city. Subsequent events showed how wrong both of them were.

A few days later the cortège reached Kherson. Catherine was so enthusiastic about all she saw there that she wrote to Grimm: 'The endeavors of Prince Potemkin have made this city and this region, where before the peace there was not so much as a hut, a land and a city that are truly flourishing and it will go on improving from year to year.' The impressions of an impartial English observer, Mrs. Guthrie, have been recorded in a previous chapter. Yet here, too, Joseph was hostile and critical, expressing his views to Ségur in the following forcible terms: 'Everything seems easy when one wastes money and human lives. We in Germany or France could not attempt what they dare do here without hindrance. The lord commands; hordes of slaves obey. They are paid little or nothing; they are badly fed; they do not dare to protest, and I know that in three years 50,000 persons were destroyed in these new provinces by the toil and the emanations from the morasses, without their being lamented, even without anyone mentioning it.' He did not disclose the sources of information that prompted him to make his sweeping statement; nor has the charge that has often been made against Potemkin to the effect that 20,000 human lives were lost during the building of Kherson ever been substantiated.

The Emperor was no more impressed by the various splendors or the launching of new ships staged by Potemkin in his honor than he had been at the time of his first visit to Russia, when Potemkin organized military parades and operatic performances for him in Moghilev. He did not even bother to dress up for all these celebrations and while Potemkin attended in full-dress uniform, bedecked with orders and jewels, Joseph preferred an ordinary tail coat. He was a morose and dyspeptic gentleman, only interested in politics and full of apprehension lest he should not get sufficient support from Russia in their joint attempt to realize the ambitious Greek project.

His mood was not improved by the sudden appearance of a Turkish flotilla near the Dniepr estuary—an alarming omen for the future, showing how perilously near the outbreak of hostilities they really were. But when Catherine's procession reached the point, where in accordance with Potemkin's plan the whole company was to disembark and continue the journey in open carriages, and Joseph saw the dazzling military escort of Cossack and native Tartar regiments following the party across the steppes, even he could not fail to be impressed. Here were these Asiatic tribes, only recently conquered, yet sufficiently safe and loyal to the Empress to be used as a guard of honor—a truly unexpected and impressive spectacle; Potemkin had scored with his daring theatrical effect.

Before long, the procession reached the Crimea and drove on to Bakhtchissaray, the ancient city and former residence of the deposed Khan. His palace was turned into their headquarters, and Catherine and Joseph occupied his former private apartments. The oriental character of the rooms, the large and smaller inner courts with the languishing murmur of their fountains, the arabesques on the walls, and the romantic minarets, all created an atmosphere of unreality, and even the most sceptical of Catherine's party came under this spell which gave him the feeling of living a fairy tale rather than paying a state visit. Dim lights, thick carpets, and heavy tapestries; in the center of every room there was a marble pool or a fountain; the only piece of furniture was a large Turkish divan; an exception was made in the case of Catherine's room, where Potemkin provided a little modern furniture. Voices of the muezzins, proclaiming the hour of prayer from the innumerable minarets; street bazaars; typical Eastern colors and smells; —it was the Orient, it was Islam which had always exercised such a peculiar fascination on him, into which Potemkin had now deliberately plunged the enchanted Catherine and her Western or Westernized guests. Tartar princes and other natives in superb costumes, accompanied by their beautiful wives, came to pay homage, and it was a severe disappointment to some of the gentlemen in Catherine's party—especially the French ones—that they could not see more than just a fraction of these Mohammedan ladies' faces.

It gave the Empress very special satisfaction that she, a European monarch, a woman, and a Christian, should now be

able to recline on the throne of a Moslem ruler who had always
been a fanatic enemy of Russia, Europe, and Christianity. She
even tried to compose a French poem in honor of the man who
had placed this new dominion at her feet; for there was no
longer any doubt that Potemkin was the hero of the day in the
Crimea and the central figure of her triumphal procession. But
writing verse had never come easy to her, and after hours of
hard and unsuccessful work she abandoned the effort, having
composed no more than the two opening lines. It is characteristic of the atmosphere, however, that verse was felt to be the
only medium fit for expressing her feelings on this great occasion. Not titles, orders, monetary or other rewards, which she
had already heaped on the omnivorous Potemkin throughout
the years, but something more personal and romantic, something more in keeping with the artistic side of his nature; and
yet, to her intense annoyance, that was the one thing she could
not do. The fact that, to honor him, she tried to overcome her
inability and worked so hard to sing his praises in verse, moved
Potemkin far more than any other form of recognition, and
they both felt mellow and sentimental. Ségur, Ligne, Fitz-
Herbert, and the others, who could turn out a neat quatrain at
a moment's notice and sometimes without the slightest provocation, were merely amused at this touching episode.

After some lovely excursions in the mountains, the company finally drove on to Inkerman, picturesquely situated on
the slopes dominating the Black Sea. A meal was served at the
newly built superb palace, and then, a sign being given by
Potemkin, the curtains were suddenly pulled back from the
windows, revealing a magnificent view of Sebastopol Bay with
a fleet of forty men-of-war in military formation, which fired
a roaring salute to the Empress. This was perhaps the most
powerful and dazzling effect yet achieved by the showman
Potemkin, and the whole party stood breathless with emotion.
Colorful Tartar regiments appeared from nowhere and paraded
before the windows. Flags, flowers, music, it was an un-

believable show, with the blue Crimean skies, the sea, and the mountains as a fantastic background. Potemkin took the Empress and the guests on a tour of inspection through Sebastopol harbor, created by him barely three years previously and yet resplendent with imposing fortifications, wharves and shipyards, barracks, churches, hospitals, and even schools. Catherine was overcome with joy, the foreigners were impressed; but this picture of a modern Russian naval base with an imposing array of battleships, all this within thirty-six or forty-eight hours of Constantinople, gave them furiously to think. The Emperor Joseph seemed almost alarmed.

More celebrations in Sebastopol, a visit to the main places of interest in the Crimean peninsula, with its ancient Greek memories that inspired Ségur and Ligne to many brilliant and philosophical dissertations, and then slowly the procession began its homeward journey. This Crimean 'fairy tale' had lasted ten days, but was so full of unforgettable impressions, that the party felt it would last them a lifetime. Back in Russia, the Empress and Joseph drove in a carriage together to Borislav, where 'Count Falkenstein' took leave of his ally and hostess. During that drive they had time to discuss their schemes and talk politics in a most exhaustive way, so that even the insatiable Emperor must have been satisfied. The return journey to St. Petersburg was made along a different route, and, as before, entertainments were staged by Potemkin at all the main points. In Poltava, for instance, he had assembled an army of 50,000 men whose maneuvers demonstrated to the bewitched Catherine the exact course of the famous battle in which Peter the Great defeated on this very spot the Swedish King Charles XII in 1709. Ségur observed that the Empress watched the performance with such burning interest, that it almost seemed as if the blood of Tsar Peter were flowing in her veins.

At Kharkov, Potemkin, who wished to return to the South, took leave of Catherine, and presented her with a magnificent rope of pearls. She, for her part, also handed him a number of valuable gifts and bestowed on him the title of 'Prince of Taurida'. Orders and presents were also distributed to his various assistants and to the officers or civil dignitaries who had taken an active part in the organization and management of the trip.

But the most moving tributes Catherine paid her hero of yore were once again not the honors and gifts, not even the medal she ordered to be struck in his honor with his effigy on the one side and a map of the progress on the other, but the tender, loving, grateful letters she sent him from practically every point of halt on the home journey and upon reaching St. Petersburg.

He too, for once, overcame his reluctance and answered her letters with great depth of feeling. Here are a few specimens of this correspondence. From Tver on July 6, she wrote to him: 'Your feelings and thoughts are particularly dear to me, and I love you and your work of service which comes from your devotion, very, very much.' In another letter she said: 'Thank God, you are well, please be careful. . . . God bless you. I am all right. . . . Your kitten has arrived with me, and is also quite well. . . . Without you we felt throughout the journey, and especially in Moscow, as if we had lost the use of our hands. . . . With the great heat you have at midday I beg of you most humbly: do me the favor of looking after your health for God's and our sake, and be as pleased with me as I am with you!' Finally, back in Tsarskoe Selo she wrote to him again and again, thanking him for all he had done, expressing her satisfaction and admiration, imploring him to be careful with his health, and, in a letter dated July 27, among other things she summed up their relations in the following words: 'Between you and me, my friend, everything can be said briefly: you serve me, and I am grateful, that is all. As to your enemies, you have slapped them on the fingers with your devotion to me and with your cares on behalf of the state.'

But this is what he wrote to her on July 17, 1787: 'Mother Empress! I have received your gracious letter from Tver. How I appreciated the feelings expressed therein, is known to God. You are more than a real mother to me, for your care about my well-being is a deliberate movement. It is not blind fate. What I owe you, what numerous distinctions you have given me; how far you have extended your favors on those close to me; but chief of all the fact that malice and envy could not prejudice me in your eyes and all perfidy was devoid of success. That is what is really rare in this world; such firmness is given to you alone. This country will not forget its happiness. It always sees you here for it considers itself your domain and strongly hopes for your favor. . . . Goodby, my benefactress and mother. God grant me the opportunity of showing the whole world to what extent I am under an obligation to you and how I am unto death your faithful slave.'

It is curious and significant that the part of the journey accomplished by Catherine and her guests without Potemkin had lost something of its dramatic tension and glamor. Of course there were feasts and receptions in all the cities through which she passed, but the spell was broken. She was no longer Cleopatra; her Cæsar, as Ligne put it, had left her. Romance was over, and prosaic dry realities had reassumed their accustomed place. In Moscow, which had never been congenial to the Empress, the atmosphere was particularly chilly. 'They are not very fond of me here, I am not fashionable in Moscow,' she said to Ligne. A few days later, from Tsarskoe Selo, she could write to her confidant, Frederick Melchior Grimm, with a genuine sigh of relief: 'Thank God, the trip is over and twenty-five years of reigning too.'

Of these twenty-five years, for half the time she had had Potemkin at her side as lover, friend, adviser, and practically as coregent.

15

SECOND TURKISH WAR

EVER since the annexation of the Crimea in 1783, the Turks had realized the extent of the Russian peril to them, and had sought to reorganize their forces for a future struggle. Despite England's professed friendship for Catherine, and the continued efforts of the British Government to make an alliance with her, it was Great Britain that took a leading part in sponsoring Turkey's war preparations. For more than 300 years France had been the principal Turcophil power in Europe, but now England assumed that role and helped the Porte not only with money and advice, but with the whole weight of her diplomatic influence. Annoyed at Catherine's tergiversations, alarmed about Russia's growing influence in the Mediterranean, the British Government embarked on a policy of adding to Catherine's embarrassments wherever it could. While numerous British and French officers were training the new Turkish army and helping to rebuild the fleet, the English and the Prussian cabinets were endeavoring to bring about an alliance between Turkey and Sweden, with a view to both these countries attacking their hereditary enemy simultaneously.

That Potemkin could see through that game and was aware of the attempted encirclement of Russia can be judged from the fact that in 1784 he drafted a program of measures to be taken in case of a war with Sweden. But in the meantime he had been busy with the building up and consolidation of the Southern Provinces, and the premature outbreak of the war forced him to abandon many of his most important projects. That, incidentally, is an essential point to be borne in mind when considering his activities as proconsul and builder; it seems to have completely escaped, or to have been deliberately ignored by his critics, who accused him of having left some of his constructions unfinished and others not even begun. Moreover, the Turks opened hostilities by besieging, unsuccessfully, the fortress of Kinburn in October 1787, or barely a few months after the completion of Catherine's great tour, which had absorbed so much of Potemkin's energy and attention.

There can be little doubt that both Potemkin and Catherine foresaw the possibility of another war with Turkey. But they expected the Crimean journey to have the effect of intimidation rather than provocation on their sworn enemies, and certainly did not intend it to precipitate events. Previous experience had taught them how much could be obtained from the moribund Porte by the mere display of force without the actual use of it. When, therefore, the Turks suddenly woke up from their apathy and declared war on Russia, the outbreak of hostilities in September–October 1787 found the Empress and Potemkin utterly unprepared.

Yet the view is prevalent among historians that both Catherine and Potemkin wanted another war with Turkey, and that this was due to their boundless ambition.

That in their dreams, especially during the early stages of their collaboration, they visualized the expulsion of the Turks from Europe, and that they wanted it there can be no doubt. But they were sufficiently practical politicians to realize the difficulties and hostilities in which any attempt to force such a course would involve them. For some reason Potemkin is usually alleged to have persuaded Catherine to have this war. But this is not in agreement with the facts. It has already been stated in another chapter of this book that the authorship of the grandiose 'Greek project' cannot in fairness be attributed to Potemkin, and that it was Bezborodko who drafted the famous document about the 'restoration of the ancient Greek Empire for the Grand Duke' Constantine, Catherine's younger grandson. Yet it is very largely on the strength of this document and also the assertions of Harris that this theory has been evolved. Helbig even went further and attributed to Potemkin the intention of creating a southeastern kingdom of his own, somewhere between Russia and the Balkans.

There are no documents of any kind in support of these allegations. From Potemkin's own letters and other papers it can be gathered that he never intended to go so far. His correspondence with the Empress provides ample evidence in the same direction. Again and again he wrote to her that the chief object of his life was the consolidation and development of Russia's new territorial acquisitions in the South. Even more convincing evidence that this was so is contained in the protocols of Catherine's Council. These show that far from cherishing any aggressive plans the Empress and her advisers were as yet mainly concerned with questions of defence.

Under the circumstances, one of the main criticisms made against Potemkin in connection with the second Turkish War falls to the ground. He was blamed for having failed in his object, because he was supposed to have desired the complete destruction of the Ottoman Empire. The truth of the matter is, that far from having been an unsuccessful attempt to realize a mad ambition, this war was to him a trial and an ordeal of the utmost gravity.

The moment the war began it was quite clear that Potemkin would have to be in charge of the Russian side. There was, of course, a string of generals senior to him, including Field Marshal Roumiantsev who had commanded the Russian Army in the previous war against the Turks. But even he, who at times had been very antagonistic to Potemkin, recognized that no one possessed similar qualifications. Potemkin had been governor general and commander in chief of all the armed forces in the Southern Provinces for a number of years. He it was who had established the various military colonies in this and the adjoining districts, created the naval bases and fortifications, studied every corner of the region that was now to become the principal scene of hostilities. Moreover, for the last fourteen years—almost the exact interval between the first and second Turkish Wars—he had been in charge of the War College, knew every detail of its organization, and had given much thought to questions of national defence, equipment, food supplies, and the various other essential problems of military, administrative, and political nature connected with the conduct of war.

He became commander in chief by right and on merit, and even the senior generals admitted that he was irreplaceable and expressed their desire to serve under him. Another innovation was that for the first time in Russian military history there was an absolute unity of command, indeed Potemkin was simultaneously commander in chief of several armies operating on different fronts. The principal front was around the Dniepr (both banks, the southern Bug and the sea-line to Perekop); there was further an advanced or protruding front in the Crimea, and finally there were two secondary zones—along the Dniestr and in the Caucasus. Thus all the regions ruled by Potemkin were suddenly and almost simultaneously involved. In addition to directing operations on land, he was also commanding the Navy, and it was left to him to create the precedent of issuing 'directions' for the co-ordination of operations on land and on sea.

The naval aspect is particularly important in view of the surprising line of attack chosen by the Turks at the outset of the war. They aimed at nothing less than the destruction in embryo of the very means of existence Potemkin had only recently created for his young Black Sea fleet, and thus hoped to wipe out the instrument with which he had been able to hold them in check and protect the Southern Provinces he was so successfully colonizing and developing. This took Potemkin by complete surprise; in fact, upon hearing of the sudden siege of Kinburn, he felt but little hope of saving anything and only longed to find the means of winning time for mobilization and the concentration of troops and food supplies.

He was in the vicinity of Ekaterinoslav when the news reached him, and he immediately sent a very full report to St. Petersburg. For his part Roumiantsev, who was in Kiev, also sent a report, and when the Council met on September 6, 1787, it considered these two documents and expressed its appreciation of the wise steps and useful precautionary measures taken by both of their authors. At the same time, the · Council so grossly underestimated the scope of the Turkish action that it assumed Potemkin's local forces in the South to be quite sufficient to stave off the Turks. The Council also · proceeded to work out instructions, saying that the war must be offensive 'since that form is in keeping with the dignity and strength of the empire, whereas the defensive position is usual for weak and exhausted powers that only think of protecting themselves and not for gaining anything.' Potemkin's army, the Council thought, should 'besiege Otchakov and, having taken it, firmly establish itself in the territory between the Bug and the Dniestr'. This move, according to the Council's minutes, had been anticipated a long time ago 'in the reasoning of the general field marshal Prince Potemkin of Taurida'.

'If God grants our armies a quick victory over this fortress, then upon its being captured operations should be expanded to Ackerman . . . so that the Russian frontier should extend as far as the Dniestr and including Ackerman' is further recorded in these minutes. And yet another passage states that 'the fortress of Bendery in Bessarabia is an important and strong point; to avoid wasting lives, if it is difficult to take it by assault, it is better in the first instance to refrain from doing so'.

Such were the views of Catherine's Council in 1787 soon after the beginning of hostilities. And it must be said that on the whole Potemkin fully carried them out, although there was, of course, a considerable delay. But the Council could not appreciate the position on the spot. The war having started towards the close of 1787, they thought that it would be possible to capture both Otchakov and Ackerman during the summer campaign of 1788. But the resistance of the Turks on the one hand and Potemkin's reluctance to storm the city and make unnecessary sacrifices delayed the taking of Otchakov by a few months till December 1788. From the very beginning of the siege it had been obvious that this city would fall; just as in his almost bloodless conquest of the Crimea, Potemkin was again relying on voluntary surrender, and was deliberately holding back. At his headquarters and in the capital both friends and enemies were foaming, putting forward endless guesses— most of them, needless to say, uncomplimentary—for the reasons of this delay. The publication of Russian state papers has established quite clearly that Potemkin was receiving regular 'intelligence' from his spies about the imminence of surrender, and was fully justified in not throwing away both human material and equipment. Finally, he yielded to pressure and took Otchakov by storm. But in the case of Bendery, where strong resistance had been anticipated, no violent action was necessary.

The siege and the storming of Otchakov by Potemkin occupy a place of special importance in Russian history. Every nation has certain battles or other events to which it looks back as landmarks in its past development. Together with the storm of Ismail by Souvorov, Otchakov has gradually acquired a legendary character and its memory lives to the present day.

To contemporaries, and especially those who took an active part in these events, Potemkin's dilatoriness seemed quite incomprehensible. Ligne, who could think only of the interests of his own master, the Emperor Joseph II—badly in need of help —was doing his utmost to spur Potemkin into action. He pestered him like a gadfly, had a new 'practical plan' every day and at times did not conceal his disappointment or irritation. 'A damned love of humanity, which is genuine but misplaced, makes him regret losses of life, which, however, are necessary for the success of this enterprise,' he said about Potemkin. He did not know that anxious though she was for the fall of Otchakov, Catherine was all the time begging Potemkin to be sparing with human lives. These requests fell on fertile ground, because with him this aspect of war was almost an obsession. Day after day, week after week the Empress was writing to Potemkin 'when are you going to take Otchakov?' 'Why have you not yet taken Otchakov?' 'When is Otchakov going to fall?' Yet she never suggested how this was to be achieved if her other request not to expose the soldiers to unnecessary dangers was also to be gratified.

She knew his own fearlessness of death and was therefore constantly worrying lest he should get killed. When he ignored her nagging letters for three weeks she decided that he must have been wounded or that perhaps he was dead. He continually exposed himself to danger, but was convinced that God was watching over him and would stave off the enemy's bullets. Ligne relates how a cannon shot just missed Potemkin, killing an officer who was standing immediately behind him: in this Potemkin merely saw the confirmation of his belief in divine protection. 'Is this not clear?' he said on one occasion, 'I am God's spoiled child.' And since repeatedly it did seem as if Providence were watching over him—as for instance, when he just missed going on a ship that was later attacked and sunk by the Turks—even Ligne had to admit that: 'Heaven seems to make a special case of him and to see to it day and night that nothing should happen to him.'

This firm belief in God must have been one of the main

causes of Potemkin's cold-blooded courage, and of the ease with which he assumed the greatest personal risks. He would appear in the line of fire wearing parade uniform, thus making himself the easiest of targets; yet he never so much as got a scratch. 'Why do you do these things?' lamented Catherine, 'Do you think I have not trouble enough?'

Yet to his men he said: 'Children, I forbid you once and for all to get up for me and wantonly expose yourself to Turkish bullets.' The soldiers loved him. They knew Serenissimus was devoted to them in times of peace and in times of war, and they saw that his tears every time he heard of their casualties were not feigned.

It is perhaps this devotion to the soldiers that finally determined him to storm Otchakov. One day they assembled outside his tent and complained about the bitter cold and their forced inactivity. He decided to avail himself of this psychological situation. He promised them freedom of action in the conquered city, and indeed when Otchakov fell it was ransacked in an atrocious manner. The actual storm was one of the bloodiest engagements in Russian military history, but the desired object was achieved. After a siege of over a year Otchakov fell.

Characteristically enough, Potemkin, who had worked out all the details of the operation himself and had personally talked in his accustomed fatherly way to the troops, felt miserable during the whole of the fight and spent most of the time in prayer at one of the worst danger spots. With his hands over his face he was beseeching the Almighty to save as many lives of his men as he could. It is said that 60,000 fell at Otchakov of whom about 20,000 were Russians.

When Catherine was notified of the event she had been longing for all these months, she sent Potemkin a note which said: 'With both hands I take you by the ears and in my thoughts I kiss you many times, my friend Prince Grigory Alexandrovitch.'

Potemkin completed the victory at Otchakov by clearing the Ukraine of stray Turkish troops and then took up a waiting position for the rest of the winter.

The delay over Otchakov also retarded other operations: Bendery and Ackerman only fell in the autumn of 1789. But even at the time of the siege of Otchakov, Potemkin had been empowered by the Empress to make peace on condition that Russia's borders were extended to the Dniestr. Negotiations, however, could not possibly start until some smashing victory had been won on the banks of the river Prut or the Danube. A plan had been considered to liberate Moldavia, Wallachia, and Bessarabia from the Turks, and turn them into an independent 'buffer state'; but the idea proved impracticable.

On the other hand, he fully carried out that part of the program which concerned the Black Sea regions. Despite occasional setbacks, due more often to stormy weather than battle, his navy played a brilliant part in the whole war. He not only used his ships for actual engagements with the enemy or for attacks on enemy transport and their coastal defences, or yet again for preventing them from landing troops and delivering food and ammunition; but he actually created a whole fleet of irregular craft, which fleet made it practically impossible for the merchant marine of the Turks to move in the Black Sea or even the Mediterranean. He sent reports to St. Petersburg after every major engagement, and these documents show how deeply he loved his navy, and how proud he was of its success.

One day he informed Catherine, who was following his activities with the utmost faith, interest, and devotion, that a whole enemy squadron had ineffectually attacked a Russian frigate and a sloop; on another occasion he described to her the operations of his privateers in the Black Sea and in the Mediterranean; or how the Russian fleet reduced to cinders the outskirts of Otchakov; or how time and again his men-of-war triumphed over the superior forces of the enemy. This predilection for the fleet was so strong that even the last report Potemkin ever wrote, only a few weeks before his death in 1791, dealt almost entirely with naval matters. When it is realized that the first Russian shipyard was built in Kherson only in 1778, and that in Sebastopol in 1783, while the Nicolaev wharves were actually completed in 1789 during the war, the glories of Potemkin's Black Sea fleet stand out as a unique achievement. They contradict in a most eloquent fashion the assertion of his enemies, both Russian and foreign, that these ships were built of putrid wood and that they would fall to pieces before they so much as went to sea.

In a similar way most of the criticisms levied against him throughout his life, but especially during the second Turkish War, fail to be convincing in the light of established facts and documentary evidence. Potemkin's detractors seemed to forget or deliberately to ignore his almost unbearable burden of multiple responsibilities, and made a point of concentrating on his admitted eccentricities. They spoke and wrote a great deal about his spleen and his indolence, his fits of depression or the oriental festivities staged at his general headquarters; they accused him of lack, not only of stamina, but also of courage, and even some of his enthusiastic admirers like Ligne complained of his dilatoriness.

If it is appreciated, for instance, to how many different problems he had to give his attention while fighting this war, and how manifold his duties and responsibilities in the Russian Empire were at the time, it appears surprising that he managed to achieve as much as he did. He was still governor general of a vast part of Russia, and in the time of war the administration of these territories—especially the newly conquered ones—was fraught with the greatest complications. He also had to organize food and ammunition supplies of three different armies, separated from each other and from the rest of the country by huge steppes; create means of communication and transport; command several armies and a navy; and attend to Russia's internal and external affairs, keeping a particularly anxious eye on the international situation in order not to miss the chance of negotiating either with Catherine's allies, or the neutrals, or the enemies.

She was as ever consulting him about everything, from serious issues to trifles, and from his headquarters he had to deal with an astonishing variety of questions. One day she informed him that she had just appointed old General Prosorovsky, under whom he had served in the first Turkish war, military governor of Moscow. To this Potemkin replied: 'Your Majesty has just moved out of your arsenal your very oldest gun which will undoubtedly shoot in your target, because it has none of its own. Only beware lest it should besmirch with blood your Majesty's name in the eyes of posterity.'

The correspondence between Catherine and Potemkin during this war is one of the most moving collections of documents that have ever been made public. It reveals on the one hand the unshakable faith and love of the woman and Empress, who displayed all her best and greatest qualities in sustaining Potemkin during these years of strain and superhuman effort; she was, as ever, by far the more stable of the two. On the other hand, it shows Potemkin, moody and fickle, it is true, but at the same time passionately devoted to the double glory of Catherine and Russia. Overworked, inadequately supported on the spot or in the more distant regions of his activities, surrounded by open or secret enemies, he was sinking under the magnitude of his task, a victim of his temperament and at times of his physique. This correspondence is not an exchange of dry official documents, where only business matters are discussed. It is the most frank, outspoken, and intimate communion between two persons so close to each other that these confidences become an almost physical necessity. That in such an intercourse fears, doubts, grief, and even despair should find their place beside the expressions of joy and triumph is only normal. No human being, especially when engaged on a great,

difficult and decisive task can avoid the alternating moods of
optimism and pessimism; in Potemkin's case this perfectly
legitimate phenomenon was accentuated by the peculiarities
of his character. But viewed in that light his letters to Catherine offer as little positive information on his military or administrative talents as the fairy tales invented about him both
during his lifetime and for years after he was dead.

Occasionally he took the trouble to answer his critics. Thus
in a letter to the Empress dated May 19, 1788, he wrote, among
other things: 'Let somebody else have the courage to repair
a fleet that has been severely battered by the storm; build, in
large quantities, rowing craft that can hold the sea; form entirely anew sixteen battalions of infantry and ten thousand
men of wholly fresh cavalry; create a large moving arsenal;
supply the artillery with a terrible number of oxen; keep going
as far as food supplies are concerned—and all this during four
months in the steppes, without proper quarters and especially
near Kinburn where more than ten thousand people had to be
provided with lodgings in one week.' He did not exaggerate
in this staggering enumeration, and these were after all only
some of the subjects of his daily routine.

At the close of last century a committee of experts of the
Russian General Staff published Potemkin's official papers,
dispatches, instructions, and other documents appertaining to
the second Turkish War. This publication destroys once and
for all the legend of his indolence and inactivity. It shows that
he dictated or wrote in his own hand daily a large number of
documents, that there are hardly any intervals in this work
except when he was ill or left the front for St. Petersburg, and
that whatever his dissipations may have been he found time
to take a personal interest in every detail of civil and military
administration. Catherine complained, as she had done
throughout her life, that he frequently left her letters without
a reply. But in this case he simply had not the time to indulge
in too voluminous a private correspondence, and only wrote

to her when he had something to say. The technical conclusions reached by the editors of these Potemkin papers are most
impressive, too. Not only did they gain the conviction after
scrupulously scrutinizing this wealth of material, that the insinuations as to his incapacity as a war leader were entirely
false, but they established that from a purely military point of
view he did some brilliant work. Moreover, they paid him
special credit for conducting this war chiefly with Russian and
not foreign commanders, using some able foreign generals and
admirals, but sharing his authority mainly with Roumiantsev
and Souvorov, who later became the greatest generalissimo
Russia ever produced.

Potemkin's relations with Souvorov form one of the most
interesting chapters in the history of the Turkish War. They
were eccentrics both of them and the various manias of Souvorov, though more limited in scope and therefore less apt to
affect third parties than Potemkin's, verged none the less on a
form of lunacy. Comparisons between the two have often
been made, and they have usually not been in Potemkin's favor.
As far as purely military genius is concerned, there is no doubt
that Souvorov was infinitely superior not only to Potemkin,
but to most of his contemporaries throughout the world. He
was, after all, one of the greatest captains history has ever
known.

Potemkin was an able, resourceful, and in many ways outstanding soldier. At the same time he was too much absorbed
in political and other affairs, and the arts of war were not his
chief interest in life. His genius as a statesman and administrator is beyond doubt, but he lacked Souvorov's quickness of
decision and his almost uncanny intuition in battle. When
Potemkin was suffering from a particularly bad fit of depression in connection with the delay over Otchakov, and even
wrote to Catherine asking to be relieved of the high command,
Souvorov's smashing victory over the Turks cheered him up
beyond measure and gave him new courage and energy. He it

was who used his influence with Catherine to obtain the most generous rewards for Souvorov, insisting that he should be given the St. Andrew Order, despite the seniority of other generals. Souvorov wrote to him in the following strain: 'Most Serene Prince, my dear Sir, only you could have accomplished it; the great soul of Your Serene Highness lights my way along the path of state service.' But when at Otchakov, annoyed with Potemkin's dilatoriness, Souvorov tried to prevail upon his chief to deal this fortress a strong and final blow, and Potemkin said: 'I give you a free hand everywhere, but in the case of Otchakov an unsuccessful effort might be harmful. . . . I will use every endeavor, relying on God's help, to get it cheaply; after that my Alexander Vassilievitch [Souvorov] with a choice detachment will precede me to Ismail. Wait till I come up to the city. . . .', Souvorov could not refrain from criticism and sarcasm. 'You cannot capture a fortress merely by looking at it', he pointedly observed to the still hesitant Potemkin.

Yet Potemkin's answer is strangely reminiscent of one attributed to Lord Jellicoe during the Great War, when the admiral too realized that a victory would mean comparatively little, while a defeat might be decisive.

Towards the end of July 1788, a Turkish sortie led to an important engagement in which the principal part fell to Souvorov's troops. Souvorov himself was seriously wounded and had temporarily to give up the command; but Potemkin even then refused to move and send up strong reinforcements to storm Otchakov, and in fact addressed a severe rejoinder to Souvorov asking him 'how it was that he, Souvorov, had dared to start such a serious action without instructions'. Souvorov's impertinent reply was two lines of verse to the effect that he was sitting on a little stone and just watching Otchakov. Potemkin himself could have easily written something similar under different circumstances. Soon after this episode, Souvorov was again wounded, through the explosion of a labora-

tory in Kinburn, and was unable to take any further active
part in the siege of Otchakov. Although he and Potemkin were
frequently having different 'rubs' there was never any serious
conflict between them and each greatly appreciated the other's
abilities. Within two days of Souvorov's new mishap, Potemkin was writing to him: 'My dear friend, you alone mean to me
more than ten thousand others', and a similar tone of cordiality
existed at the time between Potemkin and his other great
colleague, Field Marshal Roumiantsev. They had sunk their
personal differences and were all co-operating for Russia's and
Catherine's glory. To a Russian historian this side of the war is
perhaps one of its most interesting aspects, and the study of
both official and private relations between Potemkin, Souvorov, and Roumiantsev throws much light on their character
and on the period in general.

In the campaign of 1789 Souvorov, fully recovered from his
wounds, was appointed by Potemkin to a commanding position in Roumiantsev's army, and before long covered himself
with glory in the battles of Focsani and on the Rimnik, where
he routed the Turks and collected an enormous booty. At the
Rimnik alone the Turks lost 22,000 men and sixty guns, and
consequent on that defeat was the fall of their fortresses of
Belgrade, Bendery, and Ackerman.

Potemkin was exuberant with joy and not only felt no envy
but again used all his endeavors to obtain proper rewards for
Souvorov from the Empress. At his suggestion, Catherine
created Souvorov 'Count of the Rimnik' and conferred on him
the St. George's Cross of the first class, the highest Russian
military distinction. In informing Souvorov of these honors,
Potemkin wrote: 'You would, of course, have acquired both
glory and victories at any time, but not every chief would inform you of the rewards with a pleasure similar to mine; do say,
Count Alexander Vassilievitch, that I am a good man: such I
will remain for ever!' And Souvorov's reply, addressed to Potemkin's *alter ego*, Popov, read as follows: 'May the Prince

Grigory Alexandrovitch live long; let God Almighty crown him with laurels and glory; let the faithful subjects of the great Catherine thrive on his good graces. He is an honest man, he is a good man, he is a great man, and I would be happy to die for him.'

Meanwhile, the Russian troops under yet another great war leader, Prince Repnin, had defeated the Turks at Tsakhi and began the siege of Ismail. Souvorov was sent by Potemkin to this important spot and ordered to force matters to a decisive action. This is what Potemkin wrote to him: 'I base my hopes on God and on your courage, hurry up my dear friend! . . . There are many generals of equal rank there, and that always results in some sort of hesitant parliament . . . Go into everything thoroughly, give the necessary instructions, and then having prayed to God, start the action.'

Souvorov carried out these instructions and performed a feat that appeared absolutely impossible; indeed, in later years, he himself admitted that only once in one's life can a man take a decision of this sort. On December 22, 1790, he stormed Ismail and literally reduced this formidable Turkish outpost in Bessarabia to ashes and dust. After that triumph he legitimately expected a field marshal's baton, but failed to get it.

A story was current at the time that this was due to the intervention of Potemkin, who, apparently, was hurt by one of Souvorov's typically intemperate retorts. When congratulating him on his triumph, Potemkin is said to have inquired: 'How can I reward you for your great services?' to which Souvorov haughtily replied: 'With nothing, Prince. I am not a merchant and have not come here to bargain with you. Apart from God and the Empress, nobody can reward me.' Whether this story be true or not, Souvorov certainly considered himself inadequately rewarded after Ismail, and his transfer to Finland—made on Potemkin's recommendation—was meant as a reprimand for his sulky behavior. It was also hardly a coincidence that Potemkin did not invite him to his many lavish receptions during his last stay in St. Petersburg. On the other hand, it was Potemkin who suggested to Catherine that a special medal commemorating the capture of Ismail by Souvorov should be struck in his honor, and the correspondence between the Empress and Potemkin shows that all the gifts, titles, and other honors bestowed on Souvorov were due to his strong recommendations. Souvorov, for his part, bore Potemkin no malice, and after his death some years later he observed: 'A great man and a man of greatness. Not only great through his brain but also great in stature. He was not like that French ambassador in London about whom Lord Bacon said that an attic is usually badly furnished.'

From a purely military point of view it was, of course, Souvorov who was the hero of the second Turkish War, and in that respect there seems to be a great disproportion between the rewards received by him and those heaped by Catherine on Potemkin. But the truth of the matter is that the Empress would have favored the latter on personal grounds even if he had had no merits, which, however, it is impossible to deny him. For the capture of Otchakov Potemkin received the first-class St. George's Cross, a diamond bedecked sword to the value of 60,000 rubles with the words 'for valor' engraved on it, and a cash present of 100,000 rubles.

When in 1789 he paid a short visit to St. Petersburg, he received another large monetary present, a field marshal's baton covered with diamonds and adorned with golden laurel leaves, as well as a specially made cross of the St. Alexander-Nevsky Order with a solitaire diamond in the centre costing 100,000 rubles. When he captured Bendery, Catherine presented him with a huge golden laurel wreath, covered with emeralds and diamonds to the value of 150,000 rubles, a golden medal and a large sum in cash. Finally, during his last visit to St. Petersburg, after the campaign of 1790 and a few months before his death, she presented him for the second time with the Taurida Palace which she had originally built for him, and then, Potemkin being in need of money, repurchased from him for the enormous sum of 460,000 rubles. Simultaneously with the renewed gift of this palace he also received a field marshal's uniform, lined along the seams with costly diamonds and 200,000 rubles in cash.

These rewards seem enormous. But it must be realized that despite Souvorov's military exploits, the second Turkish War was essentially 'Potemkin's war'. He had had to bear the whole responsibility for it. The Austrian allies under Joseph's personal command had proved a terrible disappointment. The unfortunate Emperor's expedition into Bosnia and Wallachia had resulted in a crushing defeat of his troops. He was certainly not in a position to win the satisfaction for which he had longed all these years—that of eclipsing the military glories of Frederick the Great. He had indeed the greatest difficulty in saving his life at the battle of Karonsebes. In February 1790, Joseph died, a sick and broken man; yet his death added to Catherine's and Potemkin's difficulties, since the Austrian allies were becoming a more than ever unstable and unreliable factor.

There was also another very serious complication. While Potemkin was absorbed by his activities in the South, King Gustavus III, of Sweden, after many delays, actively joined the camp of Russia's enemies and invaded Finland in July 1788. Although he had foreseen such an eventuality and worked out the measures to be taken, Potemkin was furious at this new entanglement. As if he had not already enough to do, he now had to attend to the conducting of a Russo-Swedish War as well, sending advice and instructions across several thousand miles to the disgruntled Catherine, whose first countermove against the military operation of the King of Sweden was to write an operetta lampooning him.

As in his war with the Turks, Potemkin now had to teach Catherine how to conduct a combined operation on land and sea against the Swedes, the glamorous Prince Nassau-Siegen, who had entered Russian service, taking an active part in these naval engagements. But it is not without interest that Potemkin, who had always been partial to alien troops, told Catherine to employ a regiment of Bashkirs, and that these Asiatics greatly distinguished themselves in the Swedish War.

Peace with the Swedes was made on August 14, 1790, ridding Catherine of an invader who might have been quite dangerous, but who proved incapable of marching on her capital despite the proximity of his troops and ships to it. The following year Austria withdrew from the struggle, leaving Russia alone to face the Turks who were continuing to enjoy the support of Great Britain and all the other powers antagonistic to, or apprehensive of, Russia. Despite Prince Repnin's further brilliant victories over the Turkish armies, Catherine opened peace negotiations at Jassy and finally, through the extraordinary able diplomacy of Bezborodko (Potemkin was already dead by then), obtained most advantageous terms for Russia.

By these terms the Porte formally surrendered not only the Crimea but also Otchakov and the territory lying between the rivers Bug and Dniestr. Thus the very terms on which Catherine and Potemkin were prepared to make peace at the outset of hostilities four years earlier were now secured.

These facts made it hard to understand how the second Turkish War could be considered as Potemkin's greatest failure. His contemporaries and many historians in judging his activities in connection with it, have taken the realization of the fantastic Greek project as a criterion. That is neither correct nor fair.

With all his faults, Potemkin can claim credit for the fact that for the first time in history the whole of the northern shore of the Black Sea became an integral part of the Russian Empire.

16

THE RUSSIAN SARDANAPALUS

THE STORIES about Potemkin's life at the front during the second Turkish War could fill several books. Most of them, as indeed the greater part of the information hitherto bequeathed to posterity on this extraordinary man, appear to be based on pure imagination. There are, however, one or two accounts of eyewitnesses that deserve every credit.

Foremost among these is that by the Prince de Ligne, who obtained the permission of the Emperor Joseph, in whose service he was, and the authority of Catherine, to join Potemkin at his headquarters, and who was with him throughout the Otchakov period. Ligne, of course, was most anxious to induce Potemkin to storm that citadel, since he realized the importance of a Russian success to his Austrian master. Time and again he lost heart in the face of Potemkin's stubborn refusal to act and did not mince words when he talked to him. Yet this is what the Prince de Ligne wrote from Otchakov to his friend Ségur in St. Petersburg:—

'I here behold a commander in chief, who looks idle, and is always busy; who has no other desk than his knees, no other comb than his fingers; constantly reclining on his couch, yet sleeping neither in night nor in daytime. His zeal for the Empress he adores, keeps him incessantly awake and uneasy; and a

cannon shot, to which he himself is not exposed, disturbs him
with the idea that it costs the life of some of his soldiers.
Trembling for others, brave himself; stopping under the hot-
test fire of a battery to give his orders, yet more an Ulysses than
an Achilles; alarmed at the approach of danger, frolicsome
when it surrounds him; dull in the midst of pleasure; unhappy
in being too fortunate, surfeited with everything, easily disgusted, morose, inconstant, a profound philosopher, an able
minister, a sublime politician, or like a child of ten years of
age; not revengeful, asking pardon for a pain he has inflicted;
quickly repairing an injustice, thinking he loves God, when he
fears the devil, whom he fancies still greater and bigger than
himself; waving one hand to the females that please him, and
with the other making the sign of the cross; embracing the feet
of a statue of the Virgin, or the alabaster neck of a statue of his
mistress; receiving numberless presents from his sovereign, and
distributing them immediately to others; accepting estates of
the Empress, and returning them, or paying her debts without
her knowledge; alienating and repurchasing immense tracts of
land, to erect a grand colonnade, or plant an English garden;
again getting rid of this; gambling from morn to night, or not
at all; preferring prodigality in giving, to regularity in paying;
prodigiously rich, and not worth a farthing; abandoning himself to distrust or to confidence, to jealousy or to gratitude, to
ill-humor or to pleasantry; easily prejudiced in favor of or
against anything, and as easily cured of a prejudice; talking
divinity to his generals, and tactics to his bishops; never reading, but pumping everyone with whom he converses, and con-
tradicting to be better informed; uncommonly affable, or extremely savage; affecting the most attractive or the most repulsive manners; appearing by turns the proudest Satrap of the
East, or the most amiable courtier of the Court of Louis XIV;
concealing, under the appearance of harshness, the greatest
benevolence of heart; whimsical with regard to time, repasts,
rest, and inclinations; like a child, wanting to have everything,

or, like a great man, knowing how to do without many things; sober, though seemingly a glutton; gnawing his fingers, or apples and turnips; scolding or laughing; mimicking or swearing; engaged in wantonness or in prayers; singing or meditating; calling and dismissing; sending for twenty aides-de-camp, and saying nothing to any one of them; bearing heat better than any man, whilst he seems to think of nothing but the most voluptuous baths; not caring for cold, though he appears unable to exist without furs; always in his shirt, without pants, or in rich regimentals embroidered on all the seams; barefoot, or in slippers embroidered with spangles; wearing neither hat nor cap; it is thus I saw him once in the midst of a musket fire; sometimes in a nightgown, sometimes in a splendid tunic with his three stars, his orders, and diamonds as large as a thumb round the portrait of the Empress; they seem placed there to attract the balls; crooked, and almost bent double when he is at home; and tall, erect, proud, handsome, noble, majestic, or fascinating, when he shows himself to his army, like Agamemnon in the midst of the monarchs of Greece. What then is his magic? Genius, natural abilities, an excellent memory, much elevation of soul, malice without the design of injuring, artifice without craft, a happy mixture of caprices, the art of conquering every heart in his good moments; much generosity, graciousness and justice in his rewards, a refined and correct taste, the talent of guessing what he is ignorant of, and a consummate knowledge of mankind.'

It would be difficult to add anything to this brilliant portrait, which is also so much in keeping with those both Ségur and Harris painted of their perplexing Russian friend. They all agreed on his genius, versatility, and capacity for hard work. As to his alleged indolence, Ligne's opening remarks ('. . . who looks idle, and is always busy') seem to solve the otherwise inexplicable riddle of how a man 'who never did anything' achieved so much, and this, moreover, in the brief period of a very few years and against tremendous odds.

On this point there is also very interesting evidence in a private letter written by yet another Frenchman, Joseph de Ribas. He came to Russia in 1772 and took part in the abduction of the pseudo princess Elizabeth described in an earlier chapter of this book. He married a Russian wife and later became the tutor of Catherine's illegitimate son by Orlov, Prince Bobrinskoy. Then he entered Potemkin's service and took an active part in the second Turkish War both on land and on sea; later he became the founder of Odessa and died in St. Petersburg in 1800 having reached the rank of a Russian admiral.

Here is an extract from de Ribas' letter to a friend: 'You ask me about my present life. I have plunged into the world of work. . . . In St. Petersburg people were assuring me that Prince Potemkin here is killing time in indolence and lavishness. . . . Sometimes for several days running he remains reclining half-dressed on a couch, biting his nails and thinking. If anybody asks you: "What is the prince doing?" you can simply answer: "He is thinking." But everything here is directed by his thought, and moreover he knows everything that is happening in the Caucasus, in Constantinople, in Paris. The other day he somehow got to hear [his messengers were not only fetching rare foods or perfumes or presents for the ladies] that in France, despite the peaceful times, a new cavalry regiment was by way of being equipped. He immediately wrote a letter to the Russian embassy there instructing them to send him every information on the subject and the reasons for it.

'I also heard in St. Petersburg that apparently everything here is in the hands of Popov and Faleyev [Potemkin's favorite contractor]; this is untrue. There are no delays here that kill both things and people. The prince thinks for Popov who has nothing to do and can employ his time in playing cards. On one occasion Prince Potemkin noticed that Popov's face was tired, so he said: "You have probably once again spent the night gambling. You should be sparing with your eyesight.

When I die you will retire to some village and out of boredom you will study the stars" [this was prophetic: after Potemkin's death and upon retiring from service Popov lived in the country and studied astronomy]. . . . People are also unjust to Faleyev . . . who with extraordinary dexterity organizes food supplies for the troops. Everybody here is inspired by confidence in the intelligence and the words of the prince. It can be said of him that he could do everything himself, but he likes to share his glory with others and considers the heroic deeds of others fair compensation for part of his own glory.'

Both Ligne and Ribas observed Potemkin at very close quarters. They experienced the full gamut of his changing moods and his eccentricities. Yet both of them recognized not only his genius but perceived that behind his apparent sloth and extravagance there was capacity, action, vision, and achievement.

Potemkin's lack of balance and his love of ostentation cannot be denied; but since he was the most exposed person in Russia it is only natural that his life should have provided people with endless material for every kind of gossip, story, and conjecture.

'The Russian Sardanapalus' emerges from them as an even greater showman and eccentric than he really was.

There is, for instance, the description of his subterranean headquarters in the camp of Otchakov. A narrow, dark passage led down to it, at the end of which there was a massive door. But when this was pushed aside, visitors—petrified with amazement—could behold an enormous marble hall with gilt decorations and huge mirrors on its white walls. Rows of pillars made of the choicest stone, like lapis lazuli, supported the ceiling of this gorgeous room, and heavy curtains between the pillars separated that part of it which was intended for receptions from the more intimate apartments. Enormous chandeliers hanging from the ceiling, and also on the rows of long luxuriously decorated banqueting tables provided a warm glowing light, and the reflection of these myriads of candles in the mirrors on the walls contributed to give this hall a fairylike atmosphere. The mirrors were arranged in such a way as to convey the impression that the room doubled itself at whichever angle one looked at it. An army of lackeys in powdered wigs and golden brocaded coats was in constant attendance. It sounds unbelievable that such a thing existed at the time, but one of the beverages with which Potemkin used to regale his guests in that very hall was seltzer water. On one occasion when he entertained a party, he suggested that after the meal they should all go up into the open air again and watch some gipsy dancing. But when the guests emerged from the dark and intimidating corridor, instead of the field they had just seen they saw a paradiselike garden, with the rarest of southern plants and trees, summer houses, statues of marble goddesses and huge peacocks proudly strutting up and down the wide alleys strewn with sand of different colors. Was it reality or hallucination? When the guests expressed their enthusiasm and amazement at this unbelievable, this magic transformation, Potemkin only gave them a gloomy glance, and biting his nails, said with nonchalance: 'What? Was not all this here before?' Bored and depressed, he slowly walked towards the dancers; the fun was over and he no longer knew what to do with the effect achieved.

In one of his other camps he chose to live in a tent. This was arranged like an old Israelite tabernacle in the desert, and was divided by curtains into three parts: in the entrance, his adjutants, foreign diplomats and others, had to wait until called inside the next section, which was the holy of holies. Potemkin himself sat alone in the third and last part, like a Buddha or an oracle, lavender sprinkled all round him and blending with a strong smell of incense.

Outside the tent, his various military insignia were placed, with those of a Hetman of the Don-, Black Sea-, and New Russia-Cossacks prominently displayed among them. Guards of honor, in picturesque uniforms, changed at frequent intervals. Inside, only his faithful factotum Popov, was gliding with astonishing agility between the heavy sets of curtains separating the three sections of this strange habitation. Every few minutes the voice of Potemkin was heard roaring 'Popov!' and his secretary would run to Serenissimus. Then he would deliver some message, either by word of mouth, or more often scribbled on a piece of paper, to some person waiting in the 'holy of holies', and after that disappear either into Potemkin's section again or else into the anteroom to fetch some new visitor into the central section.

Only very few callers were actually admitted to Potemkin's presence. He did not wish to see anybody. Ligne once or twice had that privilege.

One day Potemkin happened to be sitting at a low table on which there was nothing but a few slips of paper and a pencil, a small bar of silver, a file, and a casket with jewels of different colors and sizes. He seemed deeply absorbed in strange thoughts, the expression on his face changing several times before he even uttered a word. His forehead was getting covered with wrinkles, and then he seemed to relax again; drops of sweat appeared over his brow. Suddenly he seized the silver bar and the file, and began to rub one against the other furiously. Then, after a few moments of work in grim concentration, he threw both the bar and the file back on the table, and once more relapsed into a stonelike attitude, his features this time reflecting a mood of acute disgust.

He did not remain in that position any length of time, however, and stretching his hand to the casket with the jewels he upset them all on the table and began slowly to sort them out. With his fingers, always bitten to the quick, yet long and aristocratic, he picked up stone after stone, gazed at it pensively, and then put it down—obviously in accordance with some definite and clear plan. He was making figures of odd shapes with these diamonds, emeralds, and rubies, mixing the colors, then rearranging them again and putting all the green stones together and then all the red, and finally all the white ones. He was deep in thought, and seemed to be performing some mysterious rites like a magician or alchemist, giving his jeweled figures on the table ever new shapes. All of a sudden he mixed them up again, and angrily he threw them back into the casket. His face was black with fury, his one eye gazed strangely into the distance, his large head was now resting on his fist—it was uncanny. Then, as if he had come to some final decision he once again stretched his hand to the casket, picked out two stones—a red and a green one—tossed them in the air, and caught them back in the hollow of his hand. Within a fraction of a second his face changed completely; the gloomy expression had gone, and he looked cheerful, happy, and gay. 'Popov!' he roared, and returned to the normal transaction of business. On another occasion, while talking to Ligne, he was continuously arranging his diamonds and stones, which this time even included small pieces of quartz, granite, and other less valuable specimens, and it seemed as if he were playing a game of patience with them or working out a Chinese puzzle.

No one could explain the meaning of all this, and Ligne was completely lost in guesswork. Was Potemkin playing the comedy? Was he seriously gratifying some curious superstition or mania? It is impossible to say why he did it, but he seemed to attach the greatest importance to this particular eccentricity, and indulged in it again and again.

Much has been written about his lavish entertainments in the front zone, and about his various love affairs while the war was going on. In neither of these respects does Potemkin appear to have transgressed his accustomed mode of living, and he transplanted the atmosphere of St. Petersburg and Tsarskoe Selo to his camp. That this did not prevent him from performing his duties as commander in chief, statesman, diplomat, and administrator, both his own record and the evidence of people like Ligne abundantly prove. At the same time he certainly did stage some receptions, organize artistic entertainments, and gratify his passions in a way that is not normally associated with the behavior of even an eighteenth-century war lord, although life in camp was in those days by no means as austere as in modern general headquarters.

He was supposed to have a whole harem of lovely women when he lived in apparent apathy and inactivity in the camp of Otchakov. It is true that various ladies, some of them the greatest beauties in Russia, were there, and sexual reticence or morality was not the characteristic feature of this picturesque and eccentric age. But it is hard to understand why people thought it more reprehensible that Potemkin should be madly in love with the gorgeous Princess Catherine Dolgorouky, whose husband was serving under his orders, or the enchanting Praskovia—wife of his kinsman Paul Potemkin—or a score of others, when nobody seemed to object to his open liaisons with his own five nieces or various other prominent society women, all of whom were received at court and much sought after.

His generosity to his guests, but especially to the ladies, knew no bounds. When he wanted to present one of them with an exquisite oriental shawl he staged a lottery in which every ticket had a winning number, so that each lady present drew a shawl too. On another occasion at the end of a lavish supper, some crystal cups were handed around which were filled with diamonds; he asked each lady to select a stone for herself. When one lady happened to ruin a pair of evening shoes he immediately dispatched an officer to Paris to bring her another pair from France.

Of his many romances during the second Turkish War, the one that stands out is that with an intriguing oriental adventuress of remarkable beauty—at the time the wife of an insignificant major, Joseph Witte. This major had been sent in 1778, to meet Boscamp Liassopolsky, a Polish diplomat returning from Stamboul to Warsaw, who turned out to be carrying in his baggage a very special kind of contraband—two young Greek girls he had purchased in a Turkish slave market. Liassopolsky's delicate idea was to offer these young beauties as a special present to his king, since the taste of Stanislas for feminine charm was well known to his faithful subjects. But a complication suddenly arose in connection with this extraordinary purchase, the Turkish authorities having started an international diplomatic *démarche* against this Polish diplomat, charging him with abduction. He was therefore anxious to get rid of the girls, and requested Joseph Witte to escort them back into Turkish territory and present them to the Pasha of Khotin. The major agreed, but on the way he fell in love with one of them, and decided to marry her. With great difficulty he managed to get a Catholic priest to perform the ceremony, and the little Greeko-Turkish slave became Madame Sophie Witte; the other girl was 'forwarded' back to Turkey. Sophie Witte was so beautiful and so unusually clever, that within a very short time she became a social celebrity. She and her husband invented the legend that she was of royal descent, and was a claimant to the Byzantian throne. Somebody nicknamed her 'La Belle Fanariote' and this name soon became known in every capital of Europe. One by one Sophie Witte visited the principal courts, and in every country she swept men of all ages and social positions off their feet; Major Witte was a weak and accommodating husband.

Finally, 'La Belle Fanariote', surrounded by the halo of mystery, arrived in Potemkin's camp on the Dniestr. He came under her spell at first sight, and for a long time he raved about her. He treated her like a queen, staged the most lavish of entertainments for her, and took her with him wherever he went. Contemporaries asserted that she was a Turkish agent, and that she had been sent by the Turks to spy on Potemkin. On the other hand, the late Grand Duke Nicholas Mikhailovitch, a great historian, and an acknowledged authority on the period, has described her as Potemkin's agent, whom he had not only used as a spy against the Turks, but actually sent on various delicate diplomatic missions. Whichever is true, the fact remains that 'La Belle Fanariote' was a woman of brilliant intellectual gifts as well as striking oriental beauty, and had a sensational career. She even managed to get rid of the boring Major Witte, and married as her second husband, Count Joseph Pototsky, one of the most famous and wealthiest Polish aristocrats.

But not only fair ladies helped to entertain Potemkin and dispel his spleen at Otchakov and Bendery. He kept a whole theater in his camp, and an orchestra of 200 musicians. Music had always had a most moving effect on him, ever since the days he first heard the songs of the old Deacon Krasnopievtsev at his native Tchishovo. Now the moody generalissimo found that music soothed and cheered him better than anything else. He had some of Europe's foremost artists to play for him, and at one time the Russian ambassador in Vienna, Count Andrew Rasoumovsky, was seriously negotiating on his behalf with 'an excellent pianist and one of the best composers in Germany', Wolfgang Amadeus Mozart. But Mozart died before the final arrangements were made, and it was left to Sarti to look after Potemkin's music. He composed a special 'Te Deum' to celebrate the capture of Otchakov, and that extraordinary piece includes 100 cannon salvos to be rendered by the organ. Potemkin took a personal interest in Sarti's work, debated both subjects and forms, examined every part of his compositions, and greatly encouraged the Italian *maestro* in every way. Similarly, he was interested in the works of poets, writers, scholars, and especially theologians, and liked to discuss their works with them. He has been celebrated in many odes, of which the best known one is by the poet Dershavin and is called 'The Waterfall'. In this work, pompous and verbose, like so much literature of the period, Potemkin is compared to a waterfall with its powerful stream, its foam, and its driving power that enables it to pass over all the rocks.

But the description of Potemkin as a Russian Sardanapalus is perhaps more in keeping with the legend of the extent to which he gratified his love of pomp and splendor during the second Turkish War.

17

'POTEMKIN'S APOTHEOSIS'

THE TURKISH War was over; it was only a question of finally settling terms, but the fighting was done. Potemkin was on his way back to St. Petersburg, and Catherine was particularly anxious to give the conquering hero the greatest welcome he had ever had. At every station parades, receptions, and celebrations had been arranged for him. An army of workmen were busily repairing the road from Moscow to St. Petersburg, working night shifts, and couriers, adjutants, state officers, were flying backwards and forwards just to convey to Serenissimus Catherine's love and appreciation, and bring her news of his health or of any desires he might wish to express.

But the triumphant hero was gloomy. He was not interested in the wearying receptions; for once he did not want all this fuss, he was a sick and tired man longing for peace. Moreover, he was terribly worried. For the first time in seventeen years Catherine had taken a new favorite without consulting him. And what was even worse, the passionate sexagenarian had completely fallen under the domination of her ignorant and worthless lover, who was a young man full of ambition and presumption. Potemkin knew that his enemies had at last seen a chance of effectively undermining his position, which in all these years had remained impregnable, despite their efforts and

320

intrigues. But he knew that the various court cliques who had proved powerless in their struggle against him, were now using young Plato Zoubov, the new favorite, to jockey him out of · the Empress's confidence and esteem. So far, their efforts had proved ineffective, and Catherine still appeared as strongly attached to him as she had ever been. She was still consulting him on everything, and a most important document addressed to him by the Empress on April 12, 1791, disproves the contention that Potemkin had fallen out of favor or that his power was approaching an eclipse. In this rescript she was, among other things, entrusting him with the supreme command of the Russian troops in case a war were to break out with Poland. And she gave him other most important work to do.

Yet he was anxious for the future, his own future, and that of the empire, if the influence of young Plato Zoubov and all those behind him were allowed to grow. The word 'Zoub' means tooth in Russian. 'I must pull out the tooth,' Potemkin was constantly murmuring to himself as his carriage approached Moscow: 'at any price the tooth must be removed.'

At Moscow he was met by a special delegation headed by Bezborodko, who was now the leading executive collaborator of the Empress. It is significant that this delegation to welcome Potemkin was sent by Catherine despite Zoubov's strong protests; the new favorite resented so much attention being shown to his formidable rival.

An episode occurred in Moscow which set all the gossips talking. When the old Count and ex-Hetman Rasoumovsky called on Potemkin to extend to him in person the warmest invitation to a ball about to be given in his honor, Potemkin received this distinguished visitor clad in his old filthy dressing gown with nothing underneath it. Rasoumovsky paid him back in kind by receiving him a few days later, in the presence of 'the whole of Moscow,' also in a dressing gown and with a nightcap on his head. To everybody's surprise, Potemkin, who appreciated a good joke against himself—especially when it made fun of his eccentricities—took this intended slight very well, embraced the host, and laughed the whole thing off.

From Moscow, Potemkin drove to St. Petersburg with Bezborodko, and the two men, alone in their carriage, had ample time to discuss the political situation as well as the latest developments at court. They had been in close contact for years, co-operating in many great ventures, and during Potemkin's absence they had remained in constant correspondence. Now that Potemkin had returned to the capital, Bezborodko was the only statesman he continued to see and consult.

He ignored all the others. He was not interested in them. Moreover, he was absorbed by something else. This Zoubov business had to be settled, for if it were allowed to continue it would end up by ruining the Empress and bringing discredit on Russia. But he realized that Catherine loved Zoubov with all the passion of an old woman, that she sensed in him her last lover, and that if she were separated from him it would be difficult at this juncture to restore her balance merely by supplying another eligible young man. It was no longer a case of matching his power, his unquestionable hold over her against the purely physical fascination exercised over the aged sensualist by a boy young enough to be her grandson. If the operation could be performed at all, it had to be done not by scenes and violence, but in a far more subtle way. He did not wish to procure the dismissal of the favorite in the manner he had so often used before: that was fraught with too many incalculable possibilities.

There was only one other way of removing Zoubov. Instead of using his power, as he had done in the case of Ermolov, and as he easily could do again, this man of fifty got it into his head that he could best influence a woman over sixty by trying to recapture something of their old romance. What appears even more strange, and shows that Potemkin was a subtle psychologist and knew Catherine better than anybody else, is that to a large degree he succeeded. In a letter addressed to the Prince de Ligne, and dated May 21, 1791, Catherine was speaking of her hero Potemkin with the same enthusiasm, love, and devotion that had characterized her earliest epistles about him to Grimm, Voltaire, and the others. 'When one looks at the Prince Marshal Potemkin,' she wrote, 'one must say that his victories, his successes, beautify him. He has returned to us from the Army as handsome as the day, as gay as a lark, as brilliant as a star, more witty than ever, no longer biting his nails, giving feasts every day—one more beautiful than another— and behaving as a host with a polish and courtesy by which everybody is enchanted, despite all the envious ones.'

Catherine, and indeed most women, had always raved about Potemkin's good looks. It is with the greatest of difficulty that the Empress persuaded him to allow his portrait to be painted by the Italian artist Lampi, who was paying a protracted visit to St. Petersburg at the time and was immortalizing most of the prominent men and women in society. But Potemkin, who had always been extremely self-conscious about his physical defect of having only one eye, was most reluctant to sit for his portrait. Finally, he allowed Lampi to make two different portraits of him, of which that representing him as an ancient knight in armor gives a better idea of Potemkin's features than the other and better known one, showing him in full Court dress with all the ribbons and decorations that he wore at the feasts to which Catherine refers.

Life in St. Petersburg now became an unending stream of celebrations. All the best known hosts in the capital were competing with each other in extravagance on a scale that was unprecedented even for them. The usual program on such occasions was: first a theatrical performance, a ballet or a light opera. Madame Huss, an actress from Paris, and her partner Floridor, a French actor, were in constant demand and had to appear in different houses every night. Their repertoire included plays like *La fausse Agnès*, *Le cocher supposé*, and *Bourgeoises à la mode*. After the performance supper was usually served, which was followed by cards for the older guests and a ball for the young. A few hundred guests was considered a normal gathering, and at really great receptions there was often a thousand or two.

The Swedish diplomat Stedingk describes Potemkin's appearance at one of these feasts in the following way: 'He was wearing a set of studs and a sword of the richest kind, and I have never seen a mortal being look more splendid or better groomed. Clouds of ill-humor seemed, however, to darken so much glory and observant people noticed with fear that he proceeded to bite his nails three times—a gloomy omen which immediately makes all the faces quite long.'

He had every reason to feel dejected. His stratagem to lure Catherine away from the 'child' had been only partly successful. She had aged a great deal, and although she accepted Potemkin's new courtship with tenderness and grace, it was obvious that the physical satisfaction she derived from Zoubov tied her to her young lover much more firmly than even Potemkin could have expected.

But he was not giving up the battle as lost yet. On two or three occasions he very nearly forgot all his subtle psychology and was on the point of having a violent altercation with the Empress.

It is probable that if he had persevered and had allowed his temper to get the better of him, he could have wiped out Zoubov completely. But something was holding him back. He was chary of depriving Catherine of a thing he did not see his way of replacing and which he for one was no longer prepared to give.

Yet he could not refrain from displaying his contempt for Zoubov who loathed him more than anything in the world and knew how dangerous Potemkin still was to his growing domination over the Empress. This hatred was increased by one or two public humiliations administered to him by Potemkin. On one occasion Serenissimus heard that Zoubov's father had robbed a certain major of his country seat and promptly forced the young man to put matters right. But worse was to follow.

Catherine was contemplating a gift of a large estate with 12,000 'souls' to Zoubov for his 'services to the fatherland'. At a dinner party she suddenly turned to Potemkin and said: 'Would you like to sell me your estate in the Moghilev district?'

Now, under other circumstances there would have been nothing unusual in such a transaction. On many occasions—especially if he happened to be in need of ready cash—Potemkin had sold back to the Empress estates, palaces, and even jewels with which she had previously presented him and as often as not she would give them to him once again immediately after having repurchased them.

But this time it was different. He guessed at once for whom she wanted the Moghilev estate. 'I am terribly sorry, Madam,' he said without a moment's hesitation, 'but unfortunately I cannot gratify your wish: that estate is already sold.' Catherine blushed: 'To whom have you sold it?'

'To this fellow here,' and he pointed at a young court official who was standing in attendance behind his chair. Furiously the Empress turns to the young official: 'So you have bought His Serene Highness's estate?' A furtive glance from Potemkin, and with a deep bow the young man confirmed that the purchase did take place.

That was a slight Zoubov never forgave. Even thirty years later he used to say to his friends that Potemkin had 'stolen' an estate from him.

While the festivities were continuing unabated, and while both the Empress and Potemkin were shining at all of them, it was clear that there was a growing strain between them.

According to the Swedish envoy Stedingk, Catherine's brain and physique were rapidly deteriorating. She was no longer what she used to be. Everybody and everything seemed to irritate her; it was difficult to discuss any business with her or even to approach her.

Potemkin was still the first man in the realm and for all

intents and purposes her coregent. Yet in his case personal difficulties, in addition to the general ones, made fruitful collaboration for the moment quite impossible. At no time in their long association had they seen less eye to eye on matters of domestic as well as of foreign policy.

He was trying to use up his energy in receptions, each more lavish than the preceding. He thought nothing of spending 20,000 rubles on a dinner party, followed by artistic entertainment. This hobby of offering his guests choice foods was costing him a fortune. At one feast he spent 1,000 ducats on foreign fruit; at another oysters to the value of 300 rubles were served. He engaged artists from all over Russia or even Europe. For his own diversion he brought to St. Petersburg anyone who could discuss the subjects in which he was interested.

An express messenger had to fetch a man from Moscow who was reputed to know by heart the names of all the saints in the calendar. On another occasion he, who in his younger days had himself excelled as an impersonator, sent for a man in Kherson who was supposed to be particularly good at impersonating the more famous personalities of the court. A master chess player, who was in private life a merchant in Toula, had to display his talents to Serenissimus.

He was said to have spent two and one-half million rubles during his stay in St. Petersburg. But the Empress was continually paying up for him, and when his enemies thought that in view of the reputed rift between her and Potemkin they might stop these payments, she said angrily—as she had always said—that there was no difference whether the money was required by her or Prince Potemkin. He was her consort, and she paid—admitting no outside interference.

The feast that made the strongest impression and completely eclipsed in lavishness everything that had hitherto been seen in Russia, as far as entertainment was concerned, was the great 'Potemkin feast' of April 28, 1791. The description of it has filled many volumes of Russian and foreign memoirs.

It was staged in the newly decorated palace of Taurida, where he now resided, and he surpassed himself in its preparation and its management. Three thousand guests were invited, and were all assembled when the Empress finally arrived. Potemkin was waiting for her at the door, in a red silk tail coat, with a collar of most precious black embroidery. The buttons of his coat were of solid gold, and each was adorned with a large solitaire diamond. His hat was covered with so many jewels that it was too heavy for him to hold under the arm, as was then the fashion, and a special A.D.C. had to follow him round carrying the hat for him. The huge central hall with marble pillars and a high cupola was turned into a garden. A platform was erected on one side, to which Potemkin conducted the Empress and a few other guests of honor, and no sooner did they take their seats than he gave a sign, and twenty-four couples, including Catherine's two grandsons, the Grand Dukes Alexander and Constantine, danced into the room and proceeded to perform a special ballet composed for the occasion by Potemkin himself. Then he led the Empress and 500 of the guests through the various other rooms. Orchestras and Greek choirs provided music, poets recited their verse, a French comedy called *The False Lovers* was performed, and then a pantomime, *The Merchant of Smyrna*, in which the stage represented a slave market.

A gargantuan meal, with the choicest delicacies of Europe and Asia was served, wine seemed to flow in streams. But the heat was growing almost unbearable: that was the drawback of the lighting arrangements of those days. On this occasion, 140,000 lanterns and 20,000 candles were used in the different halls, the winter garden, and the park, the wax alone costing more than 70,000 rubles. The supply in St. Petersburg had proved insufficient so that some extra wax had been hurried from Moscow just for Serenissimus.

Towards the end of the evening Catherine and Potemkin withdrew alone to the winter garden, and the Empress remarked with surprise that it was six times larger than her own;

its decorations exceeded in fantasy and beauty anything Potemkin had built before. In the midst of all these rare plants, and marble statues, and fountains, as well as innumerable other theatrical effects, the Empress and Potemkin had a most momentous conversation. Lovingly, but firmly, she tried to remonstrate with him for staying in St. Petersburg too long, and for appearing to be interested in nothing but entertainments. He, on the other hand, expressed his criticism of her new paramour and his apprehension of her politics. It was their last serious argument, but there was no violent altercation as in the days of yore. Both of them seemed to be feeling their age; they were mellow and sentimental, and both of them cried. When they returned to the scene of festivities, the ball was in full swing. Catherine stayed till two o'clock in the morning, much later than she had ever stayed at any party before. Escorted by Potemkin, she walked through the imposing hall with the cupola, and while a farewell anthem was being played in her honor, she stopped and listened to it, standing up in the middle of the room, an imposing and yet a pathetic figure, devoted to the only man whom she had admitted as her equal, and yet yearning for the young nonentity whose very existence was a sore to Potemkin. Finally, she took leave of her host and thanked him in glowing terms for the wonderful feast. He, overwhelmed with emotion, threw himself at her feet, and when he looked up to her, both of them were crying.

It was the apotheosis of Potemkin, the last great pageant he had staged before leaving the theater that is life. After Catherine's departure, Potemkin remained for a short while to talk to a few chosen guests, but soon he, too, retired to his apartments, and the party that had cost him a quarter of a million rubles ended without him.

18

THE END

HE LEFT St. Petersburg on July 24, burdened with the debts he had incurred through all his latest extravagance. His florist's bill alone amounted to the incredible sum of 38,000 rubles; he also owed 19,000 to cabmen (despite his own horses and coaches), 100,000 to the banker Sutherland, and various other large amounts; after his death Catherine paid, as she had so often done before, all his debts on her own initiative, and without a murmur.

The return journey to the South tired Serenissimus. He was sick at heart, and bodily sick as well. It is true that Catherine had been most anxious for him to return to the Army. But, apart from town gossip, there is no evidence of any kind that he had been ordered to go, and that he left in disgrace. On the contrary, no sooner was he gone than she began to bombard him with her usual letters, entreating him to look after his health, imploring him to be careful, to write more often, not to worry—in fact, nothing had changed either in the tone or the substance of her almost daily messages to him in all these years. Worried when he failed to reply, she now even took to writing to his faithful factotum, Popov, demanding news of Potemkin. Something was wrong with his health, but, as ever, he would do nothing about it; his moral sufferings, however, seemed to be even greater than the physical pain. The Zoubov interlude was obsessing him, and he could not get it out of his system.

As if she did not realize what it meant to him, the Empress was filling her epistles with references to her loathsome young lover. Not only did she invariably conclude by saying that 'the child' sends greetings, but in her desire to improve relations between Potemkin and Zoubov she dwelt at considerable length on the respect and admiration with which apparently Potemkin inspired his rival. 'The child thinks that you are more intelligent and that you are far more amusing and pleasant than all those who surround you,' she wrote on one occasion, but begged Grigory not to betray her little indiscretion if ever he happened to talk to Zoubov—behind whose back she was saying these things. The truth of the matter is that he probably never said anything of the sort and that it was just a ruse, a pathetic attempt of the aging woman to sooth Potemkin.

What he must have felt in reading all this, or in receiving obsequious and obviously insincere letters from Zoubov himself can easily be guessed. It had been enough of an effort, while in St. Petersburg, to overcome his disgust and invite the favorite to his house or to accept his invitations. He was not made for that sort of thing; whatever he was, Potemkin was never a hypocrite.

After a few days of slow traveling—the shaking of the carriage was causing him much pain—he suddenly ordered the coachman to drive at the utmost speed. Just as in olden times his procession of carriages and mounted retinue dashed through the familiar regions, and he reached Jassy within eight days of having left the capital.

A story was circulating in St. Petersburg that this sudden rush was due to the fact that on the way Potemkin had met a courier of Prince Repnin, who was in charge during his absence, and that upon opening—as he had always done—the dispatches addressed to the Empress in person he had learned to his amazement and fury that peace negotiations had been started behind his back.

Forgetting his illness and the discomfort of traveling, he had hurried to Jassy to conduct the negotiations himself and had had a violent altercation with Repnin.

That was one story. According to another version he actually knew all this in St. Petersburg and only left for the Army in order to prevent Repnin from scoring any great success.

'Serenissimus is jealous of Repnin,' people said at court, and thought they had detected another intrigue. Here again, however, official documents show that this is absolutely untrue. In the minutes of Catherine's Council there is ample evidence that far from intriguing against Repnin, Potemkin was actually supporting him. These minutes record the interesting fact that it was Potemkin who presented to the Council Repnin's draft for a peace treaty with the Turks. Yet it has been freely alleged that exactly the reverse was the case, and that Potemkin tried to prevent Repnin from making this peace because he was anxious to add that glory to his own achievements.

On his way to the South, Potemkin wrote to the Empress on several occasions, but his letters were full of melancholy, and he spoke of feeling the approach of death; he complained of his growing ailments. At times he felt a little better, but then there occurred an incident which had a terrible effect on him. While he happened to be passing through the city of Kharkov, Prince Karl Alexander of Würtemberg, a brother of the heiress to the throne, died. During his last sojourn in St. Petersburg, Potemkin had made a strong endeavor to improve his relations with the Tsarevitch Paul and his wife, and had even repeatedly pleaded with Catherine for better treatment of her son. This did not prevent Paul from loathing Potemkin, even when the latter was in his grave (which, as soon as he succeeded to the throne, Paul ordered to be ransacked); but in the meantime Potemkin wanted to continue his efforts towards better relations, and thought that Paul would appreciate his attending the funeral of his brother-in-law. Moreover, Potemkin liked the Prince of Würtemberg, who had served under his orders, and was genuinely upset by his death. Now it happened that when he had left the church after the funeral, and was waiting outside for his carriage, he was—as so often before—deep in thought. Something drove up and Potemkin, without looking at it, moved towards it and wanted to board it, when suddenly with a shudder, he recoiled: it was the hearse that had come to fetch the dead body.

To a man of Potemkin's superstititions, this episode appeared as some dreadful omen. It had a devastating effect on his mental and physical state. His illness, probably the effect of the malaria he had caught in the Crimea in 1783, was steadily progressing. The deadly climate of the region was making things worse. Moreover, Potemkin would not listen to any medical advice and refused to take the various medicines prescribed by the three doctors who were in constant personal attendance. In this respect he was not unlike Catherine herself, who—while always admonishing him to look after his health—did not believe in drugs and was firmly convinced that the best way to recovery was to leave the body to itself.

Not only would Potemkin ignore what his physicians said, but instead of dieting he was regularly having gargantuan meals and was drinking a great deal—especially his favorite Russian beverage called 'Kvass', a kind of sour cup.

Whenever the pain got worse he wrapped wet towels around his head, told the servants to spray him with eau de cologne and remained for hours completely immobile on his sofa.

Despite his lamentable state he was working very hard. He was absorbed by the various important diplomatic issues and was in constant touch with Bezborodko. There was also the Army and then there were the peace negotions. The idea that his strength might give out was torturing him. 'My strength is vanishing, there is too much to do. I am really not sparing myself . . . am tired like a dog,' he wrote.

His retinue decided to inform the Countess Branitsky: perhaps she would be more successful in persuading him to be reasonable, and to look after his health. As soon as she heard of his condition the faithful Sashenka left everything and rushed to her uncle's and lover's side. He was getting worse. Towards the middle of September he had an attack of shivering fever that lasted twelve hours. 'Am very weak. Imagine that everybody in Jassy is sick. Practically all the servants in the house. Please select for me and send me a Chinese dressing-gown—I badly need one,' he wrote to Catherine.

Meanwhile further negotiations with the Turks were taking place. Not even Potemkin's closest collaborators knew what was in his mind. Did he want to continue the war or was he anxious for peace? He was making territorial and political demands that seemed unacceptable to Turkey. Yet he was impossible to approach and it was useless to argue with him.

He became restless. He said he was suffocating in the air of Jassy and twice he drove out into the country, only to come back. Once again he was raving about withdrawing to a monastery. He talked to his staff about the healing effects of monastic solitude. Away from the world, detached from everything, relieved of the responsibilities and vicissitudes of power and government; alone with God.

Suddenly he seemed overcome with a spell. He demanded pen and ink and stationery and then locked himself in. Writing day and night he composed ten 'Canons to the Savior', or religious songs, reminiscent of the Psalms in shape and substance. They were prayers in which he was pouring out his soul to the Lord whose supreme power is destiny; they were a most moving expression of humble praise of, and fervent belief in, Almighty God.

When this religious ecstasy slightly subsided he seemed visibly better. But it had not relieved him for long. His precarious condition was growing more and more alarming. A rumor had even spread abroad that he was already dead.

In St. Petersburg Catherine was breathlessly following the developments, clinging to every report that sounded at all en-

couraging. On the one hand, as can be judged from a letter to
Grimm, she was most anxious lest Europe should prematurely
bury Potemkin; it is astonishing to what an extent even at such
a moment she kept a cool head. But on the other hand she was
genuinely and deeply concerned about the man who had been
everything to her and still meant so much. In the diary of her
private secretary, Chrapovitsky, who invariably referred to her
in the royal plural, there are frequent entries at that period:
'They wept,' 'they cried,' 'they were most upset by the latest
news about the prince.' To Sashenka she wrote thus: 'The illness of your uncle, the Prince Grigory Alexandrovitch, worries
me a great deal. Please write to me, Countess, how he is and
do try to prevent relapses as he is so weak from his ailment.'

The doctors had now made up their mind that it was gall
trouble. Together with Sashenka they made another attempt
to persuade Potemkin to take some medicine. This time the
obstinate patient suddenly acquiesced, and for a while it
seemed as if the treatment were doing him good. But shivering
returned, and with it sleeplessness, pain, and dreadful agitation.
Terrible nights followed, an almost unbearable ordeal both for
Potemkin and those around him. When he felt hot he once
more had to be wrapped in wet towels and insisted on having
masses of eau de cologne poured over him; he was also constantly swallowing cold drinks, and would jump up only to
fall back into bed again. Then he suddenly felt he was suffocating, and all the windows had to be opened or else he insisted on being carried into the garden.

All the time he was inquiring whether any messengers had
arrived from the Empress, and if there was a new letter
from her he felt moved to tears and reread and kissed it again
and again.

Too weak to sit up and read the state documents, he insisted
every morning that all the correspondence should be read out
to him and if there was anything really important he made a

superhuman effort to scribble his own signature with a trembling hand.

He tried to dictate a report on the progress of the peace negotiations for Catherine, but could not carry on. Another day, he attempted to deal with promotions and rewards in the Army in connection with the recent victory at Anapa; his strength abandoned him. Suddenly he expressed the desire to leave Jassy and to move to Nicolaev, his last and favorite establishment. With difficulty the doctors, Sashenka, Popov, and the rest of his faithful retinue persuaded him to postpone the trip for a week or so.

It became increasingly obvious that there was no hope left. Popov no longer felt justified in sparing the Empress and wrote to her that the prince was on his deathbed. Potemkin himself talked of nothing but death and the uselessness of living on. He refused to try a quinine treatment, but when they all implored him he reluctantly agreed. A few high ecclesiastics, including two archbishops, were now also in constant attendance—a natural thing, when so devoted a son of the Church was dying. They applied all their eloquence in an attempt to persuade Potemkin to desist from his unhealthy food and to listen to his doctors' advice. 'I'm not going to recover anyway,' snarled Potemkin, 'I have been ill for a long time. Jassy is my coffin. God's will shall be done. If only you pray for my soul and do not forget me when I am gone. You are my confessor,' he turned to one of the archbishops, 'so you can testify that I never wished anybody any harm. To make people happy has always been the object of my desires. I am not a bad man and not the evil genius of our mother the Empress Catherine, as has often been said. It is not true.' The archbishop confirmed all this and Potemkin—exhausted by the effort of his long speech—seemed to fall asleep.

Outside the priests met his old French physician Massot. Is there any hope, they inquired. The Frenchman told them that His Serene Highness had been so unreasonable through-out his illness that he had ruined every chance of recovery. Yet there appeared to be a slight improvement. At last Sashenka and the others got a few hours rest. But Potemkin sent for the priests and demanded the last sacraments.

After that he looked greatly relieved. Moreover, a courier arrived from St. Petersburg with a tender letter from Catherine, a beautiful fur coat, and the Chinese dressing-gown he had been asking for. He cried, but his mood was much better. In the evening with Sashenka, he felt quite mellow. He took her hands and stroked them: 'Good hands. Have often soothed me.' For a while he was silent, and then: 'Sasha, you have always told me the truth. Tell me frankly: do you think I shall recover?' The countess hastened to assure him that soon he would be well again and used a curious expression to the effect that he would never die. He no longer listened. This phrase about immortality appeared to carry his thoughts away. Was it not possible that God, who had given him everything, should also grant him eternal life? He wished to discuss it with the ec-clesiastics—even on his deathbed his passion for theological argument did not abandon him.

A peculiar process was at work in him. All the worst features of his character seemed to be disappearing one by one, as if they were melting. This passionate, ambitious, domineering, obstinate man was gradually becoming calm, humble, docile, and spiritual. Those around him were overcome by his serenity and his kindliness. Now that death was so near, his eternal nostalgia, that spleen which caused both him and Catherine so much misery, was suddenly lifted like a veil. A big, simple man, a 'Russian Colossus' as Ligne used to call him, was dying and was preparing to meet his Lord in devotion and uncom-plaining endurance. He begged all his retinue to forgive him for any pain he might have caused them. They must promise that they would convey to the Empress his deepest and hum-blest gratitude for everything she had done for him. Every

time a new message arrived from her he cried like a child. Then
he asked whether there was not anything he might do that
would give everyone present some genuine pleasure. Immediately they all retorted that the only pleasure he could give
them would be to take his medicine. He swallowed the quinine
without a word of protest, but got sick as soon as he had taken
it. A few hours later he tried it again, but with the same result.
He developed fainting fits. Insomnia, and suffocation when he
was awake, tortured him. Half the time he was no longer conscious. But when he recovered he feebly asked once again to
be moved from Jassy to his beloved Nicolaev. Its forest air
ought to do him good; his friend and protégé Faleyev who had
just returned from Nicolaev was enthusiastic about the climate.
Besides, it was October 4, or just a week from the day when
they had made him postpone his intended move.

On that day he started for Nicolaev, having scribbled with
pain the following note to Catherine: 'My dear, my almighty
Empress! I have no more strength to bear my sufferings; there
remains one salvation—to leave this city, and I have given
orders that I am to be taken to Nicolaev. I do not know what
will happen to me.' At seven in the morning he was carried in
an armchair to his carriage. A procession followed, comprising
all his faithful retinue: Baur, whom he had chased all round
the world on different missions, the merchant Faleyev, who had
been an invaluable collaborator first in the great work of building up the Southern Provinces and then in organizing supplies
during the Turkish War, the Countess Branitsky, Prince Galitsin, the doctors, and various others. The first station, Pount-
cheshta, they reached safely. The local commandant had organized a great reception in honor of the distinguished guest.
But when he met Potemkin's carriage all he heard was the
groan of a dying man. The reception and the festivities were
canceled. Serenissimus, who complained that he was hot and
could not breathe, was carried into a house. For a moment he recovered slightly: he was pleased his idea had triumphed, for

the change of air seemed to be doing him good. He fell asleep and, after three hours' rest, talked quite cheerfully until midnight. But he could not sleep at night, and appeared to suffer a great deal. At daybreak he demanded that the journey should be resumed. They had not gone more than thirty miles, when he ordered the procession to stop. 'This will be enough,' he said. 'There is no point in going on now. Take me out of the carriage and put me down. I want to die in the field.'

A carpet was laid out on the grass, and Potemkin was carefully placed on it. One of the Cossack escort was the first to realize that he was passing away. Everybody began to search for a golden coin to shut his eye—the only one that could see; the same Cossack offered a copper five kopeck piece, with which Potemkin's eye was closed. He died on Sunday, October 5, 1791, at midday.

Slowly the procession started on its return journey to Jassy. Popov drafted a short message to the Empress: 'Fate is done. His Serene Highness the Prince is no longer on this earth.' A detailed report of Potemkin's last hours is to follow.

On October 12 at 5 p.m. the courier carrying the sad news reached St. Petersburg. When Catherine heard that Potemkin was no more she had a complete breakdown and had to be bled several times. 'Now I have no one left on whom I can rely,' she said amid hysterical tears. Thus in her agony she admitted that which in her recent dealings with Potemkin she almost seemed to have forgotten: *he* was her man, her only man; the despicable puppet Zoubov, the 'child', whose intelligence and statecraft she had been describing to Potemkin in such glowing terms suddenly sank into temporary insignificance.

She tried to have a little sleep but it would not come to her. She got up and wandered about the palace like a somnambulist. 'How can anybody replace Potemkin to me?' she asked Chrapovitsky. 'Everything will be different now. He was a true nobleman, and a clever man. He did not sell me to others. No one could buy him.' She cried a great deal. Almost every day her secretary entered 'Tears and despair', or 'They wept', or just one word 'Tears' in his diary.

She felt alone in the world. Who was there among those surrounding her who had ever had the courage of an independent decision, who had dared and fought and conquered? With whom else could she have shared the responsibilities of government? With whom could she share them now?

When she calmed down a little she restored to her usual remedy. Just as after the death of young Lanskoy she had finally conquered her grief by becoming wholly absorbed in reading and writing, she buried herself in correspondence now. This seemed to soothe her and at least partly to relieve her pain.

She wrote whole days long and most of the nights. She wrote to everybody: Popov, Sashenka Branitsky, Prince Nassau-Siegen, and innumerable others both in Russia and abroad. She told them what a marvelous, rare, unique friend and statesman Potemkin had been.

But it is in her letters to Grimm, to whom she wrote on several days in rapid succession, that she expressed her feelings best. It is through Grimm that seventeen years earlier she had more or less introduced Potemkin to Europe, when she described so enthusiastically the qualities of 'one of the greatest, most bizarre, and most entertaining eccentrics of this iron age'. And now, in a letter to the very same Grimm, the grief-stricken and widowed Catherine penned an epitaph to her consort, on which it would be hard to improve:—

'A terrible blow struck me again yesterday. Towards six o'clock after dinner, a courier brought me the very sad news that my pupil, my friend, and my almost idol, Prince Potemkin, died after about a month's illness, in Moldavia! You have no idea of the extent of my affliction; he had an excellent heart and a rare understanding, together with an unusual broadness of mind; his views were always large and magnanimous; he was very human, full of knowledge, singularly amiable, and his ideas were forever new; no man ever had such a gift of witticism as he; during the war, his military qualities must have gone home, for he never missed one single blow on sea or on land. No one in the world was less led by others than he; moreover, he had a particular gift of employing others. In a word, he was a man of state, both for consultation and for carrying into effect the plans made; he was attached to me with passion and with zeal; grumbling and growing angry when he thought that one could do better; with age and with experience he cured himself of his faults; three months ago, when he was here, I said to Zoubov, that I feared this change, and that he no longer had the faults which everyone knew, and now unhappily my apprehension had turned out to be a prophecy. But his rarest quality was a courage of heart, spirit, and soul which distinguished him so from other men, and thus we could understand each other perfectly and allowed the less well-informed to babble as much as they liked. I consider Prince Potemkin a very great man, who did not take half the opportunities which lay within his grasp.'

CHRONOLOGICAL TABLE

1729 . . .	Birth of Catherine (Sophia Augusta Frederica, Princess of Anhalt-Zerbst).
1739 . . .	Birth of Potemkin.
1744 (Feb.) .	The young princess arrives in St. Petersburg as the fiancée of the Grand Duke Peter, heir to the throne of his aunt, the Empress Elizabeth.
1744 (July) .	The princess is received into the Greek Orthodox Church and changes her name to Catherine.
1745 (Aug.) .	Marriage of Catherine and Peter.
1762 (Jan.) .	Death of the Empress Elizabeth, and accession of Peter as Tsar Peter III.
" (July) .	Peter deposed and assassinated. Catherine proclaimed Empress. Her first meeting with Potemkin.
1768–1774 .	First Russo-Turkish War.
1772 . . .	Catherine breaks with her lover, Grigory Orlov, who is replaced by Wassiltchikov.
1772–1775 .	Pougatchev Rebellion.
1774 . . .	Wassiltchikov dismissed. Potemkin becomes Catherine's lover.
1774 (Autumn)	Marriage of Catherine and Potemkin.
1776 . . .	Potemkin retires from Catherine's alcove, but remains in power.
1783 . . .	Annexation of the Crimea.
1787 . . .	Catherine's journey to the Southern Provinces.
1787–1792 .	Second Russo-Turkish War.
1791 . . .	Death of Potemkin.
1796 . . .	Death of Catherine.

INDEX

343